Doing Therapy Briefly

Doing Therapy Briefly

ROBERT BOR
SHEILA GILL
RIVA MILLER
and
CHRISTINE PARROTT

First published 2004 by
PALGRAVE MACMILLAN
Houndmills, Basingstoke, Hampshire RG21 6XS and
175 Fifth Avenue, New York, N.Y. 10010
Companies and representatives throughout the world

PALGRAVE MACMILLAN is the global academic imprint of the Palgrave Macmillan division of St. Martin's Press, LLC and of Palgrave Macmillan Ltd. Macmillan® is a registered trademark in the United States, United Kingdom and other countries. Palgrave is a registered trademark in the European Union and other countries.

ISBN 0–333–94762–2 hardback
ISBN 0–333–94763–0 paperback

This book is printed on paper suitable for recycling and made from fully managed and sustained forest sources.

A catalogue record for this book is available from the British Library.

A catalog record for this book is available from the Library of Congress.

10   9   8   7   6   5   4   3   2   1
13 12 11 10 09 08 07 06 05 04

Printed and bound in Great Britain by
Creative Print & Design (Wales), Ebbw Vale

Contents

Acknowledgements

Each of the authors works in different settings, however we have been fortunate in being able to consult with one another and to facilitate our own professional development through our collaboration which has spanned continents. Our ideas have not developed in isolation and we are enormously grateful to a wide range of colleagues and friends who have supported and encouraged the writing of this book.

Our psychologist and psychotherapist colleagues at the Royal Free Hospital, London – Amanda Evans, David Glass, Debbie Levitt, Michael Sinclair, Claire Singer, Barbara Wren and Nicola Dunn; Jenifer Ball of St Paul's School, London; Teresa Schaefer of the Student Health Centre and Sue Garrett, Schimpf Carruthers and Sam Kung of the Student Advice and Counselling Centre, all at the London School of Economics and Political Science; Lucia Grun, Jonathan Sheldon, Irwin Nazareth, Eunice Laleye and Michael Cahalan of the Keat's Group Practice; all of the doctors at the Hampstead Group Practice, London, Kate Stevenson, Isobel Scher, Dr Jeannette Josse, Dr Peter Scragg and Dr Peter du Plessis, all of whose time and support have nourished and enhanced our professional and personal lives.

We are grateful to Brandon Storey for his editorial assistance.

Finally, a book on this topic would not have been possible without the numerous conversations we have had with a wide range of clients in the many different settings in which each of the authors has worked. Although we set out to assimilate as many learning points as we could from our clinical experience, we remain staunchly committed to the idea that psychotherapy can never be narrowed down to a formula and that every client has an important and valid story to tell. Our task as therapists is to facilitate the telling and exploration of their story. It is also to help to solve people's problems. Although this process should not be rushed, we believe from our experience that there are effective ways of creating intensity and connectedness with people in times of psychological distress.

This book is dedicated to all of our clients and their families, as well as to our own families.

About the Authors

Robert Bor is a Consultant Clinical Psychologist at the Royal Free Hospital, London, where he works in the Infection and Immunity Directorate. He is a Chartered Clinical, Counselling and Health Psychologist as well as a UKCP Registered Family Therapist. He is also Emeritus Professor of Psychology at London Metropolitan University as well as Visiting Professor at City University, London. He undertook his family therapy training at the Tavistock Clinic, London and is extensively involved in the training of psychologists and psychotherapists. He has many years of experience of working with individuals, couples and families affected by acute and chronic illness. He has published numerous books and academic papers on this and related topics. He is also a qualified pilot with a special interest in aviation psychology, airline passenger behaviour and pilot mental health and provides a psychological therapy service for people working in the aviation industry. He counsels individuals, couples and families and consults to organisations and also works in private practice. He is also a Churchill Fellow and a Fellow of the Royal Aeronautical Society.

Sheila Gill is a BACP Accredited Counsellor, a UKCP Registered Independent Counsellor and an accredited Member of Counsellors in Primary Care. She is an experienced systemic therapist and trainer. She holds a Postgraduate Diploma in Counselling in Primary Care from City University and a Certificate in Systemic Therapy from Kensington Consultation Centre. She has also followed a course of study in Cognitive Behavioural Therapy at the Department of Psychiatry and Behavioural Sciences at University College, London. She has contributed a number of chapters to books on the theory and practice of therapy. She works as a counsellor in The London School of Economics and Political Science and in general practice in North London. Her particular interest is to draw on systemic and cognitive models of therapy in working with individuals, couples and families and within organisations.

Riva Miller is a UKCP Registered Systemic Therapist. She has a background in medical social work. She worked for many years with people with a range of chronic and acute medical conditions. She trained as a family therapist at the Tavistock Clinic, at the Institute of Family Therapy and with the Milan Associates in Italy. She has held positions as manager, practitioner, teacher and consultant within several organisations. She currently works as a family therapist in the Haemophilia Centre at the Royal Free Hospital, London. She is Honorary Senior Lecturer at the Royal Free and University College School of Medicine. Since 1985 she has been a Consultant to the National Blood and Tissue Service, contributing to the consideration of ethical issues and instigation of counselling policies. She also has a private practice and works in the field of Occupational Health at the Royal Free and the Royal National Orthopaedic Hospitals. She has acted as an advisor for the World Health Organization since 1988 and run many workshops on their behalf on HIV infection. Her particular expertise and interests are in integrating effective approaches to treatment and care in busy medical settings. This book is the accumulation of many years of experience of practice and teaching in this field.

Christine Parrott is a BPS Chartered Counselling Psychologist. Originally from the United States, she earned a Bachelor of Arts at Dartmouth College in Hanover, New Hampshire. After moving to Britain in 1992, she earned her Masters and Post-Masters Degree in Counselling Psychology at City University, London. She also has a Diploma in Applied Hypnosis from the University of London. She now works as a counselling psychologist, devoting much of her time to writing and as a media consultant in the United States. Her special interests include the development of increased public awareness in psychology, the impact of values and ethics on the counselling process and the evolution of behaviour and emotions in people.

Note about Clinical Cases in this Book

Throughout this book, we have used clinical cases to illustrate the theory and practice of brief therapy. In order to respect the confidential nature of the client–therapist relationship, all names and facts, identifying features and most of what happened in therapy, have been altered and bear no similarity to actual clinical cases with whom we have worked. Any perceived similarity is therefore entirely coincidental and not intentional.

1 Introduction and Overview of Time-sensitive Therapy

This book explores with the reader ways of working briefly with clients in psychotherapy. We emphasise throughout this book that working briefly, as we practise it in therapeutic consultations, is more about the creation of a profound connection with the client than simply an awareness of time. The approach to therapy that is described here is ethically driven yet commercially aware. We are aware of the many challenges faced by therapists and the changing expectations that clients have of psychological treatment in the modern era. We recognise that the whole tenor of modern health care is to create a relationship of co-responsibility with the client, and to mobilise his resources and create movement in his life rather than to foster what is increasingly considered an outdated dependent, parent–child-like relationship. The approach outlined here therefore considers the client as resourceful. The therapist and client come together in a non-hierarchically arranged, collaborative relationship, in order to explore, reduce and resolve problems.

BACKGROUND TO WORKING BRIEFLY

Irrespective of the route we train as therapists (e.g. psychology, counselling, psychotherapy, etc.), the process is broadly similar. We are taught a number of skills and it is emphasised that these are embedded within clearly elucidated theoretical frameworks. Some frameworks dominate our training, while others are introduced alongside a range of theoretical approaches. Learning to practise as a therapist usually involves slowing down the therapeutic process and breaking it into manageable proportions and acquiring skills that we can learn to master. For the trainee, it appears there is so much to learn and understand. What might have seemed simple and straightforward conversations between people in a professional context suddenly demand the most careful attention as we struggle to integrate ethical issues with executive skills, theory, research and ideas generated in supervisory sessions. We must then learn to blend these with our emerging style and personality as therapists. It all feels daunting to even the most confident of trainees. What links most therapists training programmes together is that trainees are expected to work carefully and methodically with clients. They need to demonstrate competence and this is linked to personal confidence. Consequently, most seasoned trainers and supervisors expect trainees to provide more therapy in a given case than is strictly required, and to do so at a slower pace than a seasoned therapist might choose to do. In addition, the dominant approaches within the psychological therapies, as taught in therapy courses, continue to favour longer term and more elaborative work. Most graduates from therapy programmes have had scant, or no introduction to brief or time-limited therapy. Even where there is some introduction to brief therapy approaches, students are mostly taught about discrete schools of therapy (e.g. the 'solution-focused therapy' or 'brief therapy' approaches) and trainees are rarely taught how to work within their main or preferred therapy approach in a brief and focused way. Understandably, having to work in a time-sensitive way can be quite a challenge to many therapists.

CORE BELIEFS HELD BY MANY THERAPISTS ABOUT THERAPY

Certain beliefs prevail about 'brief therapy'. These may be constraining beliefs because they can deter therapists from exploring the possibilities inherent in working in a time-sensitive way with clients. The astute therapist will recognise that these beliefs do not tend to be articulated as such in textbooks and journal articles. Instead, they have become a sort of 'therapist folklore' in that they are aired in supervisory sessions, go unchallenged at therapy conferences, form the basis by which applicants might be selected for a training course and most importantly, pervade so many therapeutic relationships, irrespective of what may be best or available for the client. Some of these core beliefs are summarised in Box 1.1.

In this book, we hope to address some of these beliefs and, where possible, we present an alternative view that both validates the choice of therapeutic approach used by the reader and offers a preliminary understanding of how the variable of 'time' can be used in even more creative and interesting ways to effect deep and lasting changes in clients. This process requires keeping an open mind about your core beliefs about therapy. There are dozens of approaches to therapy and, as such, books about therapy abound. We faced a dilemma as authors in writing this book as

---

Box 1.1   Core Beliefs by Therapists about Therapy

- More therapy is better than less;
- Less is usually shallow and only touches the surface of the problem, or at best, addresses the main symptom;
- Brief therapy ignores or disqualifies the client's true emotional pain;
- Brief therapy is too active; this can result in therapy being rushed and the client feeling 'coerced' into change or being 'forced' into seeing things from the therapist's perspective;
- Brief therapy buys into a 'quick fix' culture in therapy;
- Since brief practice is not how most therapists are trained, a deviation from standard therapeutic practice could put them out of their depth; and
- Working briefly is no way for a therapist to make a living; it simply does not pay.

---

we did not want to add 'yet another' to the burgeoning list of titles. However, we have found that doing therapy briefly requires significantly more than compressing 'normal' therapy into a shorter time frame. It engenders viewing psychological problems, solutions and the client–therapist relationship differently (Box 1.2). This book is aimed at therapists and trainees who have a reasonable understanding of therapy both in terms of theory and clinical experience.

Box 1.2

An interest in working briefly as a therapist requires a willingness to re-examine:

1. The role of the therapist in eliciting and managing change;
2. The role of the client in therapy;
3. One's beliefs about psychological problems and solutions;
4. The nature of the therapeutic relationship, especially with regard to the intake process and endings;
5. The overall place of therapy in people's lives (i.e. whether the aim is for an interim solution or a permanent cure); and
6. One's attitude towards and experience of therapeutic process; it may not always be neat, orderly and predictive, but this does not necessarily diminish it's effectiveness.

The most important message of this book is that working briefly as a therapist does not require one to abandon all that has been learned thus far! On the contrary, working briefly means drawing on all of one's experience, honing and refining one's skills from an additional (and possibly novel) perspective and reviewing how to deliver what one already knows and does. If it is your choice or preference to learn about 'brief therapy' as a school, then this book may, in part, disappoint you. While we address and describe some features of the school of 'brief therapy', we have endeavoured to avoid presenting the ideas about time-sensitive therapy from within any one single theoretical approach, although we will draw on theory from several schools. Before turning our attention to why brief and/or time-sensitive therapy is an important additional skill and possibly an area of expertise for the qualified therapist, it is necessary for readers to have some understanding of the core beliefs that underpin such work. These are noted in Box 1.3.

Box 1.3   Core Beliefs about Working Briefly in Therapy

- Therapy is usually and mostly a conversation between at least two people. It is the quality, richness and intensity of the conversation, rather than its duration, that is most relevant to therapeutic outcome.
- Relationship (between client and therapist) is at the core of working briefly. The therapist listens intently to the client. Intensity is actively sought from the outset through active, positive and empathic engagement with the client. The therapist acknowledges and addresses the emotional/affective aspects of the emerging relationship by talking openly about this with the client in relation to the description of the problem.
- Emotional distress and pain is acknowledged. Contrary to some popular approaches, the therapist does not ignore the client's affective response by steering the conversation to solutions. Indeed, it is through the process of facilitating emotional expression and respecting the client's thoughts, feelings and beliefs that the therapist develops a better appreciation of his problem. This is the 'heart and soul' of therapy (Hubble *et al.* 1999).
- Less therapy should not imply a shallower or weaker form of therapy. The therapist and client can 'dig deep' over a shorter time span.
- Research has shown that most change occurs early on in therapy (Howard *et al.* 1986) highlighting issues about the 'dose effect' in therapy (i.e. a medical model term for the number of sessions required

---

to produce a 'cure'). While this research raises interesting method-ological questions (Kadera *et al*. 1996), the explicit application of a time-limited model may provide a clearer framework through which the dose effect can be measured.

- Working briefly does not mean that clients are seen only over a short period of time. Sessions may be spaced apart at intervals that are beyond the norm (e.g. weekly), and the wise, judicious and creative use of time within and between sessions can positively further the aims of therapy.
- Therapy does not necessarily nor specifically aim to 'cure' clients; the aim, instead, is to converse with clients about problems and their resolution. The therapist is not necessarily present for every step that the client takes to resolve his problem.
- Therapeutic content and process are continually addressed and discussed between client and therapist.
- Therapy is a co-partnership with clients and is therefore not hierar-chically organised.
- The therapist makes use of all available opportunities to 'connect' with the client by participating in the unfolding story about the problem. There are numerous utterances and prompts that convey to the client that the therapist is actively engaged. Listening is therefore an active rather than a passive form of engagement.
- Opportunities to affirm and validate the client and the story are never missed. Working briefly requires the therapist to 'intervene' from the outset. A tone of active and positive engagement is set from the start and continues for the duration of the therapy. The client's account of his problem is clearly valid from his perspective. There is a need, however, for the active time-sensitive therapist to introduce alternate meanings or stories to the unfolding description of a problem. For example, as we shall illustrate, the meta-message of 'I feel hurt/defeated/troubled/victimised...' and so on is some-times conveyed by the client by his very presence in the consulting room. The therapist reminds herself, and the client, that even though the client expresses hurt, defeat and so on, he[1] is also alive and aware emotionally. He is also motivated to take charge of an important part of the process of solving the problem (going to talk to a therapist), bringing clarity to a situation that seemed insoluble, externalising

---

1. The personal pronoun 'he' is used throughout the book to denote 'the client' and 'she' for 'the therapist'. This does not reflect any bias on the part of the authors but are merely convenient pronouns.

> **Box 1.3**   (Continued)
>
> both the problem and the feelings associated with it and so on. This is validating the client because it is explicitly recognised and acknowledged by the therapist. The therapist simultaneously assigns competence to the client and evokes an alternate story from the client *alongside* the story of the problem. If done with genuineness and conviction, and highlights his unique personal qualities. Empathy, at this level, is coupled with the passion of the therapist to engage with the client, his problem and possibility of solutions.
>
> • The therapist is enthusiastic and energetic with the client, conveying something of her own personality in the relationship. It is not possible, in our experience, to work briefly with a client where mutual positive feelings of engagement and a sense of security are missing in the relationship. Maintaining emotional distance, complete neutrality or making the occasional prompting gesture will not help to achieve the levels of engagement and security needed to work in a time-sensitive way. After all, intensity in human relationships is not solely determined by their duration. Hence, we do not subscribe to the view that the only way to 'connect with' and to 'properly understand' the client is to replicate family relationships (parent–child) in therapy room. Intensity, depth and security in relationships can be created and conveyed in other ways. Furthermore, we should not make the assumption that these processes or qualities are strictly necessary for change to occur in therapy.

THINKING DIFFERENTLY ABOUT THERAPY

The evolving relationship with the client is monitored directly from time to time through punctuating remarks or sentences such as: 'How are we doing in therapy?', 'Is this the sort of discussion that is helpful to you?', 'Are we going too fast or too slowly?' or 'Is this the right speed to take things?' Looking for or expecting change in the client helps us to both create forward movement for the client and measure change, as it is perceived or experienced by him. For example, one might ask:

> 'Now that we have been talking for ten minutes, what is different for you?' or, 'Now that you have put that thought into words, what difference does it make for you?'

To work briefly is to refocus and shift one's methods and goals for therapy. The overriding goals are, however, unchanged. Therapy helps people to solve problems, gain insight and deepen their understanding, express feelings and externalise problems, develop new ways of looking at issues and problems, and elicit the client's innate capability to overcome difficulties. With intensity in the collaborative working relationship, clarity of focus and an optimism that helps the client to feel that solutions are possible, without denying his difficulties or emotional pain, much can be achieved in a shorter period of time.

When working briefly, the therapist does not 'cut corners', 'patch-up' problems, trivialise or compromise on depth when engaging with the client. On the contrary, there may be more focused and intense conversations about problems at a very deep level. Furthermore, working in a time-sensitive way can help to guard against entrenched patterns pervading the therapeutic process that may otherwise thwart conversation about important issues that arise in the therapy for fear of threatening the relationship. As Hoyt has pointed out (1995), when we are time sensitive, there is no time for leisure in therapy. One does not wait for change to happen; it is induced from the first moment of engagement with the client. Opportunities for change or difference are capitalised on from the beginning. After all, the very fact that the client has presented himself for therapy represents for most clients a fundamental change or difference in their 'internal map' of how they view themselves. The therapist helps the client to re-establish his connectedness with hopefulness for the future and possibilities for the present as well as looking at the past.

Because of the structure of a brief model of therapy, motivation to attend therapy is maintained or even strengthened by the client's knowledge that the end of therapy is already in sight from the outset. How this is achieved is described in detail in the following chapters. The therapist's probing questions, considered and apt reflections, and sense of optimism further reinforce the sense that therapy is purposeful, contained and directed. In his own mind, the client can readily liken the relationship to the structure and process of other helping relationships, such as that between patient and doctor, thereby removing the apparent myth that therapy can lead to a dependent relationship or is saturated with conversations about problems, pathology and what happened years ago. Of course, a therapist working briefly is interested in these important issues and events. However, she gives more attention to how the client is coping in the present and to rewriting personal or family 'scripts' about past patterns and problems (Byng-Hall 1995) such that the problem is seen in a new light. This in itself can help prevent the same or similar problems from recurring in the future. If, however, the problem were to recur, or a related problem becomes apparent at a later stage, the client can simply call to make an appointment to see his therapist, much as he would do if he had identified a physical health problem for which he would seek consultation from his doctor. If it subsequently becomes evident that the client is a 'serial-therapy seeker' or the underlying problem is not being addressed in brief therapy consultations (e.g. chronic loneliness, poor ego strength and an inability to address problems, an unexpressed dependency or personality disorder, among other problems), then this would be a clear indication to the therapist that a different approach to therapy may warrant consideration. The therapist might then choose to provide this herself or to refer such a case.

The important point to highlight is that the therapist always first makes the assumption that the problem can be dealt with briefly and therefore engages with the client and responds to the problem with the relevant internal map. This response is irrespective of the nature of the problem as the consultative approach leaves the way open for a range of solutions after an initial session, including longer-term work or referral to another specialist. Only by engaging with the client can a more thorough assessment be undertaken and where longer-term therapy is indicated, this possibility can be openly discussed with the client at any stage during the course of the time-sensitive therapy. The approach that we describe in this book reflects a robust attitude to the full range of psychological problems that constantly present themselves in the modern work context. It does not, however, make the assumption that every problem can be worked out successfully in a time-sensitive way. However, as the approach concentrates and focuses on connecting with the individual client and not the problem, it is our experience that different people react differently to the same problem. The topic of assessment of clients for this approach is explored in detail in Chapter 5. The flexibility and creativity of the approach described allows for this difference. Part of the initial assessment must be to consider whether therapy can help with the particular problem. Evidence has shown that certain problems cannot be solved through psychological therapy (e.g. Van Emmerik *et al*. 2002) and in a few cases, can even harm the client.

Once the client has been engaged in therapy, the therapist also needs to think about how therapy will end with the client, at an early stage in the relationship. The work of the therapist begins to be done as soon as the client begins to work! This means that the therapist needs to be alert to the first signs of learning, enhanced coping, and a sense of developing self-mastery and growth (Hoyt 1995). A defining characteristic of working briefly is that the therapist develops a time-sensitive attitude (i.e. time is limited). The other defining characteristic is that the therapist adopts a stance of actively seeking out, noticing and eliciting competencies and strengths. Working thus avoids the pitfalls of having to address the question of defining brief therapy in terms of numbers of sessions.

BRIEF ILLUSTRATIVE EXAMPLES

Some ideas are best conveyed through examples, rather than lengthy theoretical descriptions. Learning how to do therapy is no exception. The following two case examples convey a sense of how doing therapy briefly is a departure from the more traditional approaches to therapy.

Case A: Max

Max was referred to therapy by his consultant neurologist. Two years prior to the referral, Max (then aged 19) travelled to Brazil during his gap year and spent part of his time abroad involved in a conservation project near the Amazon Basin. Two weeks before he was due to return to the United Kingdom, he was involved in a car accident in which a drunk driver failed to yield at a traffic intersection. Max sustained serious head injuries and was unconscious for two days. After a period of hospitalisation and convalescence, he was well enough to make the journey home. In the months that followed, he underwent physiotherapy and countless medico-legal assessments by specialists in preparation for a legal claim against the driver. Max missed the intake for university the following year as a consequence of the investigations and tests even though he felt that he had recovered sufficiently. His neurologist referred him to therapy because he had become depressed. What mostly struck the therapist was the absence of obvious signs or symptoms of head injury and just how 'normal' Max appeared and related. He communicated perfectly well. As the date for the court-case came closer, Max asked his lawyer to send him copies of the medical reports. They evidently made for depressing reading in that they highlighted the strong possibility that Max would not cope at all with university, he would be unlikely to sustain 'normal, meaningful long-term relationships' and 'he was likely to suffer permanent sexual impairment'. Max hardly recognised the description of himself which he felt consigned him to a life of dependency, misery and disability. In reality, he explained to his therapist, nothing could be further from his current situation. He was in a long-term relationship with his girlfriend; he had completed two foreign language courses that year and, he wryly assured his therapist, he had no signs of sexual dysfunction. Max had not had an opportunity to fully discuss with his neurologist this incongruity between the devastating account of him depicted in the reports and how he felt about himself. As the therapy session progressed, Max said that he might have overreacted to the information contained in the reports because they suggested possibilities in a legal sense of the chances of a person experiencing these problems after a head injury, with a slant towards financial compensation, rather than how he was functioning. Max said that reading these accounts distressed him and made him feel anxious about himself, much like some medical students feel when they first study anatomy and pathology. They erroneously believe that they are suffering from serious and sometimes rare medical conditions! The therapist identi-fied and explored Max's concern that no one appeared to have discussed with him how he was coping. The legal emphasis of his medical consultations high-lighted problems and potential deficits. Max told the therapist at the end of the session that three points stood out for him. First, she did not 'behave' as he expected a therapist to in that she was friendly, relaxed and informal. Second, he felt reassured that in spite of the accident and head injury, he appeared to be functioning normally even though the focus of most of his professional encounters was on his injuries and the possibility of permanent dysfunction. Third, he said that his sense of shame about suffering a head injury and his fear that others might treat him differently had been challenged in the session. From the therapist's perspective, a significant amount had been achieved in the first session. Max asked the therapist whether she would agree to periodic follow-up sessions, at 2–3 month intervals, at least until the legal proceedings had been concluded and for a while beyond them. He said that this would be 'for reassurance' and (with a smile) to 'keep me on the path of normality'.

Case B: Derek

Sandra brought her 14-year-old son Derek to the counsellor because she was concerned that 'he was resisting leaving home', by which she meant not willing to go to camp in the holidays, sleep over at a friend's house or sign up for an optional school trip to Europe. She had read in a newspaper sup-plement that this pattern of behaviour suggested 'attachment problems', with their origins in early childhood, and that the problem should be addressed through counselling. What emerged in the session was that Derek was an exceptionally gifted child, who excelled at most sport and was academically the top of his year at school. His main interest, apart from sport, was art and he displayed a sensitivity and self-knowledge rarely seen in boys of similar age. Careful and thorough exploration by the counsellor revealed that Derek's older brother, Steven (18), had earned a place at Oxford University and they had long been rivalrous siblings. Steven also appeared, in certain ways, to be the antithesis of his younger brother. He had travelled abroad extensively by his mid-teens, become a leader at sum-mer camps over a number of years and had earned his pilot's licence soon after his 18th birthday. There was no suggestion that Derek's physical or emotional development was in anyway delayed. He told the counsellor towards the end of the session, 'I just enjoy being at home.' The counsellor was aware that there were several pathways ahead and that she could choose to address the problem of Derek not wanting to leave home in sev-eral different ways. She chose to address Derek's sense of difference and contentment rather than explore his apparent resistance to change and his need to be at home. Since there were no obvious signs of emotional problems or family difficulties, the counsellor was able to reassure Sandra and Derek that it did not appear that anything had been overlooked in the consultation. Her advice to them was to leave Derek be and let him establish his identity through his choice to spend more time at home. Surprisingly, both mother and son expressed relief. Sandra was warned after reading the newspaper article that she might be ignoring the problem if she did not seek therapy, while Derek said that he expected the counsellor to 'encourage' him to spend more time away from home, something he feared in coming to the session. The counsellor suggested that a review session be arranged in six weeks 'to see how things have progressed'. Sandra told the counsellor during the review session that both she and her husband had resisted putting pressure on Derek to spend time away from home. Sandra said that Derek appeared more relaxed and was indeed, spending more time at home. While Derek agreed with his mother, he did, however, remind her that he booked to go to a summer camp and that he was going abroad for a long weekend with his grandparents. At the end of the session, the counsellor suggested that they contact her to arrange another appointment for some time in the future as no one in session felt the need for a further session to be booked at that stage.

The remainder of this book explores these and related issues further and, where appropriate, we also illustrate them with short case examples. The following five chapters (Chapters 2–6) describe more of the underlying theoretical ideas that inform time-sensitive therapeutic practice. This lays the foundation for some guidelines and a 'map' for conducting the initial therapy session (see Chapters 5–8). The following chapter (Chapter 9) describes a case example and helps to link the theory to clinical practice. Every therapist encounters difficulties in their practice from time to time. Apparent stuckness can also create new opportunities in therapy if handled sensitively and correctly, and without necessarily ascribing blame to the client as is sometimes done when working with some of the more traditional approaches. This is explored in greater detail in Chapter 10. Most books about therapy address how to start therapy, but surprisingly few devote any space to endings in therapy. How we end therapy is central to working briefly and therefore we devote a whole chapter to this important issue (see Chapter 11). The final chapter explores the relevance and application of brief therapy to evidence based and managed health care, given that this is rapidly becoming the most important context for the delivery of psychological care in health services.

In writing this book, we set out to describe our experience as therapists and our evolving theoretical ideas. We certainly do not seek to be prescriptive since each therapist must account for his own practice within a specific context and with each individual case. The author, Lewis Carroll, probably had a lesson for all of us in our youth to maintain a healthy scepticism towards so-called new ideas. This probably holds true for all of us as adults but is put so much more poetically in 'Alice Through the Looking Glass':

> 'That's the reason they're called lessons,' the Gryphon remarked: 'because they lessen from day to day.'

2 Exploring 'Brief' and 'Time-sensitive' Therapy

How we use the time within clinical sessions has always been of interest to therapists, while the number of therapy sessions (i.e. duration of therapy) continues to be a topic of debate. In recent years, this interest has intensified as social and economic conditions have changed and impacted the therapeutic relationship. Even clients expect to talk about the length of a course of therapy and the likely outcome. As such, the link between a therapeutic outcome, cost and duration of treatment is now one of the most important foci in psychotherapy and is likely to continue to dominate research, theoretical debate, clinical skills and perceptions of the client–therapist relationship for many years to come (see also Chapter 12).

While time in therapy is viewed by some as just another factor or variable (i.e. an artefact), within/of the process, we hope to illustrate in this book how time-limited psychotherapy is firmly embedded within a specific theoretical framework and engenders developing a different sort of relationship with the client than is the case in longer-term approaches. Working briefly means that the therapist is challenged to view psychological problems differently. This may necessitate revising some of the key aspects of one's original theoretical model. It also means viewing the client differently; there is a profound shift away from a pathology-error-deficit model to the one where the client's competence, coping, strengths and abilities are actively sought out and promoted. This is not a simplistic endeavour. The therapist takes great care to listen to the presenting problems and to acknowledge the dilemmas and emotional pain that the client brings to therapy. More and not less work is required of the therapist. In itself, this is a highly complex task to achieve. Many clients who present themselves for therapy normally know themselves to be resourceful individuals. Moreover, what has happened has introduced self-doubt and a measure of fear in their lives, which in spite of their own efforts, they have been unable to successfully sort out or remedy the problem on their own. An important and necessary part of the therapy is perhaps to encourage the client to stop persisting with their attempted (and presumably unsuccessful) solution to their problem. Brief therapy is emphatically not about 'papering over' problems or ignoring the client's expression of feelings. Indeed, the client may need to be given permission to do just that. To be distressed is not the same as being incompetent.

For some therapists, these challenges in how they practise do not sit comfortably and are unwelcome. For others, they have the opposite experience and feel that time-limited therapy appears to 'fit naturally' with their style of practice. There have always been different points of view among therapists and that is why there are so many different theoretical approaches and 'schools of thought'. Working briefly in therapy with clients is no different. Some therapists are attracted to the ideas, while others prefer to work differently.

For most therapists who make this transition from conventional longer-term therapy to more time-limited therapy practice, this change is the culmination of a process that may last many years. Each of the authors of this book has made this transition, having been originally trained in standard long-term psychotherapy models. Our experiences of transition are all different. However, we are all connected in one obvious sense; change did not happen after reading a single book on brief therapy! Therefore, rather than setting an almost impossible task in writing this book, we have chosen to highlight *what* we currently do in practice, rather than *how* to transform clinical practice. Our hope is that some ideas that you may already have had about working briefly are more clearly illustrated in this book. Perhaps you already use some of these ideas and therefore this book may confirm certain theoretical concepts and clinical skills that are already familiar to you. Of course, there may be some things that you read with which you disagree. Nonetheless, we have made an assumption that if you have chosen to read this book, you already have some interest in, curiosity about or experience with some of the ideas. Their usefulness will, in part, be determined by several key factors that are summarised below and also addressed throughout the book:

- The context of work setting(s) in which you practise and the requirements/obligations/accountabilities within it;
- The extent to which you have direct control over the number of sessions you may allocate to clients;
- The degree of 'fit' between the ideas and skills, with your own style or personality, and the nature of the presenting problem;
- Your view of the onset, maintenance and resolution of psychological problems;
- Clients' expectations of what will happen in therapy; and
- Opportunities for training and supervision in time-limited practice.

We maintain a healthy scepticism of anyone claiming to present 'totally new ideas in therapy' for it would seem that some 'new' ideas are repackaged old one's but from within a different theoretical paradigm. We do not make the claim that working briefly in therapy is a new model for clinical practice. This is clearly not the case. Our aim, in writing this book, is to highlight the importance, relevance and significance of taking into account temporal factors in psychotherapeutic practice. Furthermore, we wish to stress that, contrary to some popular wisdom, 'more' therapy is not always 'better' therapy and that there is often clear and positive benefit to the client for co-creating an intense and time-limited therapeutic relationship. How the therapist may set about practising in such a way is our main focus in this book. We will endeavour to describe and illustrate through clinical examples some of the different conceptual and clinical skills required to work briefly with clients.

WHAT IS TIME-SENSITIVE THERAPY?

Time-limited therapy has been defined in a number of different ways, but a common feature of many definitions is the amount of time available to the client or total number of sessions offered. For example, Budman and Gurman (1988) suggested that brief therapy is 'any therapy in which the time allotted to treatment is rationed' (pp. 5–6). A course of therapy that ranges from one to twenty sessions with an average of around six (Bloom 1992), or any number of sessions less than a total of 25 (Koss and Butcher 1986) have also been used to define brief therapy.

To define brief therapy with sole reference to the length of treatment is however both inaccurate and misleading. Brief therapy is significantly more than compressed longer-term work into less time; it is more accurately described as a conceptual approach in its own right (Koss and Shiang 1994). Brief therapy is not simply short-term therapy (Hoyt 1995). Indeed, it may take place over a long period of time (even several months, if the idea of 'episodes' of therapy is included) but with a sizeable interval between sessions. In some cases, brief therapy might be an unplanned or unexpected outcome of therapy, especially where the client decides not to return for more therapy and therefore, by 'default', therapy retrospectively comes to be conceptualised as 'brief' (Budman and Gurman 1988).

Before reviewing some of the key features of working briefly, it is necessary to address some confusion that might arise when making a more thorough study of the available literature on brief therapy. Some readers may be rightly confused by the array of terms used to describe this work. The literature refers variously to 'time-limited therapy', 'focal therapy', 'short-term therapy', 'solution-focused therapy' and 'strategic therapy', among other terms. It is not within the scope of this book to fully describe the similarities and differences between these terms and approaches, given their complexity. However, it may be helpful to stress that there is a sizeable overlap between the range of time-limited approaches described, although there are also important differences (Purves 2003). The total number of sessions normally associated with an episode of time-limited therapy is between six and ten meetings with the client. The common feature of time-limited therapies is the 'intentional consideration of time limits throughout the change process from treatment planning to management of the relationship and selection of interventions' (Steenbarger 1992: 404). Time is intentionally and conceptually planned by the therapist; it is not an unplanned outcome. Brief therapy does not mean 'doing less' but rather 'doing differently'.

We use the terms 'brief therapy' and 'doing therapy briefly' interchangeably in this book, rather than any of the other terms listed above. This is because we believe that these more accurately reflect what we do. Although there is considerable similarity between these approaches, there is a nuance in the terms 'solution focused', 'focal' and 'strategic' therapies that sits less comfortably with us. The reason for this is that they imply a slightly more outcome-focused and directive approach to therapy and give less emphasis to process and the therapeutic relationship.

Our interest necessarily turns to the conceptual orientation of the therapists who plans to work briefly. A summary of the main characteristics of brief therapy is given in Box 2.1.

Brief therapy tends to be clearly structured, though not rigidly so. We describe in Chapters 5, 7, 8 and 11 some of the different phases and stages in time-limited therapy and convey a 'map' for therapeutic practice. It is essential to emphasise, however, that the therapist's relationship with the client is at the core of brief therapy and for this reason, the therapist must be alert to changes in the relationship and ready to respond flexibly to the client and the direction of therapy.

Brief and long-term therapy approaches are clearly different in relation to temporal factors. There are other distinguishing features that can also be highlighted including different values (Berg and Miller 1992; Budman and Gurman 1992). Traditional long-term therapy is commonly associated with helping clients to gain insight into their problems and feelings and to develop a greater awareness of the self in relationships. Since many problems are seen to have their origins in the client's childhood and in relation to disrupted or dysfunctional patterns of attachment, long-term psychotherapy helps to compensate for or repair these early perturbations to 'normal' and 'healthy' development. The therapist working in this mode may seek to change the basic character of the individual, believing that deep and lasting changes may not be attainable without

---

Box 2.1   Main Characteristics of Brief Therapy

- The intention is to help move clients to an agreed goal in a time-efficient way; number of sessions may or may not be specified, although operationally it may be useful to have a set number of sessions ranging between six and ten meetings in total;
- Time is limited and is used flexibly and creatively;
- The therapist is active throughout and a positive, strong and collaborative working alliance is developed;
- Effort is made from the outset to engage the client as early as possible in the therapeutic process;
- There are clear and achievable goals, and a focus from the outset that is maintained;
- The therapist remains flexible and goals may be renegotiated;
- A clear definition of client and therapist responsibilities is achieved;
- Assessment is conducted early and rapidly and is ongoing until the therapy concludes;
- Interventions are introduced promptly;
- Serious problems do not necessarily require profound solutions; small changes may sometimes be sufficient;
- Solutions to problems are co-constructed with the client;
- The client's strengths, abilities and resources are recognised and encouraged rather than emphasising his pathology;
- Different skills and approaches may be used; the therapist draws on a wide repertoire of skills;
- Change is expected to occur; this expectation may be self-fulfilling – it is also recognised that some change may have already occurred even before therapy gets underway;
- Change mostly occurs outside of sessions; and
- Termination and expected outcomes are addressed early in therapy and then throughout the therapeutic process; there is a clear sense of ending right from the beginning of therapy.

Sources: Koss and Butcher (1986), Bloom (1992), Koss and Shiang (1994) and Hoyt (1995).

---

extensive therapy. It is worth emphasising that this notion of psychopathology and psychotherapy is not universally held and different cultures have different perspectives on psychological problems and their treatment. Problems and symptoms of psychological distress are conceptualised within a framework that seeks to uncover or identify pathological process or psychopathology. Indeed, some problems might mask other processes and deeper issues that require psychological treatment and the therapist might choose to focus on these rather than the problem for which the client requests help.

In a brief therapy approach, the therapist will offer a tentative and preliminary assessment of the client's issues or problems within the first session. There should be no mystery surrounding the focus and possible direction of therapy. This initial idea is then revised or expanded upon as new information or processes come to light in the course of further sessions, if these are arranged. This is in contrast to more open-ended therapies where a picture of the 'problem' builds up over time and may (or may not) be presented to the client later on in the course of therapy. In this sense, interventions and assessment in brief therapy are 'front-loaded' and given a primary focus around which the process of therapy unfolds.

It is difficult to discuss the values associated with long-term therapy through the eyes of therapists who are oriented to working briefly in therapy without implying a degree of negative judgement. As authors and psychotherapists, we all recognise the value of longer-term therapy approaches and sometimes the need to offer longer therapy within our own practices (indeed, we have all been trained in and practised longer-term therapies). What is clear to us, however, is that we would not set out to offer long-term therapy with any client without first exhausting the unique opportunities that arise when working briefly. Indeed, brief therapy might be considered a period of extended assessment for the suitability of longer-term work (see Chapter 5). The core values associated with brief therapy are essentially different to those commonly ascribed to long-term therapy.

Brief therapy is mostly pragmatic. The potential limitations of treatment (and possible harm) are recognised and openly discussed with the client. The process of therapy is not viewed as 'timeless'. The focus is on the problem that the client and therapist have identified and agreed to address, without any insinuation that there is another problem that should be considered or uncovered. Where other problems do come to light in the course of therapy, these are identified and explored if they prove relevant to an understanding of the main problem or if the client calls attention to them. The therapist does not seek out additional problems to solve. She is, however, available to discuss them if the client calls attention to them.

Change is a process and the therapist who works briefly recognises that this occurs even before therapy starts, during sessions, between sessions and after the course of therapy has ended. Therapy is not the focus of the client's life. In sessions, however, the focus is clearly on the client, and not just the problem, and significantly more on his resources, abilities and strengths so that he can view and approach his problem differently. Solutions to problems are devised and tested; attempted solutions that do not appear to work may be discarded and new ones generated. There is less likely to be so-called 'resistance' to change where the client has been helped and encouraged to take an active role in clarifying the nature of the problem and in co-creating a solution to it. The relationship is therefore collaborative and consultative, rather than hierarchical. Resources available for therapy and constraints on practice are addressed and not hidden from the client. The most straightforward and direct route to solving the problem is first followed in the shortest possible time. If this process proves misdirected or insufficient, the therapist will have already gained useful information about the client and the problem. The therapist conveys a strong sense of hope and the expectation that change can occur. Since change is inevitable and ongoing, it is important to harness and direct this to positive effect in therapy. Indeed, a positive working alliance, optimism, empathy and an ability to focus on the problem and solutions might be considered the core ingredients of brief therapy.

The client's background and history and indeed the onset of the problem and solutions attempted to date are still potential areas of exploration. They are necessary both in order to assess the problem and to learn more about the client's unique context. However, extensive and unremitting focus on the past can impede solutions in the present. The dominant focus in brief therapy is how the client is coping now – in the present – and his future orientation. As already mentioned, such a focus runs alongside a careful description and acknowledgement of the client's emotional pain. This focus also helps to bypass stuckness, resistance and other impediments to change where the client and the therapist would otherwise dwell on what 'might have been' or 'what went wrong'. We stress that this is a point of emphasis since the brief therapist is naturally curious about the client's account of his own background experiences. However, this account may focus unduly on problems and pathology, and the client might have lost sight of occurrences that were different, that is, exceptional. A summary of some of the key concepts is presented in Box 2.2.

Box 2.2 Traditional versus Brief Therapies: Key Concepts

Long-term insight oriented therapy	*Time-sensitive therapy*
• Time in therapy is unlimited and open-ended	• Time is acknowledged as a therapeutic issue and accordingly limited and structured
• Therapist seeks an understanding of the causes of the problem and of underlying or enduring traits	• Therapist facilitates a conversation about solutions and exceptions to the problem

Box 2.2   (Continued)

- Mystique surrounds therapy; the therapist is an expert
- Focus is on the client's problem and limitations

- Client is defined as having a problem that 'resides' within him

- The focus in therapy is on the past, the cause of the problem and of gaining insight; the theme is 'what might have been if things were different'
- In some approaches, goals are set by the therapist and may be instructive; solutions are outside the client
- Lack of progress in therapy is a sign of resistance and is either 'subconscious' or intentional

- Sessions may or may not motivate one to change

- Process is transparent; client and therapist work collaboratively
- Focus is on the client's strengths and competencies, whilst also acknowledging the client's distress
- Client is defined as temporarily 'stuck' in an area of his life, which might, in fact, turn into an opportunity for him to change
- The focus in therapy is on change, applying different solutions and a future orientation; the theme is on possibilities
- The goals are set jointly by the client and therapist and are measurable/observable; solutions are within the client
- Lack of obvious progress in therapy may be a sign of collaboration difficulties or the therapist 'misreading' the client
- Sessions are empowering and can energise both client and therapist

The qualities and skills of the therapist working briefly can be summarised as having ability to:

- Join powerfully and quickly with the client, but to keep an eye on the end of therapy;
- Set a time limit of an agreed number of sessions;
- Move from traditional linear assessment to interim assessments that are checked and modified as the therapeutic relationship unfolds;
- Use traditional listening skills as the client's story unfolds in therapy; his pain and dilemmas must be heard and acknowledged;
- Set goals and keep to the agenda; new goals should be negotiated;

- Tolerate uncertainty and be willing to rapidly alter the direction and pace of therapy, as indicated;
- Validate the client and seek out his competence, even in challenging and emotionally painful situations; and
- Be genuinely yourself and do not hide behind an austere professional persona – although it goes without saying that you must strive to maintain the highest standards of professional behaviour.

A constructivist or post-structuralist orientation in therapy postulates that reality is not something that is fixed (White and Epston 1990). Rather, reality is constructed and constantly changing. It is created or shaped by interaction, mostly through language and conversations between people, or with themselves, in relation to their perception of others. Since there is no assumption that there is a hidden truth somewhere waiting to be uncovered, the client and the therapist are free to engage with one another in a co-operative relationship and to generate meanings and create a reality around the problem and how best to solve it. There is no objective or standard list of 'solutions' to 'problems'. Each must be fashioned to the unique situation and reality created within therapy. To this end, the objectives and outcome of therapy must be constructed by the client and the therapist. Textbooks might broaden the ideas and expand the creative capacities of the therapist, but they do not hold the solution for a 'given' problem. Embracing a constructivist or post-structuralist conceptualisation frees the therapy from lengthy and potentially unbalanced focus on historical accounts of the problem, the search for the causes and ultimately achieving insight, with the assumption that beneficial change will automatically ensue. Instead, therapy presents a fresh opportunity to solve problems in the present and suggests ways of operationalising in sight. The therapeutic relationship helps to generate a new understanding of problems, and consequently different possibilities emerge for their resolution.

FOCUS ON A COLLABORATIVE WORKING RELATIONSHIP

Assigning competence to the client is at the core of brief, time-sensitive therapy and alters the relationship with the client, the emotional tone of therapy and brings about fresh opportunities for resolving problems. In therapies where expertise is assigned to the therapist, the client is automatically defined as lacking or deficient in something (e.g. insight, a clear understanding of the problem, or the ability to solve the problem). This may be unintentional but no less detrimental in terms of generating a climate of collaborative problem solving. To assign competence to the client in no way diminishes the role of the therapist. Indeed, the therapist must be perceived by the client as one who takes charge of the process and who knows what she is doing and why. Yet, there is arguably nothing more powerful and enabling in therapy than validating the client. We describe more fully how to validate clients in this way in Chapters 4, 6 and 9. It is essential to fully embed the therapy in a co-operative exchange between therapist and client. This is achieved in a number of ways (as we go on to discuss in Chapter 8), but especially as given in Box 2.3.

Box 2.3   Developing a Co-operative and Collaborative Relationship with the Client

- Set a positive tone, conveying genuine interest, warmth, empathy, respect and curiosity;
- Convey the notion that there is (or may be) a limit to the number of sessions available and that time will be used judiciously in these meetings;
- Focus and explore *the client's* agenda and problem;
- Ask about the client's experience of the problem, and attempted solutions, over time, and what these lead him to think and feel about himself;
- Use the client's words and terms as a way of connecting with his descriptions and experiences;
- Look for exceptions to the problem and attempted solutions (e.g. 'can you tell me about a time when you felt free of feelings of anxiety before taking a test?');
- Enhance the client's capacity to construct a realistic solution to the problem;
- Ensure that the solution or goals set are realistic, achievable, small and incremental at first (if necessary), concrete and therefore observable or measurable, and can be attained in a short period of time;
- Convey a measure of optimism and hope; instil confidence in therapy;
- Suggest tasks that can be undertaken outside of therapy sessions;
- Actively solicit feedback from the client at different stages of the therapy, and from time to time within the session (e.g. 'Is this conversation helpful to you?', 'Are we addressing your main concerns in a way that enables you to do something about them?');
- Communicate clearly and precisely; avoid jargon;
- A confrontational stance towards challenging behaviour (e.g. sarcasm, disagreement, defensiveness) often reinforces the diffidence of the client and is best avoided unless it becomes a persistent issue that thwarts progress; and
- Make it your task to bring out the best in the individual.

How Long is Brief Therapy?

Research demonstrates that clients take from therapy what they choose and leave when they determine (Purves 2003). Of course, the therapist has her own ideas about the 'average' or 'necessary' length of attendance required to solve the problem. However, the client will make this decision based on his experience of therapy or what the therapist has already told him. When working briefly, the client's view on when he thinks therapy should end is actively elicited. The therapist can convey to the client the idea that many problems can be solved in a single consultation. Often, because more information is needed before an informed judgement can be made, it may be best to put aside the issue of likely duration of therapy until later in the session. The seeds of brief work have effectively then been sown. The therapist must judge what is 'sufficient' in terms of amount of therapy to overcome the problem in collaboration with the client and not seek to 'cure' it or tamper with issues for which the client has not directly sought help. This also frees the therapist from the burden of imposing her values and norms on the resolution of problems and dilemmas, and how people go about solving them or when to end therapy.

This is, of course, the 'ideal' way of working for the experienced brief therapist in settings where there may be no precise limit on the number of sessions available to clients. Operationally, however, many work settings do impose such limits (such as in the NHS) and it may be useful to convey to the client that between six and ten sessions (with ten being the upper limit) may be needed. To have a framework for the number of sessions and to share this with the client from the start of therapy may be beneficial for both the therapist and the client for several reasons, as we discuss in more detail in Chapters 7 and 8:

1. It is containing for both the therapist and the client. It provides a real, rather than imagined, boundary. This contributes to a sense of emotional safety and containment;
2. Working within a set number of sessions requires a serious degree of discipline that contributes to keeping the therapeutic process 'on track' and focused;
3. The therapist can increase her awareness of change (or lack thereof) in the client and his problem by more closely and more frequently monitoring therapeutic process; and
4. The client is recruited into the decision-making process of and within therapy.

In our view, it is ethical for the therapist to actively work towards making herself redundant in the client's life as early as possible. Therapy is foremost a clinical matter and the therapist is duty-bound to justify her assessment of the problem and the nature of the length of therapy needed to overcome this. However, provided that the therapist acts in the spirit of 'doing the least for maximum gain' with the client, at least until a revised assessment of the problem is made, there is less chance of an accusation being levelled against her that she is guided by her entre-preneurial spirit rather than by due professionalism. One 'golden rule' of business 'never let your customer live without you' also infers, though unjustifiably, that the therapist knows more about the client and his problems than the client knows himself. This is an untenable viewpoint if the therapist strives to work collaboratively with the client. Where the therapist conveys need through lengthy contracts with the clients, this may invert the balance in the relationship that the therapist is trying to foster and therefore may indirectly subvert change. From this point of view, issues of time are secondary even when working briefly. The client will be assigned as much time or as many sessions that are necessary for him, within the resources that are available. Whilst issues of time become *paramount* in working briefly, they do not *dominate* the therapeutic process. The most significant theme of establishing a real and profound connection with the client – within the time constraints – is what ultimately defines the length of treatment. The client and his needs are at all times prioritised.

While it would be difficult to argue convincingly that 'no-therapy' is therapeutic, research has clearly demonstrated that in some cases even those on a waiting list for assessment and therapy have benefited and even spontaneously recovered (Malan *et al.* 1975). This finding suggests that taking the first steps to solving a problem (i.e. seeking professional help and being referred to a therapist) is enabling and potentially sufficient. Client non-attendance may be far removed from traditional 'resistance' or 'avoid-ance' and instead signal a capacity for self-healing where conditions allow this to happen. Length of therapy must relate to what we hope or intend to achieve. This in turn must be determined by what we discover when we begin to work with the client. All the available evidence from research (Barkham and Shapiro 1990) suggests, however, that many psychological problems can be solved in a short space of time and referral to a therapist can facilitate this, provided the therapist believes such a change is possible. The therapist must also keep in mind that the goal in this context is not to achieve structural personality change or undertake psychoanalysis, but rather to facilitate problem-solving.

Some readers may be interested to know that Freud was probably the first brief therapist of note (e.g. four hours of treatment for the composer Gustav Mahler, and six sessions of therapy to treat the conductor Bruno Walter who had a psychosomatic paralysis in his arm). However, as his theory about personality developed and became more complex, the length of his therapies increased significantly as he sought to learn more about personality through his clinical work. Interestingly, there was no direct relationship between the increasing length of the course of treatment and therapeutic or clinical outcome. Perhaps the lesson that can be drawn from this is: 'keep therapy simple and brief even if your thinking about and around the problem is complex'.

3 Emancipating Therapy

Therapy, as described in this book, is primarily understood in terms of engagement. The competent brief therapist is not a slave to time constraints. Rather, she actively chooses to impose time constraints for the positive contribution that this can make to the therapeutic process, in terms of creating an intensity of purpose, clarity of focus and a heightened awareness of interactional process. All of these processes help to foster engagement with the client. The objective of this chapter is to highlight the need to create a positive and affirming therapeutic environment which, in turn, encourages the client to see himself in a more positive light.

The client must be emancipated from feelings of incompetence if change is to take place and take hold. When this occurs, the client becomes an active participant in the therapeutic relationship. The title of this chapter is intended to convey two points. Firstly, the therapist should aim to emancipate the client. Secondly, the whole therapeutic relationship should be freed from many traditional constraints that pervade some other approaches, as listed in the first chapter of this book. The main task is to engage differently with clients rather than in predictable ways. In this regard, the constraints imposed by a managed care system (where health service managers set a limit to the number of sessions available and possibly prescribe a range of approaches that can be used) can contribute positively to the therapist, insofar as it encourages the therapist to seek new ways of engaging with their clients. Failure to achieve this may inadvertently maintain a negative self-perception within the client with predictable consequences (e.g. dependency in therapy, looking to the therapist for answers, introspection and self-absorption). The therapeutic process is compromised or at least diminished when the primary and only point of connection in the therapeutic relationship is 'the problem', 'pathology' or the 'client's past and what might have been'.

Emancipation of the therapist and her approach to therapy is unlikely to occur early in her training or career. Most therapists who work briefly have many years of clinical experience in the traditional models. Perhaps, an inverse law applies to the practice of brief therapy: to work briefly demands years of experience and intensive training. By the same token, the practise of long-term therapy can more easily accommodate therapists who are learning to practise as well as those who approach therapy from the perspective that 'more is better for the client'. Experience brings the recognition to some therapists that:

- Whilst interesting, and at times extremely valuable, longer-term therapy can stabilise the client and therapist in an entrenched pattern in which efforts to bring about change may inadvertently be hampered;
- Traditional approaches to assessment and treatment of psychological problems place an undue burden on the therapist to be the expert in problem-solving, and in coping with and managing the complexities of human relationships;
- The way in which the client and therapist engage from the very start sets the tone for how therapy proceeds; collaborative engagement is favoured by brief therapists over a client–expert relationship; and
- The mental health fraternity has a powerful collective voice. Seeking to do things differently (e.g. work briefly) might invite hostility and criticism from those who hold firm views about therapeutic practice. To cope with a measure of alienation and invalidation as a therapist demands a high level of personal and professional resourcefulnes. Advanced training and supervision in brief therapy, coupled with peer support, helps the therapist to manage her own 'internal' changes.

The therapist herself must be respectful of the client's difference and uniqueness, and his ability to address and solve other problems in his life. She must strenuously resist any conscious or indirect pull to invalidate the client. This demands in the therapist an ability to tolerate high levels of uncertainty and unpredictability. In order to overcome a 'normal' urge to settle any anxiety within herself stemming from the need to recover a sense of order and predictability in the therapy, the therapist will first need to acquire a level of confidence and competence in a wide range of therapeutic relationships. Risks are more likely to be taken in therapy (i.e. moments seized or corners cut) where the therapist feels secure in herself as a person and is comfortable improvising and working collaboratively. This is more likely to happen after the therapist has accrued a reasonably wide experience and perhaps not until many years into her career.

THE FIRST ENGAGEMENT IN THERAPY

It may take a significant amount of experience in one's clinical and personal life to recognise that change sometimes comes about quickly. In many therapeutic situations, such a belief and expectation can be powerfully self-fulfilling. It is essential, however, to engage differently with the client to that which 'normally' happens in therapy. This difference must be established from the point of first contact if the client is to have the first glimpse of his 'emancipation' in therapy, rather than for the therapist to 'spring into action later on and at the right moment' once the therapeutic alliance has been firmly and convincingly established. Even casual social chat when escorting the client along the corridor from the waiting area to the consultation room can be seen as an opportunity for some interaction and engagement.

Traditional approaches to therapy assert that therapy begins after a formal face-to-face assessment session with the client. More recently, some therapists have taken the view that therapy begins once the client is seated in the consultation room with the therapist. There is yet another variant on this theme which is consistent with a brief approach to therapy. We view the start of therapy as long before the client arrives for his first appointment (we expand on this point in Chapter 5). Indeed, the process of therapy (i.e. exploring ideas and options for change) starts when the client begins to consider the need for 'expert' help in problem-solving. Even at the point when the client and therapist are not formally established in a collaborative relationship, important things are already happening to the client that have a significant bearing on his emerging views and expectations of therapy. This is irrespective of whether he has been referred to the therapist (e.g. by doctor or teacher, etc.) or he has sought therapy on his own. The client will already be considering some of the following before he has even arranged an appointment to meet with the therapist:

> 'Is this a problem I can deal with on my own, or do I need the help of a therapist?'
> 'I wonder if therapy might help?'
> 'What might I expect to happen in therapy? How might it proceed? How might I be left feeling about what happened?'
> 'What will I talk about?' What if I don't like the sound or tone of the therapist? How will I manage silences?'
> 'What about my past do I need to try to recall in case she asks me about it?'
> 'What if I cry or if I feel worse than before I went to the therapist?'

Already, the client has started to process thoughts both about his expectations and possible doubts about therapy, and his problem. This, of course, assumes that he comes from a culture where there is such a thing as 'therapy' in the traditional Western sense of the term. Some of these expectations may have been aroused by prior experience of therapy or that of another friend or relative. For others, common stereotypes or powerful media representations might have triggered these and similar thoughts. It is reasonable to assume that in many Western cultures, clients generally expect therapists to be experts, to ask about early experiences in life and childhood, and to either interpret utterances or facilitate expression (e.g. 'uh-huh', or 'can you say a bit more about...'). Many will expect to have to engage in extended work with the therapist, possibly over many years. The perception may also be that therapy is emotionally painful and an ordeal whilst the therapist is viewed as a powerful figure.

Before contacting the therapist, the client has probably considered these stereotypes, even if fleetingly. The more emotionally distressed the client and the greater his 'problem', the more likely he is to accept these stereotypes and that he 'needs' therapy if the problem is to be overcome. Before the client even first makes contact with the therapist, a number of assumptions about psychological therapy will therefore have been made and gone unchallenged. Working briefly in therapy requires a different approach to engaging the client and demands that the therapist indirectly or even directly address some of these stereotypes and expectations. The three main points to be addressed in a brief referral (intake) telephone call with the client are as follows:

1. *Therapy must emancipate the client even at the point of first contact.* This process begins during the first encounter and is powerfully conveyed through the tone of the therapist, what she enquires about (and specifically chooses not to enquire about) and gives a small 'taste' of what the client is likely to encounter in a face-to-face session. Indeed, the act of speaking to the client before the session and asking about how he came to contact the therapist might help counter the stereotype or perception of a distant, somewhat rigid professional who maintains boundaries by not having telephone conversations with clients. The message might also be conveyed that while therapy is serious business, it does not have to be interminably painful. The client must come away from this brief phone call with a sense of hope and relief from some of the anxiety associated with encountering a therapist for the first time;
2. *Therapy is collaborative.* The relationship is professional but relaxed, the client needs to experience and hear this for himself; the therapist also needs to hear the client for herself and to make a preliminary assessment as to the nature and severity of the problem. No amount of referral information (e.g. letter or phone call from the referrer) can adequately convey this in a way that is meaningful for the therapist; and

3. *Every moment counts in therapy.* Some conversation is needed to understand how and why the client is seeking therapy and whether any (mis)perceptions need to be addressed before meeting.

The therapist might specifically enquire as to how the client came to choose the therapist, whether this was of his own volition or whether he was referred, what expectations, if any, he has of therapy and what he has already done to solve or manage the problem. Seeking out a therapist might indicate a loss of personal competence for the client as he has had to take the problem to an expert for solving. Instead, this feeling can be redressed by responding to the request for therapy as an act or measure of the client's resourcefulness. It can be very helpful to make this explicit with the client.

Possibly at no other time in the course of the therapy will the choice of actual words or tone used by the therapist on the telephone have quite as significant an impact on the client and the therapeutic relationship. For this reason, the therapist must take special care to be both professional and warmly engaging, without allowing the telephone conversation to emerge as the way forward in therapy. The induction conversation is but preparation for the face-to-face conversation(s). Warmth and respect can be powerfully conveyed to the client in seemingly inconsequential ways. For example, before asking the client to say why they are seeking therapy at this point, the therapist might briefly enquire:

'Are you free to speak now?'

This conveys respect for the client's need for privacy and also gives the client a choice in the matter. A number of orienting questions can then be asked of the client. The client might also experience relief on hearing the therapist suggest:

'Would you like to meet for an initial consultation?'

This frees him (and the therapist) to make an informed decision as to whether more therapy will be warranted and whether the rapport between the two is indicative of a positive working alliance. This also gives the client a choice which is an important intervention and conveys a message of collaboration. Even more significantly, it introduces the possibility that a single session of therapy might suffice. Collaboration is introduced by adding:

'At the end of the session, we can see what is needed and what is best for this problem.'

The emphasis is on 'we' or on a partnership in solving the problem. The message conveyed is that there will be two experts in the consultation room rather than one; namely, the client and the therapist. At the end of this brief telephone discussion, the therapist can consolidate her initial efforts to create a positive experience of therapy by stating warmly:

> 'I look forward to seeing you on Monday at 2 pm.'

This initial telephone conversation might then be followed up with a short letter to the client reiterating what has already been agreed between client and therapist, and paving the way for the first face-to-face meeting. For example, a letter sent to inform the client of the time and date of the initial meeting may include the following sentiments:

> Your appointment time is 2:00, Friday, September 5, 2010. In order for us to make the most of our limited time working together, please take a moment before our meeting to think about what you would like to achieve during that time...

or

> The number of sessions we will have will be limited. As such, I have enclosed a few questionnaires for you to complete which may help you to organize your thoughts before our meeting and for me to make a better assessment of your situation...

or even

> You may expect us to meet for one to six sessions, depending on the issues we discuss, as this is the time granted to us by your employer's programme. I am confident that you will find such time beneficial...

Giving an upper limit of sessions, as in the last example, is helpful in our experience. In this way, the client understands the maximum amount of time he will meet with the therapist but also understands that this time may be less.

This initial telephone encounter and optional letter pave the way for a different first face-to-face therapy session or consultation. A wide range of issues might be covered with the client, especially in the first session. Further assessment of the client's suitability for a brief therapy approach is necessary. This is a challenging task that must be blended with building rapport, hearing the problem and responding to the client's expectations of therapy. Given the complexity of these tasks, we devote a whole chapter to this crucial stage of therapy (see Chapter 5), and also examine the structure of the session in Chapters 7 and 8. In the following section, we introduce some of the important issues about engagement and dealing with client expectations within the first session.

Some issues in therapy are explored through questions, and the initial stages of therapy are highly conducive to the therapist's receptive openness and curiosity. By way of introduction to the first brief therapy session, readers might wish to consider the following questions (Box 3.1) that

---

Box 3.1   Orienteering the Client to Competencies and Solutions

'What made you decide to come today?'
'What is the smallest amount of change or progress that you would need to see in order for you to feel that things were moving ahead?'
'Can you tell me about a challenging situation which you think you handled well, and in a way that made you feel good about yourself?'
'What might your close friends/family/boss/teachers say about you and how you handle difficulties?'
'How have you managed to keep things going in your life in spite of these challenges and problems?'
'You have described things clearly from how you see the problem and how you feel you have tried to manage it. How might someone else who knows you view or interpret what you have just described?'
'How did you manage to "read" and understand that awful situation you described so clearly?'
'From how you see things, and as I understand it, you don't see much future in that relationship. What might you gain from moving away from it?'
'Have you been noticing and watching out for those times where you didn't feel so anxious and managed to go to the supermarket? Tell me about the exceptions you have noticed to this problem?'
'Who else was pleased to see you act so decisively in that situation?'
'What will you need to do to maintain and consolidate these changes that you have described to me today?'
'How do you describe the problem to yourself?
'Does this problem make you feel any less about yourself?'
'Who has stood beside you as you face up to this problem?'
'I assume you have been having conversations in your mind about this problem. Is this the first time you are 'going public' about it?'
'How has our conversation so far helped you to think differently about (a) yourself and (b) the problem?'

have been put to clients in real therapy sessions (these questions illustrate the dynamic of an actual session):

Readers who have some knowledge of brief therapy might be familiar with the orientation of these questions and appropriately attribute certain aspects of them to other therapists who have written about solution-focused approaches (e.g. de Shazer 1985, 1988; O'Hanlon 1998; White and Epston 1990; White 1995). The links that can be drawn from these questions (and related) and guide brief therapy practice are as follows:

- The questions are oriented towards perceptions and experiences of problem, rather than some objective reality; they acknowledge that there are differences in perceptions rather than norms that should be conformed to;
- They are mostly prefaced with 'how', 'what', 'help me to understand better...' rather than 'why'. The aim is to facilitate conversation about perceptions and not to discover the 'true cause' of the problem;
- The orientation is towards future and a hypothetical situation when the problem is overcome; it is also towards outcomes and solutions;
- The client is viewed as being confined by the problem, but not defined by the problem;
- There is a clear interest in how the client is coping and managing in spite of the problem;
- The therapist defines the client as knowledgeable, resourceful, capable and able to cope;
- A main focus is on active contribution to solving the problem; that is what can be done and achieved. It is also a goal-oriented discussion towards a positive outcome for the client; and
- The therapist is non-judgemental, non-pathologising and co-operative; she facilitates the client in building a positive and helpful description of himself.

It is tempting to dwell on the client's deficits and processes in therapy, as this forms the basis of many of the traditional approaches currently used in clinical practice. Brief therapy approaches, however, as we have stressed, draw more on the client's skills and resources. Whilst some exploration of the client's problem is necessary and appropriate, the amount of time spent on this and consequently the emphasis given in therapy is noticeably less than in traditional therapies where much greater emphasis is placed on exploring the client's problems and distress. Furthermore, the way in which the therapist explores the client's problem with him also differs in certain respects.

Rather than starting the session by asking: 'What is your problem?', the therapist shifts the emphasis to the client's needs and casts them in an active role in problem-solving from the outset. This may be achieved by asking instead, 'What were you hoping to achieve for yourself in deciding to come for this consultation today?' or 'What are your hopes for this discussion?' Most clients then choose to talk about their problem from the point of view of trying to overcome it. What is important is for the therapist to listen carefully to (a) the client's description of the problem, (b) the verbal and non-verbal clues that convey the client's experience of or attitude towards having the problem (e.g. 'exasperated', 'defeated', 'puzzled', etc.) and (c) attempted solutions to the puzzle thus far. Logically, the next stage for exploration with the client is to gain an understanding of what expectations he has about the problem and what thoughts he may have about it (also, see Chapter 8).

Posing questions to the client about what he would like to see changed, the minimum amount of change that is required to create a sense of hope and direction, and how he would feel having less of the problem helps to lift up therapy from the more problem-saturated discussions that are characteristic of longer-term approaches, especially when making an assessment. This alternate emphasis in exploring the problem is maintained by enquiring about a problem-free future with the client. Exploring the client's ideas about how he would view himself and his situation without the burden of the problem invites him to consider an alternate solution to one that might otherwise be dominated by the problem. The client might then be asked what he feels needs to happen in order to achieve or attain these changes. A major emphasis in the conversations that follow is on the client's expertise and competence in solving problems generally, and similar ones to the one presented, specifically. Assuming the client has solved many other problems in his life, it is necessary to enquire about and explore the possible reasons for why the client has yet to overcome the presenting problem. This relieves the therapist from taking up a role in which she has to generate or offer a 'better' solution. The broader question or challenge for the therapist then becomes one of how she can help the client to restore his usual problem-solving abilities. This may extend from reassuring the client that he is doing the best he can under his circumstances to helping to dispel feelings of shame, belittlement or hopelessness that the client may express or convey in having the problem.

A summary of hints for emancipating therapy, which are also explored in more detail in Chapter 7, is presented in Box 3.2.

Box 3.2   Hints for Emancipating Therapy

- Be engaging; be empathic;
- Work hard at engaging the client in the process; intensity of relationship is of greater relevance than duration;
- Remove blame; free the person from feeling entrapped by the past/his misdeeds/complaints/misunderstandings;
- Validate experiences; never disqualify the client's feelings and avoid pathologising him;
- Build up complexity; where things appear simple, invite the person to view things differently;
- Simplify things; where there is great complexity, and much detail, work with simple ideas and set small, achievable goals;
- Be aware of alternate or complementary stories of problems; seek out accounts of competence and deeds fulfilled;
- Reframe experiences; based on what you have heard, offer alternate ways of understanding events and situations;
- Be creative; perfectly reasonable solutions might come from unexpected sources or from outside of conventional frames used by therapists;
- Focus on the present and future more than on the past; project the client into a hypothetical future;
- Work collaboratively with the client and others (where appropriate); this is respectful and always welcomed by clients;
- Avoid practising as the stereotypical therapist! Create a sense of adventure and curiosity by being unpredictable;
- Learn to work comfortably with uncertainty and unpredictability; brief therapy involves improvisation and taking the lead from the client;
- Be willing to give feedback; to share openly what you are thinking can relieve anxiety in the client and help to engage him; and
- Check out perceptions of progress with the client.

As the client begins to think about himself differently and consequently feels differently about himself and his situation, new possibilities arise for solving the problem. In this way, the brief therapist's role is probably most relevant at the start of therapy. There is every chance that the problem can be solved or managed by the client himself without the need for the extended and intense involvement of the therapist. Put in another way, brief therapy is 'front-loaded' with careful and focused discussion that, from the outset, alters the client's feelings about himself and having the problem. Once he is reminded of and acknowledged for his competence in problem-solving, solutions become possible and accessible. The ultimate goal for the therapist is to make herself redundant to the client in the briefest time possible. Longer-term therapies run a slightly greater risk of not only stabilising the therapist–client relationship, but also stabilising the client's problem. The process in long-term therapy can sometimes, therefore, inadvertently be counter-therapeutic. Box 3.3 summarises the main steps taken in brief therapy sessions.

In the beginning phase of therapy, the conditions are laid for the therapeutic relationship. Effort is directed at engaging the client, developing a working alliance, setting objectives and addressing misconceptions. The client has his first glimpse into the session of the possibilities ahead. The collaborative relationship is beginning to be established and client competence is enthusiastically highlighted. In the middle phase, attention shifts to the problem at a deeper level, the meaning or consequences of having the problem for the client, and restoring the capacity and confidence for problem-solving. Seemingly unrelated issues may also have to be dealt with during this phase. For example, the client might be waiting intently to be questioned about his relationship with his mother, or be wondering whether the comfortable sofa doubles as a bed used for free associating. His own experiences or fantasies about therapy will be aroused and might need to be carefully addressed in order that the client understands how the therapy is likely to proceed. In the ending phase, the points covered should be summarised and the client's experience of the meeting explored. This is also the point at which the client and therapist together

---

Box 3.3   Steps in Brief Therapy

1. Each session has a beginning, middle and end phase; single session therapies follow the same structure;
2. Discuss the client's expectations of therapy and set outcome objectives;
3. Pose questions to the client that convey a sense of possibility about solving the problem and emphasise that his active role is changing;
4. Rapidly re-establish his confidence and competence in solving problems;
5. Utilise the client's experience in solving problems;
6. Validate the steps taken by the client to solve the problem and, if appropriate, leave him to solve the problem, while making yourself available to review progress or new difficulties;
7. Resist the urge to 'accompany' the client at all stages of problem-solving, as might be the case with traditional long-term therapy. He will hopefully seek further support if this proves necessary.

plan for the future. For some clients, a single session will suffice, while for others, follow-up will be necessary. Where follow-up is indicated, it is sometimes better to resist the pull to contract for a set number of sessions, but rather to review progress at the end of each subsequent session. A course of therapy then becomes a series of one-off therapies, with the exception of having to completely re-engage with the client each time. This degree of flexibility in sessions is consistent with the underlying tenet of brief therapy: there is no script to follow and certainly no predetermined method to solve the problem. For example, in a second session the therapist might be faced with the challenge of exploring with the client his internalised sense of failure that the problem has not been solved as he expected, rather than the contents of his mood diary or other 'homework' tasks. The moment when change becomes most possible can seldom be predicted, though we have found that it is more likely to occur when therapy is collaborative and affirming. Hence, a genuine collaborative atmosphere is cultivated in the brief therapeutic environment. This translates into the therapist explaining the reason behind many of the interventions, questions and/or exercises chosen by the therapist. For example, a therapist using a cognitive-behavioural approach may explain:

> 'Sam, I want to ask you to keep track of some of your thoughts over the next two weeks, especially those that occur at the time of any panic attacks. You see, often the thoughts that we have unknowingly add to the stress we may be experiencing physically. So the reason behind tracking these thoughts is that we may be able to then work together to manage these thoughts and to ultimately foster a more resilient coping style.'

A therapist with a special interest in families and systems may precede an exercise with:

> 'So often, the problems we face in our life are maintained through the various verbal exchanges we have with our friends and family – in the language, in the tone, even in the body language we use. As such, I'd like for us to model an exchange that you may have with your partner over this issue. In this way, we may be able to uncover some of the patterns of communication that are contributing to your difficulties and we may be able to discover new ways to approach this situation.'

A therapist working from within a humanistic perspective might begin a line of questioning with:

> 'Jess, when I hear you talk about the challenges you are facing at work, I seem to hear a lot about what other people expect of you. I am

concerned that you might be neglecting your own feelings about the situation. As such, if it is OK with you, I'd like for you to close your eyes for a moment and focus solely on your feelings over this issue, and then I'd like to ask you a few questions which I hope will help you to focus even more on what is important to you. Often people are so overwhelmed by the expectations and demands of friends and family and co-workers, etc. that over time we get confused about what we truly want. I think this exercise will help us to re-establish that.'

No matter what one's theoretical orientation, the relationship between client and therapist when working together needs to be collaborative and as such, the power difference inherent in all therapeutic relationships will begin to diminish. Power is continually being handed to the client to enhance client competence in this context. The client becomes a driving force in the process of therapy rather than simply a participant. In this way, the conditions are set, or re-established, for self-healing and self-sufficiency. With a more limited time frame, the goal of care must become client autonomy.

The greater collaboration between client and therapist and the immediate problem orientation of therapy will greatly affect its course. Both may be enhanced by frequently requesting feedback from the client. For instance, when introducing the time landscape to the client, the therapist might request the client's feelings about it:

'I know that many clients I have worked with have initially expected a longer course of therapy, but I was wondering how you felt about it?'

Therapists must be ready to address any concern raised by the client. Feedback is beneficial to the client and therapist especially when it is used to positively direct the course of therapy:

Elan: Actually, it makes me kind of nervous. I mean, I've always thought therapy was a long-term thing so I guess I kind of figured I'd have a long time to sort out my feelings.

Therapist: You know, I think that is a perfectly natural reaction and expectation to have. Yet, how would you feel if we were able to sort out your feelings in less time?

Elan: Well, that of course would be great. I guess I just feel like 'the pressure is on'.

Therapist: Yes, I can see it feeling a bit pressured, but remember just because we have ten sessions doesn't mean that we have to have them back-to-back. We have the opportunity to space them out according to the progress we are making. If we feel that more time between sessions will benefit your ability to sort through your feelings then we can certainly do that. Also, we can aim to work hard and in a focused way in our sessions together, and there may even be a bit of 'homework' to keep up the pace between sessions.

For the client who has had some form of therapy previously, one might comment on the difference in length expected this time:

> 'I understand that you worked with Dr. Selim for twenty sessions three years ago. We won't have the liberty of such an extended time together, however I have generally found that if we use our time wisely we can make substantial progress in creating the changes you would like in your life…'

When working briefly, a therapist may also want to inform her client that sessions may not be spaced out at regular intervals as traditionally expected:

> 'To get the most out of our time, we may not meet at a regular slot. Depending on our goals, we may allow some time to pass between meetings so that we can better determine how the changes you make are working for you. Sometimes, allowing 2 to 3 weeks between sessions allows time for you to either consolidate what has been discussed or discover the need to have some new ideas as to how you might proceed. You and I can discuss the options as we go along.'

In every case, time must be addressed with the client. To ignore its influence, is to be irresponsible in one's practice. A client who does not know that he has only four sessions to address his problem may feel like a contestant on a game show who is unaware that he only has ten seconds to answer a question. However unnerving or jarring limited time may seem to a client, it is certainly less problematic to be aware of that time from the beginning than it is to find out that one's next session is the last. It may ofcourse come as a relief to some clients to know that the number of sessions is limited.

When a client is informed, time becomes a tool. A client's feelings about limited time can be impacted by the manner in which a therapist introduces the idea. For example, think about the difference between the following two presentations:

> 'Unfortunately, we only have six sessions to work together, as provided by your insurance company. I do wish we had more time but such is the reality of our situation. However, I am sure we can make substantial progress during this time.'

or

> 'We are privileged to have six sessions to work together, as provided by your insurance company. I am delighted that we will have this time to meet as I am sure that within that time frame we will be able to make substantial progress on the challenges you may now be facing.'

The language used within brief therapy is critical in setting the tone and pace of the therapy. The first presentation frames the limited time as a disappointment to the therapist despite his final optimistic outlook. This creates the belief that the therapist would ultimately have liked more time, *no matter what the presenting problem*. Time then has become a negative factor. Yet, in the second presentation, time is presented as a positive factor. Indeed, from the therapist's language, the atmosphere is filled with anticipation for the time available while the time landscape has been clearly set. Time has thus become a friend rather than an enemy. Gathering feedback will help to keep therapy on track. The therapist should be aware of the client's feelings about time not only when the session limit is introduced but also during the course of therapy:

Therapist: Today, we have reached the mid-point of our time together and so, I thought this might be an appropriate time to take a few minutes to review what we've discussed and to figure out what has been the most helpful so far.

and near its end:

Therapist: As you know, the next time we meet will be our last session. I was wondering how you felt about our time coming to a close and if you had any concerns about it.

Feedback is central to the progression of therapy when working briefly. It is the most direct path in addressing the immediate concerns of the client. As such, besides requesting feedback on time issues, feedback should also be attained for the effectiveness of sessions, exercises, homework assignments and any information that has been given. Even the value of outside resources and support systems should be examined:

Therapist: I know that you have met with Dr Sedat on several occasions and regularly see the nurses to help you manage your illness. How do you find those meetings?

Jay: Helpful for most of the time. Sometimes though I just feel like I am just another 'number' for them to check off on their to do list.

Therapist: Are there certain people or nurses that you prefer to see? That makes you feel less like a 'number'?

Jay: Sure, there's this one nurse, named Betty, who talks me through everything she is doing. I like that because it makes me feel like I am learning more and more about my illness and how to handle it.

The expectations of client and therapist will be different in a brief therapy context. Requesting feedback on a variety of issues is one way for the therapist to help manage those expectations and to make sure that they are in keeping with the present limitations imposed on some work settings. This may be a more direct approach than with which many therapists are familiar. However, the entire engagement style of a therapist may need to be altered to accommodate the evolving demands of modern mental health care.

By the end of the initial consultation at least, the client should have experienced therapy as:

- Respectful of both his problems and his capabilities;
- Accessible and collaborative;
- A relationship in which he actively participates rather than relaxes or languishes;
- Having value, in that every moment counts; and
- Goal directed and purposeful.

Brief therapy is a dialogue, rather than a monologue. The therapist and the client converse equally as in 'normal' conversation. The therapist, no matter how experienced, cannot possibly 'read' or mentally register every nuance or utterance. The conditions within which the client feels comfortable to talk and volunteer his opinion need to be actively created by the therapist. Feedback from the client must also be actively sought within the session from time to time. It is useful to check whether the client is following the direction of therapy, whether the pace of therapy is comfortable, versus too fast or too slow and whether the issues being explored are helpful to the client. Even if the feedback requires the therapist to make certain adaptations to the process, the client will, at the very least, hear the message that his views and feedback are essential for collaborative practice; ultimately this respects the client's needs. The following chapter describes more fully the idea of therapy being conversation. A chapter then follows in which we expand upon assessment of the client for brief therapy and another on the central notion of client competence in brief therapy. The chapters following these describe how to structure therapy sessions.

4 Therapy as Conversation

> Conversation is a meeting of minds with different memories and habits. When minds meet, they do not just exchange facts; they transform them, reshape them, draw different implications from them, and engage in new trains of thought. Conversation doesn't just reshuffle the cards, it creates new cards.
>
> (Zeldin 1998: 9)

Therapy is brief when it becomes collaborative. This idea is based on the simple understanding that work can be done more effectively and efficiently when there are two people instead of one at work. For this reason, this book assigns importance to developing a collaborative relationship between therapist and client. Chapter 6 suggests ways of creating just such collaboration. However, the fact that a therapist sets out to establish a collaborative relationship is not the same as being successful in that task. A critical question to consider is: what is the hallmark of collaboration? How does one know when therapy actually becomes collaborative?

Therapy happens in language. This chapter considers the assumption that the moment that monologue becomes dialogue, or put differently when talking becomes conversation, therapy becomes collaborative. Thus, from a postmodern perspective this is the point at which therapy becomes therapy.

To talk is at the heart of therapy. How many times have you heard someone say or have said to yourself, 'I never realised that until I said it'? Talk comes before thought (Anderson 1996). Traditionally, the context of therapy is understood as a place where the client comes and talks through his distress and is listened to sympathetically. This process is believed to have a therapeutic effect. When a client talks through his problem, his talk is often a monologue, with the therapist making a few interjections. The client has to organise his thoughts in such a way that they make sense for the therapist to understand. During this process, the client's understanding of the problem can change. He may begin to feel more in control as opposed to being overwhelmed by his distress. However, talk as such 'does not necessarily change one's own or other people's feelings or ideas' (Zeldin 1998: 1). Indeed, the fact that talk in the therapeutic context happens does not mean that a therapeutic effect has been achieved. Therapy is more than talk or mere monologue. From a postmodern perspective, therapy is an interactional process expressed in language. This chapter endeavours to explain, identify and illustrate through the use of case vignettes, the moment that talk or monologue becomes an interactional dialogue, or put otherwise, a conversation.

Lest this notion sounds strange or complex, it may be helpful at this point to state that for the alert and perceptive therapist, the moment in the therapeutic process when talk turns to conversation is usually not difficult to recognise. Such a moment is not a special kind of occurrence different to what happens in everyday conversations. The client may become more alert and animated. His stance may become more upright. This can be accompanied by direct eye contact being made by the client or the client may actually look away. A renewed focus and clarity of thinking is normally present. The language the client uses may become more accurate, intense and focused. This moment is frequently accompanied by a verbal response from the client, such as 'You're right', or indeed, 'That's it' or 'Hey, I never thought of it like that' or a moment of silence may occur.

The primary characteristic of the moment talk turns into conversation is the moment of mutual engagement of both client and therapist. The characteristics described above in terms of the client can be equally true of the therapist. Present to both client and therapist is a sense of mutual sharing, creative thinking and above all a sense of enjoyment in the mutual genuine connectedness of this moment. This can occur even if the exchange is in the context of emotional pain. It is this sense of sharing or deep connectedness that is at the heart of therapy as understood in this book.

A profound listening to the other characterises a conversation that flows. Both partners are alert to each other so that cues as to when to interject or finish are received and understood by the other. As the conversation develops, new meanings are constructed depending on the responses of one participant to the other. The expertise of both partners is being utilised. More is then accomplished. It is in the response to the other's response that newness arises (Gergen 1994).

Case Example: Barbara

Barbara, married for 21 years, came on her own to therapy to discuss her relationship with her partner. When the therapist asked her whether she would like her partner to be present at counselling, she hesitated. The question provoked Barbara into thinking about why she had come on her own, without her partner. This led to the reflection that what she wanted was time out from her relationship rather than more time within it. For her partner to be present at the sessions would have been more of the same. The above question had been posed by the therapist as an invitation for consideration. It seemed an appropriate question to ask as the problem presented for therapy was the relationship between both partners. The question triggered the realisation that what Barbara wanted was to explore herself as a separate human being. The decision to do this put the remainder of the therapeutic endeavour on a different track.

Bateson's incisive citing of the phrase: 'the difference that makes a difference' (Bateson 1972: 45) can be understood afresh when used in terms of the therapeutic conversation. The therapeutic task may be understood in terms of voicing appropriate responses or asking questions in dialogical exchange. It also includes an acute sensitivity to the effect of any intervention on the client. This is in fact a specific skill. To notice, at any given moment in therapy, the client's response to what has gone before is a skill which is often given scant mention in therapy training manuals. This sensitivity on the part of the therapist to the responses of the client and responding in turn to the times when the client manifests signs of a deeper engagement is frequently what shifts talking into conversational mode. It is the responsibility of the therapist to notice when the client is being different. The client cannot do this for himself. After all, not being different is what makes him a client. In the conversational process, the client may display both verbally and non-verbally signs of the difference that are apparently out of his reach.

As described above, such an expression of difference may last for just a fleeting moment manifested only perhaps by a moment of silence, or there may be a pause in the flow of the conversation, or the client's attitude may change. He may become alert and animated and sit more uprightly as already suggested. His breathing may change; he may grip the arms of his chair. He may begin to say something quite different. Unless the therapist is watchful of such moments and allows them space, they can be missed and opportunities may be lost. Such moments are fragile and may be transitory. If such expressions of difference are noticed by the therapist and addressed, they can gain both definition and significance. They can aid the flow of the therapeutic process and put the dialogical interchange on a different track. These moments arise directly out of the living verbal exchange between therapist and client and can signal a turning point in therapy. This of course is the reason as to why they are being scrutinised here. It was the very moment that Barbara was invited by the therapist to reflect on whether or not she wished to have her partner present that the possibility of difference emerged for her. Barbara stopped speaking for a moment, caught her breath, sat upright and fixed her gaze on the therapist. It was only a fleeting moment, that might have been lost had the therapist not responded, not paused in order to give Barbara's new pose, space. It was a moment of vivid self-awareness for Barbara that led to further pathways of increased self-realisation and self-definition. The therapist invited Barbara at that moment to say what she was thinking,

'I need time out!' Barbara exclaimed in response.

At this moment, Barbara moved from talking about her life, her pain, her confusion to a clarity of vision that projected her into a position of active management of her own life. At that moment, a multiplicity of new possibilities became available to her. Barbara began to talk about her hopes of forming new friendships outside her marriage relationship; embarking on a course of physical fitness and signing up for a college course. Her face and voice had taken on an alertness and energy as she spoke that was new and palpable.

When talk becomes conversation in the therapeutic context, or when client and therapist become co-participants in the dialogical process, we believe that therapy becomes most effective. When such a connection occurs between therapist and client, it is like a shortcut through the many issues that often present themselves and may at times overwhelm both therapist and client. For example, in Barbara's case, much time might have been allocated to exploring such issues that had been identified earlier, including her low self-esteem, feelings of being stifled within her relationship and feelings of emptiness as her children had begun to depart. However, Barbara now imbued with a new energy began to map out alternative pathways for herself in the future. Former negative descriptions of herself became redundant.

Such an approach is also anchored in the time-honoured tradition of an empathic regard for the client (Rogers 1951). Indeed such a deep connection, as described above, between therapist and client can arise only from a profoundly empathic orientation towards the client by the therapist. New possibilities arise directly out of the verbal exchange between therapist and client, which the client on his own cannot reach. New meanings are generated depending on how new expression by the client is treated by the therapist either by privileging it or by ignoring it. If the therapist does not notice or respond to a display of difference on the part of the client, its significance is likely to be lost.

Affirmation and acknowledgement aid growth. As Barbara began to describe her plans for the future, they were given encouragement and validation by the therapist. As the conversational exchange continued, it began to be clear to both Barbara and the therapist that as Barbara's active engagement in her own life grew, her need for therapy reduced. A joint agreement to end therapy earlier rather than later was reached. This is a very logical conclusion as the emphasis in this approach is noticing client difference or put differently, noticing, acknowledging and validating the aspects of the client's life that represent that which he wishes to develop and make grow in his life. Thinking thus, therapy does not necessarily have to be a drawn-out process as it sidesteps unnecessary pathways and does not waste time exploring blind alleys. Such moments as described above are not products of time. They have little to do with a pedantic adherence to a particular step-by-step model of therapy. It is possible for them to emerge at any moment in any session, whatever the model being used. We believe that they are most likely to emerge from a context in which the client feels free to express his point of view without any sense of being judged or censured. The hallmarks of such a context are the positive encouragement of spontaneity and the expression of difference and individuality. This is the opposite of persuasion or coercion. Such an orientation represents an approach to working briefly that is discussed in detail in the introductory chapters of this book.

Case Example: Alison

Sixteen-year-old Alison had a history of frequent and severe panic attacks that had confined her to her home for two years. These panic attacks had begun when her parents divorced, two years earlier and somehow, although the youngest, she had become the family carer. She had the feeling of being burdened and overwhelmed. In response to the question:

'From where do you get your strength to keep going?'

posed by the therapist, Alison sat bolt upright, gazed directly at the therapist and replied

'I don't know.'

Alison's response, although a seemingly innocuous negative statement, embodied the expression and acceptance of her strength, a strength she never realised that she possessed before it was named as such by the therapist. The fact that she expressed uncertainty as to its origins was relevant. The uncertainty implied in the statement 'I don't know' was the first sign of her accepting a different view of herself. Indeed uncertainty of itself is often the herald of difference. Once it had been named, Alison recognised it and began to own it. Prior to this, Alison had only ever thought of herself as weak and without resources. As the conversation progressed and the idea of Alison as a strong person grew, she became more and more animated. At one point she laughed out loud and declared: 'I would never have realised all this about myself if we hadn't talked.'

Such a moment is the moment of excitement in therapy – the moment of real engagement and deep connection between therapist and client. Paradoxically, this moment may also be a moment of separation from the therapeutic context. Alison had moved from the position of being a client to being herself, Alison. This is the moment that makes therapy brief. It arises directly out of the connection that is formed through dialogical exchange. It is the moment that talk becomes conversation. Two people instead of one were at work here. Alison had begun to connect with her own competence, her own self-agency. She was energised and began playing an active part in creating new possibilities for herself. She began to talk about her new college course and how much she was enjoying it; how it represented a new world, apart and separate from the family. As she continued to express herself, a new definition of being Alison grew into being.

The recognition of such a moment by the therapist as significant and pivotal is critical to therapeutic work. When talk becomes conversation, the client becomes invested with dignity and a sense of self-mastery that makes him an equal partner in the therapeutic dialogue (Shotter 1998). In the very moment of verbal connection, the client simultaneously becomes connected with his own competence and paradoxically separates from the therapist. It is through deep connection that disconnection or separation is possible. It results from therapist skill and expertise, when the therapist's attitude is characterised by a real curiosity about the client. The client is invited to consider and express himself differently to the habitual and accepted view of himself. In a very real sense, Alison found herself at the moment of dialogic response. She was able to take on board this new idea of herself as a strong person, which had opened up the possibility of a myriad of new connections for her. She began to think differently about herself. She was not the parent in her family; she was 16 years old, with the excitement of her life ahead of her. Logically too, this moment may well herald the end of therapy – such moments in therapy, if they are attended, make working briefly and profoundly possible. The changes that occur are real and significant.

The intervention on the part of the therapist as described arose from a genuine and empathic response to her client. The therapist was impressed with 16-year-old Alison. It might also be described as intuitive and risk-taking. It was an intervention that put the therapeutic endeavour on a new plane. Once one becomes watchful of the difference manifested in the client, it begins to be easy to recognise the moment when talk becomes conversation. As in the case of Barbara and Alison, at a certain moment both became visually more animated. Their words became clear and fluent and they changed positions from being clients to masters of themselves in their own lives. This change happened through the therapeutic dialogue. It can only happen when there is a genuine connection between the client and the therapist. It is in the therapist noticing the change and naming it that it is brought into being and given definition. It is usually too difficult for the individual to do this alone. This is the work of therapy as understood from a postmodern viewpoint. It is essentially a two-way process. Therapy happens within a relationship expressed in language. The client cannot do therapy as such for himself.

Case Example: Stella

Stella was a 25-year-old professional woman with a history of childhood abuse. During the first interview she recounted the experience of being abused as a child. Whilst she talked, Stella assumed a foetal-like posture. The therapist noted that her gaze was averted. She sat on the edge of her chair with her arms clenched tightly around her. She spoke hesitantly. As she began to retell the story of the day she walked into her home and announced to her family that she had decided to leave, Stella's body language changed entirely. She unclenched her arms, assumed an upright pose and looked directly at the therapist. She clearly recounted the events of that afternoon.

Before the end of the interview, the therapist commented on both body postures and expressed the view that the change in body positioning and the assertive pose Stella had exhibited and maintained throughout the remainder of the interview was very striking. She invited Stella to comment on whether she thought that the changed body pose was significant. This intervention turned out to be the turning point in the therapeutic encounter as Stella was later to reveal to the therapist. Stella felt that it had contributed to placing the story of the abuse in its correct, current context. The current context was that Stella had become a strong and independent woman. The fact that this had been noticed and acknowledged by the therapist was of vital importance to Stella. She was not being perceived only as one who had suffered. It had restored a balance to Stella from seeing herself as an abused person to someone who had at one time suffered abuse but who had picked herself up and got on with her life. It was the act of noticing that had given the revelation an 'entity' or definition, a reality that could be used by the client.

Stella's pain was not ignored. Indeed it had been responded to – as the client had 'flinched' at the beginning of the interview. It was the client's ability to change from the stance of being in pain to a different stance of alertness and energy that had struck the therapist and was voiced by her to Stella. The therapist invited the client further into the dialogical exchange by asking Stella if she felt it was significant that she had changed her body posture and mode of expression. The client said that in her previous experience of counselling, only her pain as a victim of abuse had been the subject for consideration. This was of course essential work. However what happened here invited therapy to move to a new level. The therapist had taken seriously the client's own description of herself as successful and independent as reflected in her alert and upright pose. This act by the therapist made this therapy different. Stella explained that this challenge to begin to see and talk about herself in terms other than as abused was what excited and engaged her. She began to think of herself as a successful and active professional with exciting options in her life as well as someone who had suffered abuse. Excitement and energy were developed at this point in the conversation. Suddenly the future was being thought about differently. Such energy and excitement is experienced by both therapist and client. It had arisen directly out of the dynamics of the therapeutic conversation.

In a subsequent session, Stella added validation to the change that had occurred in her by being able to recount that a friend had recently asked her: 'How come you are so full of life?' It is essential for the therapist not only to recognise the process whereby the therapeutic conversation gains endorsement outside the therapeutic context but to encourage it by asking questions directly about it such as:

'Has anyone noticed that you are different?'

In the case being described, Stella did this work for herself.

When the client connects with the vitality of life outside the therapy room and gets support and feedback through the normal routine and contacts of ordinary life, then therapy really begins to bear fruit. The service of the therapist can accordingly be withdrawn and therapy can terminate. This is often the significant moment that indicates that therapeutic work is complete. Indeed, there is a case to be made that there is no place for further therapy at this point.

Part of the essential skill of being a therapist is to be able to judge the moment to end therapy in partnership with the client. This skill can be developed when careful attention is paid to the nuances and development of the dialogical exchange as illustrated by the above case examples. What is required of the therapist is to notice the moment the client shifts out of the client position to become an active collaborator in the therapeutic conversation. The moment the client becomes an active participant in the therapeutic conversation is coincident with the moment that he is back in the driving seat of his life. We believe it is important, especially when working briefly, to be alert to this moment. To miss this moment is to not see that the objective of therapy is being approached.

This chapter considers the idea that connection occurs in language and that language is the vehicle of relationships in the therapeutic context. When a client reports on another conversation, during the process of therapy, that has occurred outside the therapy room, it is often wise to consider it carefully. Twenty-four-year-old Cynthia, studying for a Masters degree, was not feeling confident about her approaching examinations. At one point she described a conversation with her tutor in which she had rated herself positively relative to other students in one particular module of the course. At this point in the conversation, Cynthia's whole stance, bearing and facial expression changed. As described at the beginning of this chapter, Cynthia sat up in her chair and made direct eye contact with the therapist. She smiled broadly for the first time in the session when she recollected her remark to her tutor about the other students' failure to pass the statistics paper:

'Statistics is not my subject, yet I passed. The other students must have worked very hard indeed to fail that exam.'

The therapist interjected at this point and asked Cynthia if she had noticed her changed attitude. She had moved in the conversation from an unconfident to a confident stance in relation to herself, even if in the guise of humour. The therapist discussed in some detail with Cynthia how this experience of self-confidence might be useful to her. The therapist enquired as to whether the confident voice adopted by Cynthia might be resurrected and utilised by her at times when she was feeling most unconfident about her impending examinations. Cynthia was pleased with the idea of utilising the positive thinking displayed by her in the course of this therapy session. Her concluding remark was:

'Hey that's quite a funky idea...you know I might just be able to use that.'

THERAPY IS CONVERSATION

The approach described in this chapter differs from traditional psychotherapeutic approaches whose models are prescriptive. This approach is demanding of the therapist in terms of training, skill, experience, focus, creativity and scrupulous attention and monitoring of the variety of expressions of the client. Identification of the skills and endeavours on the part of the therapist that lead to change in the client has implications for the training and supervision of therapists which too often lay emphasis on teaching the model of therapy. Focus is placed frequently on the difficulties experienced in the application of the model. As well as active listening, genuine curiosity and a non-prescriptive attitude, to achieve what is being described here, the therapist must be alert and open to difference. Such an attitude is directly embedded in the therapeutic conversation.

Case Example: Savoula

Savoula came to therapy because she was feeling stifled by what she thought was an overly close relationship with her mother. She was unemployed and had recently experienced a steep rise in her anxiety following an episode of serious illness in her mother. She was terrified and said that if anything happened to her mother she wouldn't be able to cope. She said that she, 'wanted to get herself a life'.

Savoula began to feel better quite quickly. She got herself a part-time job. She signed on for an IT training course. She had begun a relationship with Brian, through a dating agency. 'I've got myself a life', Savoula said at the beginning of the fourth session which was two months since she had begun therapy. She spoke animatedly about the beneficial effects of her relationship with Brian. Marriage had already been mentioned. Savoula was very keen to get married. However, a question eliciting her feelings about married partners being free to have other sexual relationships, posed by Brian to Savoula, had greatly perturbed Savoula. This question had reminded her of earlier anxieties felt when Brian, on another occasion, had described his interest in what Savoula felt were rather dubious sexual practices. The therapist allowed Savoula to voice her anxieties, without comment or interruption. The therapist was aware that this on her part took some restraint. She had experienced some sense of potential danger in this relationship of Savoula's. She was aware that Savoula was inexperienced with members of the opposite sex.

The therapist simply asked Savoula the following question:

'How come you are not so overcome by your warm feelings of affection towards Brian that you are still able to voice your anxieties about him?'

Savoula's response was unexpected:

'I think I'm beginning to believe that I have a mind of my own and that should anything happen to my mother, I might survive.'

This response rather surprised the therapist as there was no obvious logical link between the therapist's question and the client's answer. However, a pivotal leap had been made by the client. Perhaps the understanding of such a leap in the therapist's mind is not always the critical issue. What is critical to track is where the client has arrived.

The therapist continued:

> 'What is it you are really saying when on one hand you describe your feelings of pleasure in the relationship with Brian but at the same time, you express your misgivings about it?'

Savoula responded:

> 'I guess what I need to do is to see this relationship as an enjoyable life experience, not to expect too much of it, and be somewhat on my guard in it.'

Savoula was not so overcome by her emotional response to Brian than she was unaware of the hazards of the situation for herself. Savoula was beginning to think for herself and form sound judgements. She was developing the ability not only to take care of herself even in an apparently tricky situation but to make the best of it despite the risks.

The attitude of self-guardianship displayed by Savoula was a welcome outcome in the therapist's opinion. Savoula was also developing a new self-confidence reflected in her statement about her belief in her ability to survive should anything happen to her mother. This quite unpredictable outcome emerged out of the conversational responses as described above between therapist and client. Much depends on how the therapist orients or positions herself in relation to the client, to allow unpredictable possibilities to occur.

The therapist's attitude is characterised by a profound respect of the client based on the principle that underlies this book that the client is able, resourceful and competent even in distress (Gill 1999). What the therapist needs to do is to attend to the client with great care, to listen to what he says, to notice his demeanour and non-verbal communication, and respond with a genuine curiosity reflected in the use of a questioning approach. In addition, the therapist needs to have the capacity to allow herself to be surprised by the client, indeed to be delighted by the client. The hallmark of the conversational exchange described above is a deep sense of connection that is accompanied by both pleasure and enjoyment in the fresh discovery (or rediscovery) of new skills and resources as they emerge in the client. In the above interchange between Savoula and the therapist, the therapist gives Savoula the time and opportunity to integrate and reflect on the two aspects of her experience of the relationship between her and Brian, which in turn yielded the unanticipated result.

The therapist's experience of this particular excerpt from the therapeutic process between the client and herself was entirely unhurried. Space had been allocated to the client to make sense of her experience in her own time. The conclusions she arrived at were both adult and profound. There was no sense of this process being hurried. This is one of the hallmarks of working both profoundly and briefly. Working briefly does not imply working in haste. Working at a profound or deep level is not a product of time. It did not take a long time for the apple to fall to the ground, an event that according to legend, triggered Newton to construct his scientific theory of gravity!

CONCLUSION

This chapter has attempted to highlight the seemingly unusual notion, but not an uncommon occurrence, that when talking turns into conversation, therapy is at its most effective. Effort has been made to illustrate the detail of this idea through a number of case excerpts. As already stated, there is nothing new or magical about this phenomenon. It happens many times in the course of many conversational exchanges both within and outside the context of therapy. At the risk of repetition, the principles that underlie this chapter are simply that therapy happens in language. The paralinguistic expressions that are part of the therapeutic dialogue, often the precursors of difference, are an essential part of the dialogical exchange. What is required of the therapist is sensitivity, a degree of openness and freshness at every moment in the therapeutic dialogue to be able to receive and respond to the numerous and various expressions of the client and to be able to notice and select those responses in the client that are helpful to privilege. It is the belief of the authors that when the therapeutic encounter does not result in a therapeutic conversation as understood in this chapter, therapy is not happening. It is therefore essential for the therapist to constantly monitor the process of therapy as it reveals itself moment by moment. If active engagement between therapist and client as manifested in conversation is not occurring, it is essential feedback to the therapist which, if ignored, may endanger the effectiveness of the therapeutic encounter. The many and various reasons that contribute to lack of engagement in the therapeutic process are addressed at length in other chapters in this book.

What is being described here is an orientation towards the client that is not dependant on any particular model of therapy. The therapist needs to be aware that it is the reciprocity of the process that is its strength and essence. Out of the dialogic interaction, newness and the experience of something different can emerge. At the very moment when talk becomes conversation, the therapist and the client do not withhold from each other. It is a moment of connection experienced by both. It becomes an experience that has an effect on both client and therapist. Conversation becomes a shared experience.

The qualities required of the therapist, described above and illustrated in some detail in the chapter, are the key to working briefly as considered in this book. Such qualities in the therapist require a degree of humility in order to sidestep the role of expert and to firmly place the client centre stage. This requires skill, choice, experience, commitment and conviction on the part of the therapist.

Once again, our belief is that when true connection occurs between therapist and client in the conversational process as illustrated by the many examples above, therapy is most profound and effective. Therapy allows people to engage deeply in a safe and professional environment. Connecting with another person affirms that we are real and alive. Clients, when they come to therapy, frequently feel isolated and insecure. In a work-driven modern workplace, people often neglect their social lives and sacrifice relationships. To connect deeply and meaningfully with a therapist, even for a brief period, begets a warmth that can be energising and life giving, as illustrated by the preceding case examples. Out of the experience of engagement can come the moment of awakening of the client to a sense of his own competence and resourcefulness. When this realisation takes root in the client, therapy can end, sooner than might have been anticipated. The client is now able to see, be different and assume mastery in his current situation. He sees beyond his problem, and may no longer require the services of the therapist. It can be appropriate to end therapy at this moment.

As already stated, the moment at which conversational connectedness occurs is not, in our experience, necessarily a product of time. It can happen at any moment in the therapeutic process. The point being made here is that to miss this moment, to let it slip by unnoticed, is to prolong therapy unnecessarily. Seizing these moments means working efficiently, effectively and, most importantly, denotes an attitude of absolute respect for the client.

5 Assessment for Brief Therapy

The approach in this book is operationally underpinned by the notion that the client is able, active and resourceful even in psychological distress. Since people react differently to the same challenge or problem, it is always necessary to assess the problem and it's impact on the client. It is also necessary to assess the client's suitability for brief therapy. It must be emphasised that in this approach, the process of assessment is viewed as intrinsically linked to the process of therapy itself (Keeney 1979). This is distinctly different to a linear, medical model approach that is sometimes used in psychotherapy where the client is first assessed within a self-contained phase of the overall contact with the client, followed by therapy designed to 'treat' that specific problem. We have already discussed some aspects of client assessment in the previous chapters. In this chapter, we expand upon these and focus more on the nature, purpose and approach to client assessment for brief therapy, with an understanding that there is some overlap between the ideas contained here and elsewhere in this book.

Our approach to assessing who might or might not be suitable for brief therapy is perhaps more inclusive than most other models. Suitability for therapy is not based solely on the definition of the client's problem, but also on a dynamic process, which includes the client's willingness and motivation to participate in the process of therapy. It is also based on the client's perception of the counsellor and of therapy, depending on the setting in which therapy is provided or previous experience of therapy. A further factor is the therapist's self-assessment of her skills and confidence in dealing with the problem and the particular client in front of her.

Assessment is a two-way process. It occurs from both the therapist's and the client's points of view. The therapist has to make a professional judgement as to whether she can work with the client in front of her. Accordingly, she begins her assessment by engaging in what might appear to be a simple conversation with the client. If the client, from the initial stages of this process, manifests signs that he can freely engage in the therapeutic dialogue, and is at least open to change or improvement, it becomes likely that the therapist will be able to continue to work with this client. From the client's point of view, his assessment of the therapist or therapeutic process is expressed by his continued presence in, or absence from, the therapeutic process.

The therapist's first aims of assessment in and for brief therapy are to find out whether the client (a) wants to use therapy to overcome a problem; (b) is willing to do so within a time-limited and intensive therapeutic relationship; (c) is able to co-establish with the therapist specific and attainable goals for the therapy; (d) has realistic expectations of both the therapy generally and the therapeutic relationship, specifically (see also Weber *et al.* 1985); and (e) that his problem is an appropriate one for therapy. Working in a time-sensitive way defines a new role for the therapist in the modern health care environment. Much as one visits a GP for a sprained wrist and its care, clients can look to the brief practitioner as someone from whom they can seek treatment for a current issue. Moreover, just as a patient may return to his GP long after his sprained wrist is healed for a new problem or even an associated one, so too can the client of a brief therapist return for consultation on a new issue or one related to past treatment. Therefore, therapy may be appropriate for specific issues and problems at different times throughout the client's life cycle. Assessment is therefore not primarily conducted with the aim of discovering some static or enduring personality or state of client, as useful as this might be to the overall process of therapy.

The initial task of the therapist at the start of each new episode of care (as distinct from each session) is therefore to assess and understand the client's problem at that time and, in collaboration with the client, determine how best to address the problem. Therapists today may better serve their clientele by applying the model of doctor–patient relationship to the client–therapist relationship, where a relationship may build up between the two over time and where the door is kept open for future visits. The relationship differs, however, in that the brief therapist is not prescriptive.

A brief therapist may or may not necessarily claim *expertise* in treating specific problems for a particular client (e.g. fear of flying, Post Traumatic Stress Disorder, bipolar affective disorder, etc.), though she may claim specific experience and therapeutic *skills* for dealing with these problems (such as, say, cognitive-behavioural therapy). The therapist's most useful expertise is initially to engage with the client; to hear his account of his problem; to understand what solutions have so far been tried and which have been useful or have failed; to understand how the problem has emotionally affected the client and how best to help restore the client's confidence in himself. This lays the foundation for resolving the problem. The therapist's skills and expertise in treating specific psychological syndromes or problems may well become useful at a later stage in the therapy as an adjunct to the intensive process of engagement and assessment. It is, however, a matter of priority in the approach to therapy outlined in this book, to first form a positive relationship with the client prior to working on solutions to the so-called problem. In our experience, the engaged, intense and collaborative relationship that forms between client and therapist may be sufficient in some cases to restore the client's confidence and competence in solving some of his own problems. Indeed, this might be described as a major objective of this approach.

An understanding and sound training in psychiatrically defined categories of mental health problems is essential to the therapist. It is important, however, not to equate such knowledge with how to practise therapy. Working briefly in therapy is about engaging the client in specific ways so that he becomes an active agent in creating desired changes in his own life. If the client becomes positively engaged in the process of therapy, unrealised or unexpected results may emerge. If clients are simply categorised according to their problem, much opportunity for change may be lost.

We live in a society and practise within professions where there may be excessive use of psychiatric diagnoses. This focus places attention on the pathology of the individual and avoids consideration of what might be an alternate or preferable explanation for the client's problem, thereby reducing the options for 'better' or more creative solutions to problems. While DSM-IV (Diagnostic and Statistical Manual of Mental Disorders) and ICD-10 (International Classification of Diseases and Related Health Problems) categorisations may alert the therapist to possible problems the client may display in his relationships, thinking and overt behaviour, these taxonomies may be of only partial value to the therapist who is assessing a client for brief work. These medical model categorisations give little guidance on how to engage with the client and give scant clues as to the client's motivation to confront and overcome the problem. They offer only limited insight into how the individual relates and forms connections with people and ideas; how he feels about his problem; his unique attributes and limitations; his motivation for therapy and incentive to change; the potential impact the problem has on the client's relationships with others and his self-identity; the relevance of social class, gender, culture, sexual orientation and other demographics to the onset and maintenance of the problem; and trans-generational family patterns relevant to the 'cause' and possibly to overcoming or coping differently with the problem. The client's core beliefs and narratives about himself, the problem; and therapy itself and its possible role in his life at this particular moment are also relevant. All of these are critical to assessing the client for therapy. A multi-layered and systemic assessment is always necessary if the complexities of a client's situation are to be fully appreciated

(Combrinck-Graham 1987). This requires the therapist to work hard at every step of the therapy in order to invite and engage the client to be a part of the therapeutic process. Whilst much emphasis is placed here on how to engage with the client, it is imperative to remember that part of the objective of assessment is to recognise from the outset of the therapeutic process the point at which therapy can or should end. The objective of assessment and brief therapy itself is therefore both to engage with and to prepare to disengage from the client at the earliest possible moment that consolidates the client's feelings of competence and ability to cope.

We do not suggest that formal assessment and psychometrics should be disregarded. However, we need to be reminded in the context of brief therapy that psychometrics is not a precise science and diagnostic categories do not predict behaviour in every situation. Formal assessments should be viewed as only *one reality* or version of the client's problem; they are by no means the only one. Indeed, accepting psychiatric diagnoses at face value without attending to some of the other issues, as previously listed, may deny the client's possibility and hope for the future. This, in turn, brings into question the extent to which it is even ethical to work psycho-therapeutically with a client if their situation is deemed hopeless. The extent to which a problem is even amenable to change in therapy may need to be openly addressed to the client based on current evidence (Seligman 1995). Where problems are deemed 'intractable' or 'insoluble', the emphasis in brief therapy may need to shift to how the client can be helped to cope better with his problem. Formal assessment and diagnosis also places undue emphasis on the therapist as 'expert' creating an imbalance in power in the therapeutic relationship.

A client who has been diagnosed with a psychiatric illness is not neces-sarily always unsuitable for brief therapeutic treatment. Brief therapy for these individuals may be suitable for specific problems they encounter or for crisis intervention. For example, a colleague of ours who works in a psychiatric prison ward was asked to see a client who had been physi-cally abused while in the ward and subsequently suffered from nightmares. The client had a history of being uncooperative with other therapists using an open-ended therapeutic approach designed to help the client resolve issues pertaining to his imprisonment.

Upon the client's arrival at his session with the therapist who chose to work briefly, she simply stated: 'Rather than talk about why you are in the ward, it may be helpful for us to focus instead on what happened to you on the ward over the last few weeks and for us to help you reflect on those events so that you can more effectively cope with them.' This approach with the client was engaging for him. Here was someone who did not want to focus on his past, but who wanted to engage with him in the present, and moreover wanted to help improve his quality of life rather than focus on how he had destructively influenced others. As a result, our colleague found that this client readily engaged with her. They met four times focusing strictly on the crisis at hand. When significant progress had been made, the client was discharged from her care.

This example illustrates a striking feature of brief therapy: it can be used as crisis management or contained problem-solving for a wide range of clients. Psychiatric or clinical diagnosis does not preclude a client's suitability for therapy – brief or otherwise. What contributes to an assessment for brief therapy are the objectives of the client and his willingness and ability to engage in the process. In the above case, the objective was contained (to restructure the nightmares). The client's motivation to work was what made therapy possible.

Evidence-based health care can help guide the assessment of a client's suitability for therapy (Goss and Rose 2002; Sackett *et al.* 1996). However some caution may be necessary in this regard. For example, existing research evidence suggests that the Cognitive Behavioural Therapy (CBT) model is the most effective approach to use when working with clients with some of the more commonly presenting problems to therapists, such as depression, anxiety and phobias. However, the notion that there is a formulaic approach to such problems that automatically guarantees a successful outcome is misguided and does not accord with our experience. The success of the specific model and associated therapeutic interventions also depends on the nature of the relationship forged by the therapist with the client. In fact, CBT relies upon an empathic relationship with the client to be effective. This underscores our point: if the client feels he has been judged by the therapist, misunderstood, pushed to change too fast, prescribed to or simply does not trust the therapist, no amount of homework tasks or carefully kept mood and activity diaries is going to solve the client's problem of anxiety or depression.

CONTRAINDICATIONS TO THERAPY

As we have already stated, it is important that the therapist assesses the client's suitability for therapy. In our experience, it is not possible to do effective time-sensitive therapy with everyone who is referred or requests it. There are several contraindications to therapy, although these cannot normally be properly assessed until one encounters and interacts with the client. The most common problems that interfere with the viability and course of brief therapy are listed in Box 5.1.

There are, of course, other or unforeseen problems that may occur either at the point of first contact with the client, during the course of

---

Box 5.1   Common Problems that Interfere with the Viability of Therapy

1. Those clients whose mental or physical health state prevents them from comprehending the questions that the therapist may pose to them and who are therefore also unlikely to benefit from any therapy while these problems are evident.
2. Those who are not free to enter into a therapeutic relationship (such as clients who are coerced into attending therapy or who find that undergoing therapy is a condition forced upon them, such as by a court of law or as a condition in order to preserve a relationship). This is not to suggest that therapy cannot work with these people, but that the client's own motivation for therapy must become clear otherwise a conflict over the aims of and agenda for therapy may emerge.
3. Clients who have no real motivation to change or who simply do not want to be in therapy, with no particular purpose or goal (apart from, perhaps, 'analysing themselves'); also included are those clients who misuse or subvert therapy and relationships and are not genuine about seeking help.
4. Those whose expectations and previous experience of therapy are rigid and who are not open to a different approach to therapy (some may also have a masochistic side to their personality and only feel that therapy is properly working when they have been 'pathologised'; some may feel 'defrauded' by 'less' therapy; or wish to dwell exclusively on past 'causes' of problems).
5. Clients who cannot relate or engage in therapeutic conversation; this includes those whose cultural or national background is so different to that of the therapist that it precludes them from understanding the therapist, and vice versa.

---

therapy or that only become apparent at the point of termination that are poor prognostic markers for therapy, or prevent a satisfactory outcome from being achieved. By definition, these may not be recognised until much later into therapy or even at the end of therapy and therefore may not be entirely preventable. It is for this reason too that we stress that assessment is an ongoing process. In this way of working, the process of assessment is intrinsic to the process therapy. The alert therapist will be aware that no change is occurring at an early stage and therefore no undue wastage of time and resources need occur. As professionals, we all accept that we will work with some clients with whom therapy ultimately fails. Working briefly is simply not appropriate for every client in every context presenting with any problem. As an approach to working with clients, it is also not the preferred way of working among all therapists. Indeed it is important to stress that if the therapist believes that she cannot work with a client for any reason, then therapy cannot successfully occur.

PHASES OF ASSESSMENT

The list of the key contraindications to therapy helps to shed light on which clients or patterns in relationships may be less amenable to brief therapy. So what exactly is the therapist looking at when she is assessing? It must be restated that assessment is not simply a phase in therapy: it is continuous. For the therapist, it starts when the client first makes contact with her and continues after the client has left the room at the last session and she reflects on the whole course of therapy. For the client, the assessment begins even before he makes contact with the therapist as he will have already made some preliminary assessment about his problem and presumably have felt the need (or pressure) to seek more specialist help to solve it. For purposes of clarity, assessment can be depicted in phases as given in Box 5.2.

The approach to assessment in brief therapy, although apparently simple and naïve, is complex in nature and is centred on processing feedback not only during every session, but at every moment of the therapeutic process. Assessment in brief therapy is embedded in the whole process of therapy.

In the previous chapters, we introduced the idea of therapy being 'a conversation' and how therapy actually works – a topic sometimes overlooked in books about therapy. Only when this process is actually understood can accurate and appropriate assessment occur. The essential feature suggested in this chapter is that therapy is a dynamic and interactional process between therapist and client. If the client can interact creatively and productively with the therapist, as co-partner in the process, then therapy can occur and change should follow. This is the desired outcome. The ability of the client to be actively engaged in the process of therapy is therefore core to the assessment for brief therapy. We now focus attention on those factors that help to assess the client's suitability for therapy. This is presented below in 'phases' of assessment. However, this sequence is presented for purposes of clarity and does not accurately reflect the ebb and flow of 'normal' conversation with a client in the first session. Rather, these ideas are drawn on at appropriate moments and the therapist may choose to 'switch' between topics that aid the assessment and the respective questions that help to effect the assessment.

Box 5.2   Phases of Assessment

1. The client first experiences a problem that he feels he is unable to solve on his own and he starts to consider therapy, or therapy is suggested by someone else, as an option to help him overcome the problem. The client has therefore made some preliminary assessment of his problem either to himself or has disclosed it to another.
2. He then sets about finding out whom he should consult. This may involve talking to friends, family, work associates, his doctor or looking on the Internet in order to find the name of a therapist. The client now assesses his options for therapy; whether this has been his own idea or an idea suggested by another to which he has responded positively.
3. A telephone conversation with a prospective therapist might be his first encounter with someone who is a specialist in dealing with psychological problems; this is obviously the therapist's first opportunity to briefly assess the client and his situation. The therapist may have received information about the client in written form from a referrer. It is also the client's first opportunity to assess whether he has made the right decision – based on what happens in that initial encounter – to approach that therapist.
4. Provided that an initial consultation has been arranged between client and therapist, the face-to-face encounter will permit further discussion and assessment of the problem and the client's motivation for and expectations of therapy; (the therapist's 'normal' assessment of the client's mental state, social and family background, relationships, social conditions, etc. is blended into the assessment for brief therapy. As this is likely to be familiar to most practising therapists, the nature and format of this is not detailed in this book); the client also continues to assess whether the therapist meets his expectations in this first session.
5. During the course of the session and any subsequent therapy sessions, further assessment can be made of the nature, direction and extent of change and whether this meets the expectations of the client and the therapist.
6. At the end of the course of therapy, both the therapist and the client will assess the outcome of therapy; the therapist will then reflect on what has happened in that session as well as in the course of therapy after the session has ended.

Assessing the Client's Suitability for Brief Therapy

Client's motivation to be in therapy: is the client here of his own volition?

The orientation described here is based on a willingness to talk to all clients who seek therapy, perhaps with the exception of certain categories of clients already mentioned. Our understanding is that if a client chooses to talk to a therapist, he wants to change something. This may sound simple, but it is our experience that not all clients who are present for therapy actually want to change. Furthermore, someone else may have referred them. They may have chosen to attend the first therapy session in order not to let down the referrer or with some motive that is not immediately clear to the therapist, or even to the client (Selvini Palazzoli *et al.* 1980). The problem may not even relate to the client although he may be affected by it. Instead, the problem may relate to other systems (e.g. professional or family) with which the client maintains contact (Van Trommel 1983). To elicit the client's motivation and to orient the therapist at the start of the first session, it is common practice to begin with a series of questions about the client's referral and motivation for therapy. These may include some of the following:

'Whose idea was it that you come for therapy?'
'If it was someone else, to what extent do you agree with the referral?'
'What is going on in your life that brings you here?'

If the client replies that it is his own idea, then therapy can begin immediately. For us, this seemingly naïve and simple question is crucial to the process of the therapy that follows. It orients everything that follows.

Part of our remit as therapists is to encourage or augment the client's desire to change, based on an understanding that change might be perceived as difficult for him. Hence, if the client before us implies or states that he is there at the suggestion of another – be it a friend, family member or a professional (such as his doctor) – then the client can be helped to claim ownership of his presence by the therapist asking the client what he made of the suggestion to come to therapy. He can be asked what he thought were the concerns about him that his referrer might have had. These questions are at the core of assessing a client's suitability and readiness for therapy at this particular moment in his life. Such questions can introduce a tone of reality to the therapeutic endeavour as the questions touch on the immediate experiences and beliefs of the client, without 'contaminating' the therapy with discussion about the client's 'problem' from the outset. Indeed, the brief therapist never asks the client at the beginning: 'What is your problem?' as this fixes the conversation and relationship in a 'problem' mode which is not conducive to forming a positive relationship.

To quote Shakespeare's Hamlet (Act 5, Scene 2), 'the readiness is all' is entirely applicable to the process of therapy. If the client is not ready to change, for a myriad of different reasons, therapy cannot occur. This does not, however, preclude some discussion with the client about what conditions would need to be met or established for therapy proper to commence. Of course, the fact that a client is seated opposite a therapist in a consulting room does not mean that therapy is either possible or necessary. The time-sensitive therapist, drawing on a consultative map, will first need to determine whether therapy can start or proceed. In order to do this, a number of points have to be considered. These are set out in the algorithm (Figure 5.1).

What is the client's definition of the problem?
What are the client's objectives for therapy?

Although some client's goals may be vague at first, a definable problem or goal is necessary for therapy to proceed. The task of defining the problem may involve extensive discussion about what the client is experiencing. Normally, the therapist would take a lead in inviting the client to share his feelings and perceptions about the problem. In our experience, identifying the problem, naming it for the client and examining the effects of the problem on different aspects of his life is a core task in brief therapy and should be allocated the time it needs. It should never be rushed. Indeed, it is a process that can take several sessions with the client. The respect and sensitivity that is conveyed through this careful exploration of what is happening to the client is itself part of the therapeutic process in brief therapy. Setting goals immediately begins the work of therapy which is to define and contain the problem, by breaking it down into more manageable stages or tasks. Examples of questions that can be used to help to explore and define the client's problem are:

> 'Can you say what has happened or what you have been thinking about that you wanted to discuss in our session today?'
>
> 'Is this how you want to live, or do you want to live differently?'
>
> 'How has this problem taken a hold on these aspects of your life? And how has it influenced these parts of your life?'
>
> 'What are the effects of this problem on [the client's contexts, such as work, friendships, other family members, school, his community, his identity, etc].'
>
> 'Which aspect of the problem(s) troubles you the most?'

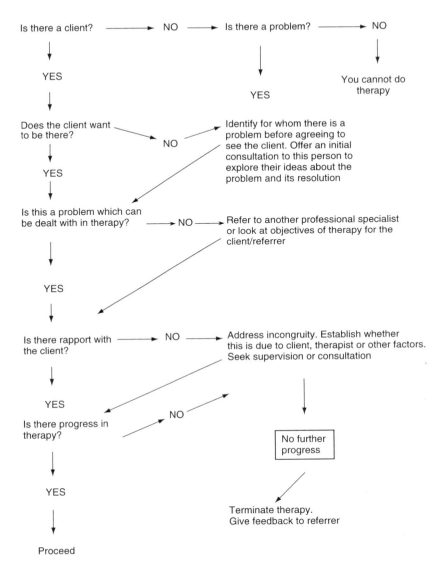

Figure 5.1   Algorithm for Deciding whether Therapy can Proceed

We recognise that some clients may not be seeking exploration of and solutions to specific problems. They may instead be seeking better self-understanding and a more in-depth self-examination. Such self-exploration is admirable and a worthwhile endeavour. If long-term self-exploration is the client's goal, a brief therapeutic approach may not be appropriate. Brief therapy can, however, be useful in helping some clients to prepare for longer-term work by enabling them to clarify their goals and expectations for this, as well as giving them 'a taste' of a therapeutic relationship, without a particular commitment to continue beyond a single or a few sessions. Brief therapy may also be a useful context in which the therapist can better assess the client's personal suitability for longer-term work.

Questions that might be considered in initiating discussion about progress (or lack thereof) at different stages of therapy include some of the following:

> 'Now that we have been talking for 10 (30) minutes, what is your experience of our conversation? What difference has it made to you so far?'
>
> 'How are we doing in therapy? Is this what you were expecting or is it different?'
>
> 'Is this discussion useful to you?...What aspects are useful and what aspects less so?...Can you say why?'
>
> 'Is the pace of therapy too fast; too slow; or about right for you?'
>
> 'You say that you feel unsure as to how helpful therapy has been with this problem. It is really helpful to have this feedback so that we can reflect on what has happened and perhaps we can think about what we can change. Can you say more about what has not been helpful to you?'
>
> 'I am not clear that we are moving towards the goals that we discussed in our last session. I was wondering how you felt about what we have been discussing and whether you might be able to suggest some ideas for keeping on track?'
>
> 'Do you think that trying to change or maintain the problem as it is demands more effort from you? Where do you think that your effort will be most helpfully directed at this stage?'

Feedback on these and similar questions helps both the therapist and the client to assess what has been achieved in therapy and whether more of the same or a different style or approach to therapy might need to be considered. Open discussion with the client about progress in therapy also stresses the collaborative nature of the relationship and reduces the burden on the therapist to carry out all the 'mapping' of therapeutic process and progress on her own.

Using a time framework as an instrument of assessment

Assessment in a brief therapy approach is also linked to the notion of working within a set time framework. Research suggests that change happens earlier rather than later in the therapeutic process (Hubble *et al.* 1999; Miller *et al.* 1997). A practitioner who works in a disciplined way within a time framework of an agreed number of sessions – perhaps between 6 and 10 – has at hand a framework for measuring progress or improvement. If change does not occur in the early stages of therapy, it challenges the therapist to do something different in therapy. This may mean re-evaluating the client's motivation, reflecting on the therapist's skills or revising the definition of the problem. It may also invoke thoughts about the so-called 'client resistance' (see Chapter 11) which may need to be explored and addressed. This review and assessment of progress needs to be an ongoing activity whilst working briefly. The therapist working creatively and actively within time constraints does not wait till the final session to address the fact that no change has occurred.

In traditional psychotherapeutic practice, the client's 'inability' to change is assessed differently. The client is often described negatively. Lack of change may be attributed to client resistance. One consequence of this is that the client may be invited to attend more frequently or the overall duration of the course of therapy may be extended. From the brief therapist's point of view the initial experience of no change occurring acts as an incentive to the therapist to work harder to find ways to connect with the client. As assessment, as we understand it, is a dynamic concept and is not just about the client's motivation and willingness to change. It also includes the skill of the therapist working in a given context, her training, experience, background and her ability to work productively and creatively with a particular client at that stage in the life cycle of that client's problem. Hence, when change is either slow to occur or undetectable, the brief therapist's response to this may be many and varied. It is not simply a question of arranging more sessions for the client. It may be liberating for those therapists who are more reticent about openly discussing progress with their clients in therapy to find that in brief therapy, this is precisely what is encouraged and is viewed as integral to the therapy.

The client's perception of the therapist's role

The client always has some expectations of or ideas about the therapist before they have actually met, based on folklore, stereotypes, previous experience of therapy, information passed on by the referrer, or through an image that builds up in one's mind based on an initial encounter over the telephone. More importantly, the client may have certain expectations of therapy. Some of the more common ones are:

> 'The therapist is the expert; she knows best about this issue';
> 'The therapist will solve the problem';
> 'I will do most of the talking; the therapist will want me to "free associate" and she will interpret what I say to her';

> 'We will meet at a fixed time every week (or several times in a week) for an extended period'; and
> 'I will be expected to talk about my childhood generally and about my relationship with my mother in particular'.

These expectations are not entirely unfounded since, if they were untrue of the experience of most forms of therapy, they would have disappeared long ago. They are clearly appropriate and accurate to some approaches of contemporary therapy. An image that builds up in the client's mind about therapy may be that the therapist is the expert and will solve the problem; the client need only be active in the session insofar as he brings material or content for the expert to analyse and interpret. Therapy in this framework 'works' when the therapist instructs the client or prescribes a solution to the problem.

The brief therapist should obviously not assume that the client holds this view of therapy or the therapist's role. Indeed, a feature of working collaboratively with clients is to avoid making assumptions, explore perceptions and openly discuss with them roles and relationships in order to guard against therapy becoming a hierarchical relationship. Exploration of the client's expectations of the therapist's role is an important aspect of the overall assessment so that misperceptions can be identified and addressed. This need not be a lengthy discussion but rather a few well-placed questions can help to highlight key areas about the client's expectations. The most helpful, in our experience, is a question about the client's previous experience of therapy and how the client views the role of the therapist. Some of the following questions to the client may help to explore these issues:

> 'Have you spoken to a therapist before? Did you find this helpful or unhelpful?'
> 'How do you think talking to me about this problem may help you?'
> 'Who else have you tried talking to?...What else have you tried?... Why do you think this was not successful?'
> 'What expectations did you have of therapy before you came along today?'

The client who conveys through his responses that he believes that the therapist has all the resources and expertise necessary to solve the problem will need to be challenged in this belief, otherwise there is a danger that he will be confused and ultimately disappointed by the process that follows. This can be achieved by exploring with the client concepts and experiences relating to his competence in problem-solving, as previously discussed in this book. Examples of questions include:

'In which other areas of your day-to-day life do you get to solve problems?... What is that like for you?'
'How would you feel about us trying to solve this problem together – drawing on the idea that "two heads are better than one"?'

If the client then persists with the notion that the 'therapist knows best' and renders himself a passive recipient of the therapist's expertise, this will need to be discussed with the client before moving ahead in therapy. Indeed, it is probably a contraindication to brief therapy and indicative of the need for a different approach to therapy with this client. In which case, a decision will need to be made as to whether to adapt the course and style of therapy accordingly, or to refer the client to another colleague.

Working collaboratively with other colleagues and agencies

In the 'world' of health care, we have access to (and are sometimes surrounded by) a wide range of colleagues on whose support we can draw to help us with a particular client and problem. Colleagues can be a resource to therapy and their contribution may be both desirable and necessary to effect change. Sometimes, their presence or contribution helps the goals of therapy to be reached more rapidly.

To practice in a positive and collaborative way with other professionals can increase the range and number of clients with whom we can work, whatever the context in which we practise. The question for the therapist is: 'Can (should) I work on my own on this case, or would it help to involve another colleague?' This is not only a question about the therapist's skills and competence, but also suggestive of the need to monitor the therapist's stress levels about a particular case. If these are too high, because the therapist cannot address every aspect of the problem on her own, help is needed. When working as a school counsellor, the therapist should build links with child psychotherapists, family therapists, remedial teachers, child psychiatrists and other professionals, such as the school doctor and nurse. Similarly, when working as a therapist in a busy GP surgery, there will be colleagues working within and outside the practice with whom cases can be discussed and referrals made.

To work closely and collaboratively with our medical colleagues is important in terms of holistic client care and management. In our experience, the prescribing of psychotropic medication (such as antidepressants and anti-anxiolytics) is sometimes necessary and helpful to effect change. Medication and therapy are not mutually exclusive. Indeed, it may be considered unethical not to raise the issue of the possible benefits of medication with some clients, which the client can then discuss with his doctor. When medication is appropriately prescribed and adequately monitored, it significantly increases the number of clients with which we as therapists can work. Again, with clients at risk, access to doctors and statutory services can create the conditions in which therapy can at least be initiated with clients who might otherwise be unreachable. A range of other services and specialists (such as financial, educational, alternative therapies, skills training, recreational and leisure activities, childcare facilities, etc.) may also increase our capacity to work with clients in therapy and also create the conditions for clients to optimise their participation in the therapeutic process.

It is up to the therapist not only to be knowledgeable about local services that can be directly helpful to the client in her care, but also to be aware of the contribution that others in the client's world (e.g., friends or family members) can play in the client's recovery from distress. To 'recruit' such people into the therapeutic dialogue either directly, or simply by acknowledging or validating their presence or role in the client's life, helps augment the assessment of the client's suitability for therapy. Such awareness directly influences the issue of assessment of clients suitable for therapy.

CONCLUSION

The assessment of client's suitability for brief therapy can be seen to be a complex issue. As we have seen, there are a large number of different factors to be addressed. However, consistent with the approach to therapy described in this book, a simple question can help to orient and simplify the issue: can the client and therapist succeed in having a productive conversation together? If the answer to this question is in the affirmative, it is likely that therapy can take place between that client and therapist at that moment in the client's life. However, since assessment is an ongoing process, the final outcome is never guaranteed and the therapist and client will together need to monitor progress for the duration of the therapy. In this context, assessment will become integral to the therapy. We now turn our attention to validating and reframing the client's experience and then how to organise and structure the first therapy session.

6 How have you Managed to Cope so Well?

Traditional models of psychotherapy are hierarchical and expert oriented. Expertise and competence are assigned to the professional. The implications of assigning competence to the professional means that the professional takes charge of the therapeutic process and assumes responsibility for the client and his problem. As such, the client adopts a position of incompetence and passivity. Likewise, the client assigns responsibility for the resolution of his problem to the professional. This position of the therapist arises from the traditionally held view of the client and the professional that is deeply embedded in the western modern culture and typified in the medical model. The medical model as such has been found to be both valuable and appropriate. If a bone is fractured, the client wants it to be fixed by a competent professional skilled in orthopaedics. Roles are clear and defined. The underlying assumption is that if the client places himself in the hands of the professional, his pain can be ended. Out of this rigidity of thought emanates a whole protocol of professional practice which has had a powerful influence on traditional psychotherapeutic training and practice.

Different approaches and models of therapy abound, frequently underpinned by the belief that the secret of successful outcome lies in perfecting therapeutic technique. The role of the client can often be ignored when assessing therapeutic outcome. The assumption is that the client is inactive and passive, incapable of clear thinking, befuddled by the strength or loss of his emotions, and somehow cut off from his lifetime of experiences, skills and resources. Indeed, frequently he is defined by the nature of the problem he is experiencing. This viewpoint prevails especially today in an empirically driven culture. Much emphasis is placed on techniques utilised by therapists and problem definition that may be measured objectively. Questions that challenge such traditional thinking are as follows:

- Is the traditional model, where power and competence lies with the professional the optimal one?
- What are the implications of such a relationship for the client who begins therapy feeling inadequate, confused, deskilled and defined by the nature of his problem?
- Might such feelings as mentioned above be intensified when the client assumes a one-down position to the professional?

Such questions may lead to another question:

- What kind of relationship would be more conducive to problem resolution, client growth and successful outcome?

Developments in thinking as embodied by the systemic and narrative approaches to therapy help shape a different therapeutic response to such a question. These viewpoints suggest that although the client may be in pain and distress because of his current situation or difficulty, he remains active, resourceful and responsible. A powerful and positive belief associated with this modern perspective is that problems are a common and 'normal' part of the process of life. Moments of difficulty and distress can also be seen as moments of change and possibility. This perspective of the client and his problem is a radical reframing of the traditionally held view of the client as one who is passive and unable to think clearly. To 'reframe' a situation is to see it differently to the commonly held view of it (Watzlawick *et al.* 1977). To reframe a situation does not mean changing any of the facts but alters the point of view through which these facts are perceived. To an enthusiastic gardener, a rainy day may well be considered a blessing, to another it may be seen as a miserable occurrence!

This chapter attempts to consider the implications for therapeutic practice in the context of a session of therapy when the traditional view of the client is altered. The client is now approached as someone who is capable, competent and an active participant in the therapeutic process. As such, all his actions and reactions are worthy of appropriate respect and regard. Such a view changes the relationship with the therapist and elevates the client to a position of co-partnership. The skill and expertise of the therapist accordingly demands that the focus of her efforts must lie in eliciting the skills and expertise of the client.

IMPLICATIONS FOR PSYCHOTHERAPEUTIC PRACTICE

The Therapeutic Relationship

The therapeutic relationship is considered by almost all models of therapy to be critical to the therapeutic endeavour. To maximise the potential of the therapeutic relationship by adopting an approach that treats both partners as equal might not just be useful, but indeed optimal. An approach that is profoundly rooted in client competence implies that to attempt to actively engage the client in the process of therapy becomes a major and priority objective. Indeed the client's active participation in the process of therapy is the single most accurate indicator of successful outcome in therapeutic practice (Miller *et al.* 1997). It therefore becomes imperative for the therapist to consider what she can do to foster the client's participation in the therapeutic process. This challenges traditional thought patterns with regard to the assessment of treatment outcome based on an evaluation of therapeutic technique. The basis of therapy shifts to becoming a relationship based on collaboration with responsibility for problem resolution shared between therapist and client.

The Therapeutic Conversation

To hold the view that the client is able and responsible in the midst of pain and distress challenges the therapist. It increases the range and scope of the therapeutic focus and conversation. The therapeutic conversation must now include all aspects of the client's life, not just the problem. All the client's efforts to survive and endure, as well as the problem, pain or distress he chooses to share with the therapist, are of immediate and equal interest to the therapist. The therapist's attitude now becomes characterised by a positive curiosity about the whole of the client's life. This curiosity is conveyed in language through the use of a questioning approach to the client. A questioning approach is respectful of the client and his abilities. It is not demanding or inquisitional but invitational in its attitude. The objective of the therapist is to elicit the client's understanding of his problems or his situation and not to impose his own! This modern attitude frees the therapist to work creatively. It demands high levels of skill, focus, alertness and availability to the notion of possibility.

Using a Positive Approach

The very nature of many therapeutic settings in which we see clients contribute to prioritising the problem and its cure as opposed to seeing the client as a person who happens to have a difficulty. Clients themselves also only too readily succumb to slipping into the role of passivity and inactivity in the presence of the professional. Not all clients are able to articulate the pain of being defined by their problem as the one who exclaimed: 'I am more than my problems!' Consequently, the first task for the therapist working from the approach described above is to find ways that heighten the client's awareness of his coping abilities and to bring forth the story of not just his distress, but also his endurance and his survival. The objective of this is to introduce the client to new possibilities about how he might see himself differently. Working thus inevitably increases the range and number of clients with which it is possible to work.

Fundamental to many modern cognitively based models of therapy is the notion that there is always another way of looking at things, no matter how fixed or stuck the situation may seem. Consequently, any display of uncertainty and anxiety that is manifested by the client is welcomed into the therapeutic arena as the first signs of a departure from certainty or fixity of thought (Mooney and Padesky 2002) which lie at the heart of distress. Anxiety and uncertainty can therefore be understood in positive terms. As such, they can be handled as the precursors of change. Inducted by traditional patterns of thought the client may think of himself as incompetent and helpless. By utilising an upfront positive approach to the client as able and competent, this negative mindset is reversed. Possibility arises, and the therapist and the client's aims converge. This chapter suggests how to create such possibility for the client.

THE FIRST SESSION

Every session provides unlimited opportunity for the therapist who is prepared to work hard and whose orientation is grounded on the belief as outlined above that the distressed and upset client in front of her is at the same time displaying other qualities that are illustrative of his endurance, creativity, sticking powers and decision-making capacities. A basic belief to guide the modern therapist is the understanding that a client is only able to recognise that he is overwhelmed by grief or pain because he has already experienced or has within himself a vision of life without misery. The words of one illustrates this idea: 'life does not have to be this miserable. I just know it'.

Allowing the Client Express his Point of View

Allowing the client to express his grief or distress is of course initially the most pressing task to be addressed in the therapeutic process. This is essential work and the traditional starting point of the therapeutic process. The therapeutic qualities of empathy, unconditional regard and being genuine, as outlined by Rogers in 1951, are as relevant now as then. If the client does not feel that the expression of his pain is heard, taken seriously and understood, he will not become engaged with the therapeutic process. Modern research supports the traditional view that a client must feel understood, respected and not adversely judged for improvement to occur.

An invitation to the client, which may be utilised in the pursuit of the expression of pain and distress, is as follows:

'Tell me about the things you think are significant that make you the person you are today.'

This is an open-ended invitation for the client to tell the story of his problem in his own way. Beginning thus establishes the baseline for the therapeutic encounter. It is an essential first step for the therapist to gain a clear understanding of how the client understands himself.

The moment in the therapeutic encounter to ask questions about coping and endurance may come only after much expressed empathy on the part of the therapist. Clients who are severely depressed need space and time to express the depth of their misery. However, even with such clients the elegance and delicacy of the upfront, empathic style of questioning as described in this book does not have to be abandoned. The therapist can begin by asking for a detailed description of the client's depression by saying:

'Depression means different things to different people. Some people get agitated, move about a lot, cry, others put on their pyjamas close the blinds and pull the blankets over their heads. What do you do when you feel low?'

Such a direct approach may startle the client and indeed engage him in the process. The idea that he does not have a monopoly on how depression is 'done' may begin to erode his conviction that his misery is complete and absolute. Such an approach may even inject humour into an apparently humourless scenario. When one client's complaint was excessive tearfulness, the therapist was able to elicit a smile with her absolute genuine exclamation: 'So you are skilled in tearfulness!' (The therapist's previous client had complained that she was unable to cry!) Encouraging the client to give a detailed description of the problem in terms of behaviour or interactional patterns in itself can reduce the experience of the problem from seemingly overwhelming proportions to being more manageable. Any sense of the problem being reduced in size can elicit in the client the beginning of a sense of mastery of the situation.

A sense of mastery can be further encouraged into existence by inviting the client to prioritise his concerns. Utilising the simple question 'What bothers you most?' (Quick 1996) helps the client to organise his thinking about his current experience. It accesses the client's own expertise. Any experience of mastery is valuable in helping the client resume control of his life. Such questions epitomise the elucidative and tentative approach described in this book. It is respectful of the client and is based on the fundamental belief that incompetence is rarely global.

By following such an empathic and non-judgemental approach to the problem, the therapist can then venture to ask the client the question as articulated by Strong (2000): 'How did you come to understand yourself just this way?' This question encapsulates the spirit of almost all the following interventions aimed at eliciting the coping skills and resourcefulness outlined in this chapter. The implication being that other ways of understanding oneself exists.

Using Time as a Measure of Coping Ability: How has the Client been Coping before the Session?

From a systemic perspective, therapy begins at the moment the client makes the first contact with the therapist. This is a useful fact to keep in mind. Research supports the view that once the decision is taken to begin therapy, considerable improvement in the problem or distress often accompanies it (Miller *et al.* 1997). To find out how the client has been managing before the first session is important therefore for the therapist. The first contact may have been on the telephone, by letter or via a third party, for example, an agency or doctor. During the time period between the initial contact and the first session, the client may have tried to reduce his distress or solve his problem. Whatever level, or lack, of success he has reached in this regard can be included in the therapeutic conversation. Inevitably, the client will begin most initial sessions by talking about his problem or pain. However, to proceed differently and more constructively than the simple retelling of his story, the client will need prompting in order to uncover the ways in which he is also managing to cope in the midst of distress. The following questions may help to do this:

> 'How do you feel today in comparison with how you felt when you first made the appointment to see me?'
> 'Has anything happened during this time that has changed things for you?'

These questions invite the client to be reflective. The client's current situation is being validated and indeed becomes the focus of enquiry. Time is being used also as a relative measure to elicit any changes or differences in the current situation. Changes may well have occurred. These should be acknowledged and explored. The most dramatic could be that the problem has disappeared completely. If this has happened, in our experience, we have found that clients will not necessarily volunteer this information at the beginning of therapy. They may need prompting to do so. Clients come to therapy to discuss 'a problem'. The therapist needs to lead the conversation in such a way that the client will share the fact that the problem may have diminished. It is by being selectively alert to the client in front of her and not influenced by past experiences of the same 'problem' that the therapist may be able to recognise that this client has in fact accomplished much and is very much 'on track' in terms of problem resolution. If this is so, therapy may accordingly end sooner than anticipated. If the problem has got worse recently, the client's effort to survive may also be acknowledged and commended. No effort on the part of the client in this respect need go unnoticed by the therapist.

Case Example: Nisha

Fifty-four-year-old Nisha, an Asian woman, who had been married for 23 years, had discovered that her husband was having an affair. From the moment she had decided to see a therapist she had initiated a series of events. Having ascertained that her husband had no intention of leaving her she had decided that she too was going to stay in the marriage. She had, however, imposed a number of changes and conditions on her husband. Some of them were as follows: her husband was to cut off contact with his mistress; she and her husband were to spend each evening together; they were to go out for lunch on Sundays and discuss the situation with their three daughters.

All this information emerged in the course of the first session when the therapist having listened to Nisha's story asked about any changes that had occurred since she had made the appointment. Nisha's pain and distress were very much in evidence. However, as she described her plan of action, a sense of her own self-agency and competence emerged simultaneously. Nisha's spontaneous response to this realisation was: 'You know I hadn't appreciated how much I'd done till you asked me!' Subsequently, Nisha was successful in her attempts to get her marriage back on track. Asking questions as suggested above emanates from a completely respectful and positive view of the client that engenders a sense of possibility and self-agency in the situation. As a result therapy was both effective and briefer than it might have been if Nisha's pain and distress alone were the focus of the conversation.

How is the Client Currently Coping?

From the moment the therapist encounters the client, she must be on the alert for signs of coping and resourcefulness as already suggested. Just the fact that the client has arrived at the session can demonstrate his ability to cope and take control of what is happening to him. If the client arrives neatly dressed and on time for his appointment, this could be seen as a reflection of his effort and desire to do something about his current difficulty. To make these observations explicit early in the therapeutic endeavour can have a powerful effect on the client. In the above situation, the therapist may choose to say something along the lines of:

> 'Given that you are so distressed, it impresses me that you have arrived on time, and that you have taken care over your appearance.'

Firstly, this statement acknowledges the client's pain. Secondly, it creates the context for a conversation where the client is noticed and spoken to as a person, separate from his pain. Such an attitude introduces the basis of a respectful and collaborative relationship. The client may benefit by being given a moment to process the above statement. This moment can serve to slow the client down and allow him to pause, which may be therapeutic in itself. This kind of statement frequently takes the client by surprise, which may help to engage the client. To be addressed so positively can have an impact: it challenges the client's idea of who he is from the very beginning of the therapeutic encounter.

Operating from this stance, the client can be encouraged to describe anything that he is currently doing that relieves or moderates his distress or that makes him feel less overwhelmed by his problem. The following questions may be useful in this respect:

> 'What do you do that helps reduce your anxiety?'
> 'What have you done to bring about this improvement/change?'
> 'How did you learn to do this?'
> 'Is this something you've recently learned or have you always been someone who copes?'

These questions based on ideas developed by de Shazer (1985), may take the client by surprise, especially if they are asked with deliberateness and certainty conveying the attitude that what is being asked about already exists. Indeed this very certainty of approach challenges the client's fixity of thought. When uncertainty emerges, hope may be generated. As the client has probably been experiencing himself as hopeless and deskilled, he is unlikely to recognise or acknowledge responsibility for changes or

improvements in his life. The effect of such questions can be very powerful as they attempt to highlight and positively commend the client's
efforts to cope and survive. In fact, they imply that his attempts to cope
already exist. The therapist may need to encourage the client in this
regard. The following prompts may help to do this:

> 'You've told me that you manage to get yourself into work on time
> most days. What do you do that helps you to do that?'
> 'How come you managed to get yourself up in time to come here this
> morning, given that you've been telling me you lie late in bed almost every
> other day?'
> 'Has the conversation with your friend that you've told me about
> encouraged you to feel a little more positive about your own efforts to
> work through this problem?'

Whilst recounting his story, the client will have given the therapist much
material that can be used to construct the type of prompt illustrated
above. If the client not only accepts that this new version of himself is so,
but starts adding to the list himself, a sizeable step has been taken in terms
of the client beginning to see himself in a new way. The result of this may
be that in place of hopelessness, hope may be engendered. At this point, the
client may begin to become more positive and begin to perceive options
and possibilities that were, hither to, hidden from view. If and when this
occurs, it orients the remainder of the therapeutic conversation differently.
Hence the therapeutic conversation is at every moment a dynamic and
unpredictable process. It is informed, supported and cross-fertilised by
feedback from the client at every point along the way.

Progressing the Session: Eliciting Evidence of Coping

The therapist must give the client time and space to recount his story at
his own pace and in his own way. The first session may be the first
opportunity the client has had to do this. This allows him to put the
'jigsaw' pieces together and make sense of seemingly fragmented and
unconnected experiences. During this phase, the therapist may feel that
she is not contributing very much. However, she is doing essential work!
The work of therapy can often involve adding complexity to what the
client sees as a 'simple' problem. It is equally true that the work of therapy
may be simple – even seemingly uneventful. Sometimes the simple recounting of his story may be sufficient for the client. This may be a new experience for him. For example, a parent may not want to burden a child with
news of a terminal illness and so keeps his distress to himself. A young

person may not wish to disclose troubles he is encountering in school or college to parents that may themselves be enduring some emotional distress. An adult who has been sexually abused as a child may require the time and the space to be able to recount the event in order to be able to begin to come to terms with this traumatic experience.

The recounting of the story with a few prompts or suggestions from the therapist may be enough for some clients to get a fresh view on their situation. This may be enough to mobilise them into positive action, as with 17-year-old Isobel.

Case Example: Isobel

Isobel, a 17-year-old student, was referred by her tutor to the college therapist because of her poor performance on the course. At the beginning of the session she was tearful. She said she felt a failure and could not see how she could possibly tackle the amount of work she had been set. Having listened to Isobel's negative description of herself, the counsellor asked her to list the individual pieces of work and select the least difficult assignment. Isobel was happy to carry out this request, and was quickly able to identify the simplest tasks. The counsellor asked Isobel to describe the piece of work and decide what she would need to do in order to complete it. Isobel explained that she needed to speak with her tutor to clarify the task. She also knew that the task required her to do some reference work in the library. As she talked, Isobel sat up in her chair, her tears stopped and her face looked brighter. She exclaimed, 'Oh goodness, I hadn't realised it was so simple.' She seemed revitalised and shyly asked the therapist if they could end the session early as she said she wanted to begin working on her assignment immediately. The therapist subsequently learned that with hard work and effort, Isobel had managed to set herself back on track with her college course. Therapy is rarely this simple or straightforward. However, one must be alert to the times that it is just so.

The therapeutic model that the therapist follows informs the next step in therapy. Continuing with the belief that the client is able, resourceful and responsible, the appropriate interventional response will now be explored. Accordingly, when the therapist has gained enough insight into the client's problem and situation, she may elaborate and move things to a different level psychologically. Certain questions may be useful in this regard:

'From where do you get your strength to keep going?'
'Given all that you've been through, how have you managed to survive/cope as well as you have?'

With such responses, both the person and the pain are validated, yet a distinction between the two is drawn. They are expressions of positive curiosity that do not coerce, but invite the client to think differently about himself. Once again the effect of such questions can be dramatic, as the client may not expect this response from the therapist. Clients are often surprised when the focus of the conversation does not limit itself to a discussion of their pain. Such questions can foster engagement early in the therapeutic encounter, which in turn, can intensify the pace of the therapy process.

Much of professional training focuses the therapist on how to intervene, interpret and question the client. Too little attention is given to noticing the effect of any intervention by the therapist. Client response is always unpredictable. The therapist needs to be selectively alert, focused and flexible. The therapist must recognise the moment when the client ceases to be a 'client' as traditionally understood in terms of being passive and incompetent and becomes actively engaged in the therapeutic conversation. Chapter 4 considers in detail this moment of therapy when the therapist and the client connect at a deep level. The effect of this is that therapy becomes a meaningful conversation between two equal participants. This is the 'litmus test' for this approach to therapy. Our experience indicates that a client cannot accept a positive description of himself if it does not echo, in some way, with his own view of himself. Once a client begins to accept the new, positive description of himself, hope has been engendered, possibility is encountered and therapy has taken a quantum leap forward. This is the moment that may also herald the end of therapy – the moment the client has begun to be both creative and responsible, capable of thinking and acting differently. The skill that is now required of the therapist is firstly, to recognise that difference has occurred and secondly, to assign space and validation to this new expression of the client. The therapist must see beyond the initial sense of uncertainty and anxiety that may arise in the client when he first begins to think differently however challenging.

The objective of therapy has been achieved at the moment when the client becomes reconnected with his own resources. This may occur at any moment in the therapeutic process. For the alert therapist this moment is not difficult to recognise. This moment is not necessarily a product of time and is not specific to any particular model of therapy. To lead the client in a discussion as to whether he thinks that the work has been completed or not, or how much more time he needs is respectful of the client. Ethical practice demands that therapy ends as soon as the work has been accomplished. In doing therapy briefly, the end of therapy may be indicated not when the problem has been solved but at the point whereby the client considers that he is able to manage and solve the problem unaided by the therapist. After all, the more the client is able to do for himself the more competent he becomes.

How has the Client Previously Coped?

One of the ways the client can get to the point of being reconnected with his resourcefulness is by helping him to recollect other times in the past when he felt low and distressed. Part of the nature of suffering is the sense of isolation, impotence and immobilisation that often accompanies it. Not only can the client feel cut off from others, he frequently feels disconnected and cut off from the person he used to be – someone who was able, resourceful and active. Pain can so engulf him that he may not easily recall other times in his life when he felt distressed (Hewson 1991). To elicit the recall of other such times can benefit the client, as part of remembering such periods may also include recall of how the distress ended. The client can benefit from being encouraged to remember his role in contributing to the end of his distress. It may be something he actively did or simply that he sought out support on that occasion.

Case Example: Sandra

Twenty-eight-year-old Sandra was having difficulty in facing decisions about ending her relationship, immobilised by the fear of being on her own. She then remembered how she had overcome her fear of scuba-diving. She had separated herself from the group and took the plunge 'in her own time'. 'In her own time' was a phrase that seemed to symbolise for Sandra the marshalling of her resources at her own pace. She became convinced that she could marshal her resources yet again in her current situation.

On this theme, the client can benefit by being asked simple, direct questions about the other times when the client has felt low or distressed:

'Have you felt like this before?'
'Have there been other times in your life that things felt as bad as this?'

If the client responds in the affirmative, the therapist can ask him to describe these other occasions. Other questions the therapist might utilise include:

'How did you manage to get through that time?'
'How have you survived and coped?'

The therapist needs to work creatively and sensitively when encouraging the client to describe these past times. The client may feel that his current distress is worse than anything that has happened to him in the past. Taking these two points into account, any enquiry about past coping skills needs to be asked from a stance of positive curiosity and with sensitivity. The client should always be given sufficient time to fully respond to any enquiry the therapist makes. Using a questioning approach allows the client the freedom to accept or reject the suggestion.

When Sandra had begun to remember how she had got herself through an earlier frightening experience, she became alert, animated and more engaged in solving her current problem. Such a turning point in the process of therapy can be very valuable. It can help reconnect the client with his own particular method of coping. This can powerfully help the client achieve a shift in attitude towards his current situation and help distance himself from a sense of inactivity and passivity.

How can the Client be Helped to Cope Better in the Future?

Our experience suggests that while the expression of pain, misery and depression in the course of therapy is imperative, too much dwelling on negative thought and behaviours may hinder a therapeutic shift. One way of helping clients who feel stuck is to begin to talk about a future time. Much has been written about the well-known 'miracle question' (de Shazer 1985). The belief is that future-oriented talk may encourage the client to think more creatively about how he would like things to be and about what changes he would like to make in his current situation.

In our experience clients have difficulty in talking in general terms about their 'miracle' or preferred future. This is not surprising. We have therefore found it more useful to limit questions about the future to a particular situation or context that he finds is particularly troublesome for him, rather than asking in general about a preferred future scenario. For example, a client may want to change his angry response to his teenage son's refusal to get out of bed on time for school in the morning. The father has tried his best to control his temper as he can see it is not productive, but he has not yet been successful. Adopting an idea suggested by Mooney and Padesky (2000), we invite the client to think of someone he admires. This can be a friend, a work colleague or any fictitious character from film or television. We then ask the client how he thinks that that person would act in the situation he wishes to change. This use of a role model in our experience can free up the client's own creativity and enable him to conjure up a preferred behaviour or way of behaving or being in a given situation. When the above-mentioned client was invited to think of an admired role model, he immediately smiled and exclaimed: 'I can just imagine what Tony would do in that situation. For one thing he would work out, in advance, a plan of action.' The very thought of this friend Tony seemed to introduce the client to a variety of alternative behaviours in the previously 'stuck' situation.

If the client is asked to conjure up details of a miracle future, the question that we have found most useful to ask is as follows:

'Which bit of the miracle, if any, currently exists?'

This question helps to bring the future into the present. It can help to validate whatever is valuable in the present. Just such a question led 28-year-old Mabinti to the awareness that although one brother had sexually abused her, currently she was forging a rich and mutually satisfying relationship with her other brother. This realisation was particularly therapeutic for Mabinti as part of her current distress had been based on the fear she could not make relationships. Such a question can encourage the client to realise that he is already some way along the pathway of making the miracle happen.

Questions that Help the Client to Experience a Sense of Movement

Any intervention that helps the client to feel less 'boxed in' by his current situation and introduces the possibility of movement or options is useful even if the herald of this is an initial increase in anxiety. Any sense of movement that the client may experience can generate a sense of hope, reality and possibility that further change can happen. Hope has been identified by research as a critical ingredient for positive change to happen.

A simple scaling exercise can be used to achieve this. Point one on the imagined scale represents the time when the client felt at their lowest and point ten the best they could ever feel. The client can then be asked to select a point on the scale, which most accurately represents where he currently judges himself to be. Whatever point the client chooses can be utilised. He can be questioned as to what he has done to get himself to that position. This can take effort (and a good memory!) on the part of the therapist to help the client recognise and acknowledge his own self in this regard. It took just such an effort to get Sam, who had been feeling low for a long time, to recollect that it was he himself who had troubled to respond to an e-mail sent by a friend informing him of a new job opportunity that he had subsequently realised for himself.

It can be useful to ask questions such as:

'How did you manage to get yourself to point 4/5 on the scale?'
'What did you do to help you arrive at that position?'

Such questions can challenge the client to think of ways that he has contributed to his own progress. Frequently clients will require encouragement, even coaxing, to begin to think in terms of change or improvement as already having been accomplished and their own contribution therein. Clients frequently attribute change to outside factors such as medication other than their own efforts.

The scaling exercise mentioned above can be used at different times in the course of therapy. One such occasion is at the end of a session. Point one on the scale can represent the way the client was feeling at the beginning of the session. Point ten, again, represents the optimal position. Whatever point the client selects today to position himself releases new information that can be utilised by the therapist. If he is feeling a little better, the therapist can help the client to be quite specific. She can make suggestions such as:

'How come you feel a little better now at the end of the session?'
'What has brought this change about?'
'Was this change due to some thought you had?'

Helping to make explicit how any improvement has occurred, even if it is simply the client's ability to use something the therapist suggested, is valuable. It can be used as evidence of the client's ability. If made explicit, this can be very affirming and can contribute to the client's sense of mastery in the situation. If the client is not feeling better, this situation needs to be addressed too, particularly if the client has moved 'down' the scale in the session. Taking feedback is intrinsic, at every point to this way of working. It is what informs the next step of the therapeutic process. If things are so extreme that the client is actively suicidal, appropriate action will need to be taken.

OPPORTUNITIES FOR COLLABORATIVE WORK THAT ELICITS AND VALIDATES CLIENT COMPETENCE

To work collaboratively with the client is validating the client's ability to be a co-equal partner in the therapeutic process. This is a serious departure from traditional approaches to therapy. In theoretical terms, it connects with the idea of seeing the client as expert and competent in his own life as expressed by Anderson and Goolishian (1995). Only the client can know what he really wants.

Setting Goals

One of the major areas in which such a collaborative approach is manifested is in the setting of mutually agreed goals for therapy. Without the client's help in this process, therapy will inevitably be off track. For example, the therapist cannot possibly know that when Gayle is referred by her GP with problems of self-esteem, what this actually means. For Gayle it means that the next time she goes out of her way to please her mother, and her mother complains instead of acknowledging Gayle's effort, Gayle will be able to point this out to her mother. Mutually agreed goal identification and goal setting between therapist and client is a topic outside the remit of this particular chapter, however, this activity is at the centre of collaborative activity. Having stated this, this chapter in its entirety could be understood in terms of a continuous process of goal definition and redefinition.

Timing and Spacing of Therapy Sessions

Another example of collaborative possibility within the therapeutic process is the timing and spacing of sessions of therapy. Clients have lives, families, jobs and responsibilities. They also, for the most part, have decision-making ability and sound judgement about what is possible and what fits them. If invited to be part of the decision-making process of the timing and spacing of sessions, clients are usually very well equipped to do so. It is a validation of their co-partnership in the therapeutic endeavour. To allow the client to be part of this process is a challenge for any therapist. It is a very deliberate displacing of herself as sole expert in the therapeutic process. Such an approach is a direct challenge to a fundamental belief inherent in traditional treatment models that the therapist knows best. Traditionally, the therapist prescribes when and how often therapy should occur.

The timing and the number of sessions in therapy are critical issues and are highlighted in the introductory chapters. The topic can be introduced at the very beginning of the first session. The therapist can start by suggesting that she and the client will have a conversation, at the end of which, they will both decide together whether today's session is sufficient or if they should meet again. Such a statement alerts the client not only to the possibility that therapy may end imminently but, significantly too, that the client has a part to play in the decision as to whether this will happen or not. Such an approach can foster the client's participation in, and responsibility for, the process early in the first session. It is consistent with the approach being described to share co-responsibility with the client for the therapeutic process. It affirms the client's decision-making capacity and his increasing sense of mastery and co-equality in the therapeutic process. This in itself can keep therapy relevant, focused, on track and brief. A therapist new to this approach may be surprised that the client may sometimes choose to opt out of therapy earlier rather than later. Surprisingly often, if invited, clients are well able to express that they have got what they want and that they can now manage by themselves. This can be understood in terms of a successful outcome when the object-ive is more about the client's ability to cope rather than solving the problem.

Talmon (1990) suggests that clients who leave therapy early frequently do so because they have got what they need from it. Therapeutic research suggests that change most frequently happens earlier rather than later in the therapeutic process. The alert therapist who is confident in the client's resourcefulness and ability to manage on his own is always vigilant to ending therapy earlier rather than later. This is both ethical and likely to be one of the most powerful therapeutic interventions she can offer the client. It is a powerful message for the client to hear from the professional: 'I think you're okay; it seems as if you can now manage on your own.' This is the ultimate validation of the client. Such a decision is only ever taken when based on sound judgement, clinical experience and appropriate skill.

For clients who state that they think they need many more sessions than are available in a specific context, such a desire can be creatively examined as part of the therapeutic conversation. The topic of referral elsewhere must, of course, be part of this consideration. If referral is not considered appropriate, time should be assigned to the careful exam-ination of examples of the client's proven skills and ability to endure and survive. The fact that the client survives between sessions can be explained in terms of this interval being like a practice run for when therapy ends. Sessions can be spaced over longer periods of time to increase the client's confidence and ability to survive alone. Skill and determination are necessary on the part of the therapist to recruit the client into this way of seeing things and to be at least willing to try out going it alone. Time is at all times a tool of the therapeutic process and is available for creative use. Here it is utilised in the search for client competence.

Lest criticism be levelled suggesting that an approach characterised by actively seeking out client competence is an approach that lacks rigour and discipline, the opposite, in fact, is true. The subject of attendance at sessions can exemplify this. Clients at times fail to attend sessions. Things happen to clients: they sleep in; they get ill; cars get punctures; public transport lets them down. However, clients, who are invited to participate as co-equal and responsible partners in the process of therapy, in our experience rarely fail to attend pre-arranged sessions of therapy. This of itself is validating of the collaborative approach. When clients are freely engaged in the process, they turn up for the sessions. Time is then optimally utilised by both participants. The therapeutic process becomes a working alliance. It finishes when the negotiated targets have been reached as mutually agreed by both partners.

When Therapy Gets Stuck

Brief therapy is a continuous process of assessment and re-evaluation of the therapeutic interaction moment by moment. The alert brief therapist is acutely aware of when the process is not progressing. This occurrence is considered in detail in Chapter 10. In the context of eliciting client competence it is worthy of brief comment. It can be confronted by the therapist, as any other problem might be. Many alternatives are available at this point. For example, the client may need to be referred elsewhere. However, frequently the impasse can be utilised as a moment of therapeutic opportunity and possibility.

Case Example: Susan

Twenty-six-year-old Susan, a married woman with a young child, whose high profile husband was frequently absent from the home, repeatedly voiced the complaint that she did not feel appreciated. Despite the therapist's every effort to encourage and help Susan, Susan's story remained the same. The therapist felt compelled to point this out to Susan. She explained that she had every sympathy with Susan's distress but that since Susan was still voicing the same complaint after a number of sessions, it might be that she could not help Susan. The therapist invited Susan to reflect on this. Such an upfront approach startled Susan into the awareness that she herself had a role to play in bringing about change. The question that Susan then voiced was how could she begin to value herself more. The therapeutic process assumed a new direction and impetus at this point. The client's competence in the situation had been called upon and the responsibility for progressing the process was shared between client and therapist.

TOWARDS ENDING

Eliciting Evidence of the Client's Contribution to Change

The task for the therapist towards the end of the therapeutic endeavour, be that a single session or a number of sessions, is discussed in detail in Chapter 11. From the perspective of this chapter, the task is to find ways to help embed the new story of competence and resourcefulness into the client's thinking. The scaling exercise already described is one very useful intervention in terms of highlighting and re-enforcing the client's own contribution to any change or improvement that has occurred, either during a specific session or throughout an episode of therapy. If such an intervention is utilised towards the end of the session, time needs to be allocated in order to reap its therapeutic benefit. This exercise is best placed at least ten minutes before the end of the session in order to maximise its therapeutic effect.

Another powerful way of re-enforcing changes the client has managed to make is to ask the client directly to search for evidence in his life that supports this new view of things. He could be asked:

'Has anyone noticed that you are different?'
'Who else notices the changes you have made?'
'Who else has said similar things about how well you are managing?'
'Who in your life would be least surprised at how well you are managing?'

Again, such questions often come as a complete surprise to clients and their own answers to them even more so. Frequently when change begins to happen in clients, it is noticed by those living or working close to them before it is acknowledged by themselves. People often remark on such change, and yet clients on their own may not attribute significance to such remarks. For example, 30-year-old Usna was a political asylum seeker who had witnessed a number of atrocities in her own country. In time she began feeling less anxious and tense. Her appearance reflected this change. She began wearing face make-up. To this her aunt had remarked: 'You look so much happier.' Such a statement had a particularly significant impact on Usna who had previously lamented how people would notice her sad face. Complete strangers would approach her and ask what was troubling her.

If the approach to therapy is grounded on the firm belief that the client is capable even in distress, inevitably therapy may end earlier than with traditional treatment models. This does mean that certain issues in the client's life may not have been considered in detail. To avoid the omission of any serious relevant issues, the following question can be asked:

> 'What could we have discussed that you might have liked to have discussed more or indeed have not mentioned at all?'

If an area is identified by the client, the client can be encouraged to think about how he might now address this issue or topic, or with whom he might consult in order to resolve it. Such an attitude is not avoiding the issue, but is firmly grounded on the belief that the client has skills to cope with or without the therapist. As one such client said: 'I don't need to come to see you again; I know the questions you might ask me and I can use them myself to help resolve whatever may be a problem for me in the future!'

CONCLUSION

This chapter has attempted to illustrate the viewpoint that the client is capable, resourceful and responsible even in times of distress. Effort has been made to describe what the implications for therapeutic practice are, based on this assumption. One of the major effects of this assumption is the creation of a new collaborative way of working with the client. To engage the client becomes a primary objective. Accordingly, the therapeutic contact becomes a dynamic process informed by feedback at every step of the therapeutic endeavour. Positively viewing the client as competent does not side-step or negate the presence or experience of problems and distress. The objective is to privilege both aspects of the client's story and to connect the client with these two different aspects. Effort is made to elicit what else besides the problem is happening in the client's life that gives witness to the client's ability to cope. In this way the client begins to see himself as more than his problem. In our experience, one of the most therapeutic interventions the therapist can make is to help the client to differentiate between his distress about whatever has happened and his ability to cope and function.

Giving space and support to the client to express his negative emotions and distress is a normal and essential part of the therapeutic process as emphasised many times in this chapter. Many people who come to see therapists are those who feel a pressure to cope both at a personal level, and in their family and professional life, with whatever life throws at them. As a police officer exclaimed, 'Just because I'm a police officer, it doesn't mean that I don't suffer pain and am not in need of help myself at times!' Such distress can be reframed. Clients can be told that to be able to feel and express distress and pain is a normal response. Moreover, it is a measure of their resourcefulness to be able to seek help in this regard. Such an understanding should always be relayed to the client.

To normalise negative emotions experienced by the client and explain that they are appropriate to the situation is a powerful therapeutic intervention in itself and can help the client to maintain a sense of balance. For example, to feel one is on an emotional roller coaster experiencing a wide range of conflicting feelings following a traumatic event is a normal and understandable psychological state. It does not mean that the client is either 'mad' or 'bad' – which is frequently what clients in this state think about themselves. To be given reassurance in this regard by the professional can have both a calming and hence, a therapeutic impact on the client.

Attempting to work in the way described in this chapter, therapists may feel at times as if they are going against the thrust of traditional treatment models. This is not so. The approach described here aims to combine the richness of traditional practice, whilst at the same time forging ahead in adopting new attitudes towards the client that powerfully influence therapeutic practice across a range of models. With these new attitudes the client is elevated to a position of competence and partnership, and the therapist is freed from the position of being the expert. Treating the client differently informs the process of therapy itself. The therapeutic conversation becomes transformed into an enlivening experience for both the client and the therapist. Both participants have significantly contributed to and jointly hold responsibility for the therapeutic process as it unfolds moment by moment. The objective of the whole process is for the client to see and understand himself, differently. When that is achieved, therapy may end for the individual client. If a client can be helped to understand himself as more than his problem and be able to engage productively with the therapist, therapy can happen with many more clients in minimum time than if clients are categorised simply in terms of their problem.

7 Preparing for the First Therapy Session: What to Consider

When meeting a client for the first time, many factors come together that influence the encounter and its outcome as described in Chapters 1–3. In this chapter, some concepts and parameters that are pertinent to doing therapy briefly will be considered in more detail. These include the contexts of therapy, the pace of therapy, a framework for practice, guiding practice principles and finally some challenges and dilemmas that face the therapist, using a brief approach to therapy.

In doing therapy briefly, decisions have to be made by the therapist about what to include in therapy, what to leave out, when best to intervene and how. These can be viewed as decisions that the experienced therapist appears to make confidently and without apparent effort. The client, likewise, also has to make decisions about what to prioritise and what to bring (or omit) to sessions. However, what is unique in practising brief therapy is the recognition that one focuses on what is most important for the client. These decisions are influenced by the context and parameters brought to the session by both therapist and client and are characteristic of a collaborative relationship.

CONTEXTS OF THERAPY

The context in which therapy occurs has a direct impact on the therapeutic process. As such, it is a 'parameter' of therapy that must be kept in mind by the therapist. Context is defined as the parts surrounding a word or object that can throw light on its meaning; the interrelated conditions in which something (person, ideas, beliefs) exist (Penguin English Dictionary 2002). In therapeutic terms, the context is a recognisable pattern of events or ideas that is created by an individual in interaction with his environment. Defining a pattern as context gives meaning to the thoughts and behaviour of the individual. In this sense, therapy cannot be conducted without taking some account of the conditions that surround an individual and thus contribute in some way to his problem. Beliefs, traditions, hopes, expectations and limitations all arise out of the context in which therapists operate and their clients live. Thus, throughout this book the client's specific culture, gender and religion as well as other relevant factors are recognised as being part of the broad context. Each individual also has a set of personal circumstances and responses within these broad contexts.

The therapeutic context, in the broadest sense, can be divided into three levels – the macro, mezzo and micro. These levels are relevant to all therapy, but are particularly pertinent when the approach to therapy is brief. Each level contains conditions that impact on service delivery and the pre-session, engagement and ongoing assessment of the suitability, process and outcome of therapy. Appreciation of all three contexts serves to enhance a collaborative approach between therapist and client.

The macro level represents the 'world' of people from different cultures and socio-economic backgrounds. From a practical point of view, this context is specifically defined and thus given meaning and direction by the country in which therapy occurs. The word 'therapy', and its practice, as described in the traditional Western sense is a concept that does not have meaning, as we understand it, in many parts of the world. Even in cultures where it is now an accepted approach to dealing with personal difficulties, it is understood in a variety of different ways. With immigration and migration taking place with greater ease throughout the world, therapists have to be prepared and equipped to work with people from different cultures and who hold different personal and core beliefs. It is helpful for therapists to consider this wider context before starting therapy, especially if working briefly, as there may be less time to unravel assumptions or iron out misunderstandings once work has started.

The mezzo level represents the setting in which therapy takes place (health care systems, social welfare, education, workplace health, private practice, etc.). Practical issues (how referrals are made, where the therapy takes place, how many sessions are allocated, how it is paid for, etc.), beliefs, expectations and limits of the particular setting have an impact on the therapy that is offered. In the UK National Health Service, for example, therapists are accountable both to medical practitioners as well as to the system in which they operate, and to their professional bodies. They might have to work with and accommodate other members of a multidisciplinary team. In the education system, therapists have to tailor their approach to the needs of the school as well as to the child and his family. Such constraints, although challenges in themselves, can afford opportunities for the therapist and the client to focus on maximising their time together and to achieving optimal management in terms of joint care with other professionals (see Chapter 12). At the mezzo level, resources for therapy have to compete against other health, social welfare and education services in the allocation of funds (e.g. for prescribed medication, housing, social welfare benefits). A series of questions may help to consider how therapy might fit into a particular context (Bor and Miller 1991):

> 'How does therapy fit into the need for other services in this setting?'
> 'What is the role of therapy in that context?'
> 'Who are the natural "helpers" or "healers" outside professional therapy?'
> 'What additional resources are needed to include psychological care into the setting?'
> 'What is the least that can be done to bring about the most difference to the client, the context and other interested parties (school, medical care, employment)?'
> 'How will referrals be made and processed?'

At the micro level, the client's particular circumstances and context are the primary focus of attention. At the same time, the therapist's awareness of her own influences (training, experience, strengths, difficulties) is also vital to effective work with clients. These factors have an impact on how the aims and outcomes are agreed and evaluated between client and therapist. They also contribute to the initial assessment of what that client requires and how that can be matched within the boundaries of a limited time. Learning about the client's beliefs, relationships and behaviour can enhance the possibilities of change and strengthen the alliance between therapist and client. Some questions that relate to the client's unique context and help to focus on relationships are:

> 'What is your main concern right now?'
> 'Who else knows about it?'
> 'For whom is the problem the greatest?'

The use of diagrammatic representations for work and social contexts is a way to clarify hierarchies and relationship issues. These can be a rapid and easily accessible way of depicting complex information that represents the macro, mezzo and micro contexts. Genograms (family pedigrees or family trees) are tangible and graphic representations of situations that help to bring the 'context' of the client's problem into therapy (McGoldrick and Gerson 1985), as are diagrams representing the client's work system and relevant players.

The brief approach to therapy puts a great emphasis on the context, firstly in making assessments and then in evaluating the process of therapy (see Chapter 5). The context acts as a yardstick against which to assess if brief therapy is appropriate and then whether it is helpful and on the right track for the client. Evaluation is thus a necessary part of taking a brief approach to therapy (see Chapter 12). Evaluation of the effectiveness of therapy is provided by feedback from the client, as well as carrying out more formal systematic outcome research (e.g. Du Plessis and Bor 1999).

THE PACE OF DOING THERAPY BRIEFLY

Doing therapy briefly raises issues about the pace of therapy. Brief therapy does not mean that the pace during the sessions is hurried! However, it does mean grasping the moments of connection that occur in the therapeutic relationship, and utilising events and possibilities when they arise rather than storing them for later use or interpretation. Sometimes these moments are demonstrated in reply to a question posed by the therapist. At other times, the client might think about an issue in a different way and acknowledge openly that this idea is being prompted by the discussion. The alert therapist will use these moments of possibility to facilitate a change in perspective for the client. Some problems change and are relieved through the dialogue and others through practical steps taken by the client outside the session. This means that in doing therapy briefly some issues may be dealt with immediately. Conversely, the pace in doing therapy briefly might, in some sessions, be deliberately slow, allowing the client to follow a train of thought or clarify feelings about something particular. Skills and techniques can be used to achieve a pace that suits each client. These are developed over time and with experience.

PREPARING FOR THE FIRST SESSION

In all fields of practice, therapists need to know why they are doing therapy, what they are doing and which specific theoretical ideas inform their practice. Having a theoretical framework for thinking about and addressing problems is even more necessary when working briefly. The initial interview with a client sets the direction and tone for future therapeutic help. In doing therapy briefly, the therapist needs to be adept in engaging the client, making an assessment and intervening all in the same session. This is coupled with developing an awareness of the context in all its dimensions and how this specifically influences the therapeutic process. Sometimes, ongoing contact with the client will be indicated. At other times, this first session is a 'one-off' consultation session. By itself, this first session may have the potential to be therapeutic and sufficient for the client (see Chapter 3).

Therapists are inevitably prejudiced by their experience and training. However, the therapist should listen to and endeavour to reach an understanding of the client's problems, allowing for the richness of difference that every client brings. If this is done in a manner that does not allow prior experience to prejudice her to the full meaning of the client's description of his experience, the chance of the session being effective for the client is enhanced. Making no assumptions, choosing small goals, using words carefully, respecting the client's capabilities and balancing reality with hope are the guiding principles that ensure that collaboration is achieved and that the session is effective.

The approach to therapy described here aims to encourage therapists to conceptualise problems in a framework that will be a springboard for doing therapy briefly, no matter what one's primary theoretical orientation is. This framework includes some guiding principles, a review of the main aims of doing therapy briefly and an outline for the session as described in the next chapter. Vignettes from several different cases will be used to illustrate points made in this chapter.

Guiding Principles

Whichever theoretical stance is adopted, some overall guiding principles are fundamental to thoughtful brief practice. They give the therapist the foundation from which to focus on the tasks of therapy. These principles are more broadly described in Chapter 3. Guiding principles form the 'bottom line' from which to consider the ethics, legal requirements and values for collaborative work with clients. The main guiding principles are listed in Box 7.1.

Box 7.1   Guiding Principles for Brief Therapy

- *Avoid making assumptions* about a client's concerns, reactions, beliefs, cultural background or wishes. This means not jumping to conclusions about issues that might not hold true for the client. By not making assumptions, the therapist reduces the tendency to make judgements, for example, that some behaviours or thoughts are 'abnormal'. This means respecting the reasons the client gives for continuing with behaviour that might seem 'abnormal', rather than labelling them as pathological immediately;

- *Have small, achievable goals* for each session, as this helps the client focus rapidly on those issues of most importance. Setting small goals for the session is a way to achieve maximum benefit, as solving one problem can lead to an ability to address other difficulties more easily. Ranking problems in an order of severity facilitates choosing a single, main concern and is thus another way of achieving small goals. Having small goals is also a way to help clients reduce anxiety to manageable proportions, giving them a greater sense of control over their situation. Sometimes the client presents only one problem concern, but more frequently there is more than one interrelated difficulty. If the therapist tries to address all the client's problems that are voiced at the same time, neither client nor therapist is likely to have clarity about what has been achieved. Lack of clarity impedes the collaboration necessary for doing therapy briefly;
- *Use language carefully*. Everything said during the session has an impact and may alter perceptions and responses. Problems exist in the language used between people and are unique to each dialogue. Words themselves, the emphasis placed upon them, and the intonation may be understood and interpreted differently. The way the therapist enquires about the problem, the tone and the emphasis given to the words brings forth different reactions. For example:

  'What *brings* you here *today?*'
  'What is it that made you *decide* to come here today?'
  '*Whose* idea was it that you came today?'

- *Respect and reinforce the client's competence and own resources* for dealing with issues (work collaboratively). For example, by acknowledging that the client has taken the first difficult step in seeking help and has been able to clearly express what is of main concern to him conveys respect and validates the client's actions;
- *Balance reality with hope*. Be realistic about the client's situation (what can be achieved from a therapeutic point of view, the therapist's availability, etc.). There may be 'miracle' questions that help change perspectives, but there are no 'miracle' cures for many of the problems faced by clients. Help the client to find the smallest difference in perspective that gives him the hope, no matter what the prevailing problems might be;
- *Share responsibility with clients and appropriate colleagues*. For example, if the client presents a problem that is of concern to the therapist, such as expressions of deep depression or a medical condition that has not been discussed with a doctor, the therapist should seek consent from the client for referral to other appropriate

---

Box 7.1   (Continued)

specialists or encourage the client to do so himself (as appropriate); and

• *Seek regular consultation and supervision* from appropriate professional colleagues to review difficulties or decisions made during therapy with a client. Consultation enhances skills, avoids 'burnout', audits practice and ultimately determines effectiveness.

CHALLENGES AND DILEMMAS: THE FIRST SESSION

In taking a brief approach to therapy, the first interview with a new client can present some particular challenges for therapists new to working briefly and also to those who have greater experience. Many clients experience some anxiety and apprehension prior to this first meeting, some being unfamiliar with the notion or process of therapy. When the focus of therapy is brief, the client's anxiety has to be addressed or dealt with rapidly so that time can be spent on the issues that brought the client to seek help. The challenge to most therapists in the first session is to achieve a balance between:

• Establishing rapport;
• Describing the parameters for therapy;
• Obtaining a history from the client;
• Making an assessment about the appropriateness for brief therapy;
• Exploring the problem;
• Establishing a plan for ongoing work (if appropriate); and
• Ending effectively.

Achieving this balance can be difficult. A number of factors may contribute to this difficulty:

1. There may be internal or external pressure for the therapist to 'succeed' and 'get it right'. These pressures depend on the context of therapy and referrer, especially if the client is only able to have a few sessions of allocated therapy time. Time constraints are common in the setting of general practice and in other contexts where sessions are limited for practical reasons. The need for a brief, yet effective therapeutic approach is critical. In doing therapy briefly, we view these constraints as opportunities for heightened collaboration between client and therapist. Difficulties about succeeding in the task are also related to having clarity about whether

this 'success' is to meet the referring person's expectations or whether it is attending to those problems of the client. A feeling of being judged by the client and referrer can be a constraint and interrupt the creative flow of conversation. Being aware of these pressures, and how they might impact on the therapy, prior to the first session helps bring clarity to the situation. An example of the therapist's pressure is illustrated in this case:

> John, aged 44, was referred by an Employee Assistance Programme (EAP) for therapy to help him deal with work stress. The therapist was aware of several pressures. She felt she had to succeed in helping John for his own sake, and that of the referring EAP. She also felt she had to be cost effective for John's employers who were paying the EAP for the sessions provided by the therapist. The therapist knew that there would be an audit at several levels at the end of therapy.

2. The first encounter with a new client is a time when a diversity of factors converges. The number, nature and complexity of problems presented by clients may at first seem overwhelming. It is therefore important for the therapist to take charge of the process and help clients to set their own priorities.

3. If time is to be used effectively, the therapist has to take the lead in starting, continuing and ending the session. At times this can pose dilemmas for the therapist as the different stages of the interview present different challenges. Calculated risks might have to be taken at any stage about what to include, what to note, and what not attend to. This is part of the assessment process. In beginning a session the therapist may have questions in mind such as:

> 'How do I greet the client?'
> 'How will I start?'
> 'How appropriate is my theoretical approach in dealing with this client?'

As the session progresses questions might arise such as:

> 'What issue is the most important for the client?'
> 'What if I get stuck?'
> 'How will I keep going?'

As the time to end approaches questions might be:

> 'Will I know when to stop?'
> 'How will I end?'
> 'What about the follow-up?'

Such reflective questions, as outlined above, are considered in greater detail in other chapters of this book. They can help the therapist to keep an open receptive stance, whilst being actively involved in conducting the session.

4. The mood of the client when first greeted may transfer itself to the therapist and set the tone for the session. In the early moments of the session, or at any other time, the therapist can inadvertently be pulled into the client's 'despair' or view of the problem. If this happens, it could cut the client off from his own strengths and resources. Uncertainty about how to respond in the session to the client's mood and responses (anger, sadness, anxiety, silence, depression) can be inhibiting to the flow of conversation. Under some circumstances, matching the response may be quite appropriate. For example, if the client appears confident and outwardly cheerful, it would be inappropriate to appear very sombre before establishing some relationship. However, if the client is clearly anxious and nervous, the therapist might feel a greater onus to create an atmosphere in which the client is enabled to talk. For example, she could simply state that she appreciates how hard it is to start telling his story and that he should take his time. This can help the client to feel more comfortable. If the client talks rapidly and incessantly, the therapist might try to set a calming atmosphere by slowing down the process. This might be achieved by interrupting the flow and picking up on words for clarification. Part of the expertise of the therapist doing therapy briefly is to be 'in charge' of the session, including the mood. A questioning approach, and eliciting the client's views of his strengths and resources, ensures that the therapist is working collaboratively towards achieving the client's wishes.

5. Age, gender and cultural differences can impact on the therapeutic relationship. Therapists may be younger than their clients and may be required to deal with issues related to a life stage of which they have no personal experience. When working with children and adolescents, the therapist will be much older than the client and this can equally be difficult. Awareness of age differences and having methods to address any difficulties can help overcome these barriers. For example:

'Help me to understand the hardest things about being older and well, for you?'
'Remind me of just how it is for someone of your age to feel bullied.'

In some circumstances, gender and cultural differences have to be overcome in order for therapy to take place. This means exploring client's views. Raising the topic is often sufficient to enable a conversation to take place and for barriers to be overcome. For example:

'In your culture as I understand it, men don't talk to women, especially alone. How might this affect how we might be able to work together given that I am a man?'
'How do you suggest we talk about what is of concern to you?'

In some instances it might mean respecting their boundaries by referring them to other therapists.

6. The therapist's credentials. Sometimes clients ask about, or comment on, the therapist's training and experience. The increasing need to monitor and evaluate the effectiveness of therapy makes such enquiries more likely to occur. The therapist should feel compenent and able to respond to such enquiries. Having a client who is a therapist can be a particular challenge. The therapist may feel that she is being tested and observed. Under these conditions, the therapist might be self-conscious and find it harder to proceed with her normal confidence and creativity. With these clients it is helpful to address expectations and wishes, and to clarify any areas of difficulty.

7. Defining the time available and the methods of payment (if applicable) have to be dealt with clearly if they are not to detract from the session. Setting time limits when clients present with anxiety and pressing concerns can be difficult as the therapist is trying to establish sufficient rapport for the client to begin her story. At the same time, imposing time limits can also help to establish rapport by focusing the contact between therapist and client. In brief therapy, adjustments may occasionally be made to traditional times for therapy, such as the 50-minute session. For instance, an hour, or more, may have to be given to the first session, whilst subsequent sessions may be briefer. Dealing with practical issues such as fees can be difficult to introduce when seeing clients for the first time, especially if they are in distress. In both these circumstances, clarity at the outset is best. Dealing with such issues over the telephone, as the details of the first meeting are arranged can be appropriate.

8. Clarifying the number of sessions at the outset is an issue in brief therapy (see Chapters 2 and 3). Some therapists give clients contracts for a number of sessions. Such contracts may or may not be appropriate in brief therapy. The first session can usefully be defined as a 'consultation' to find out what the client wants and how the therapy might be able to meet his needs. For example:

'We are able to have up to eight sessions together. Today we will meet to consider together what might be most appropriate for you and how you might wish to proceed.'
'Today we will meet to consider what is best for you. If more than the four sessions is required we will look again at the contract and what is possible.'

Prescribing a number of sessions to the client at the start might defeat the objective of defeat effective brief therapy. For example, in some situations a 'one-off' session might be sufficient. In others, it might be during a follow-up session that the therapist becomes aware that an issue has been resolved, or that the client has gained sufficient ground to help him deal with difficulties alone. The client might say, 'I feel better now.' Labouring time to fill allotted sessions can be detrimental to the achievements made. Knowing when to stop is an essential skill to develop in doing therapy briefly. For this reason, it is important not to raise expectations in the first session that might 'imprison' client and therapist in a number of sessions. The first session should focus on engaging the client, by showing that his story is being heard rather than deciding the number of sessions required. The key to brief, effective therapy is recognising the moments when therapy starts and should end. Thus, fixing the number of sessions prior to beginning therapy is in some way contraindicated. Sometimes, however, this may be required within the particular context in which therapy is provided. On the other hand, in some rare circumstances indicating a number of possible sessions may help the client to feel 'contained' and 'focused'. In other situations therapy might take place over a length of time but not involve many sessions. What is important to achieve, given the constraints of a particular context, is having a flexible approach, within the parameters set by that setting.

9. Uncertainty about the number of people who should attend the first session may add to decisions for the therapist, particularly when doing therapy with time limitations. The choice of who attends from the client's system depends on the therapist's theoretical approach and expertise, as well as on the client's wishes and the nature of the referral. If the presenting problem is about relationship difficulties, to have a couple or a whole family present in the session may sometimes be advantageous. The presence of other family members may enhance the chances of rapidly clarifying relationship patterns. In doing therapy briefly, where the most effective use of time is a crucial factor, this is a decision that needs careful consideration. There are many options that can be considered, and maintaining a flexible approach is key to using available time well. For example, the individual can be seen for part of the session alone and then with the partner. Alternating sessions alone and with significant others is another possibility. The important factor is to collaborate with the client by giving careful attention with whom to start.

CONCLUSION

Therapists are helped to meet the challenges of doing therapy briefly through training, experience, ongoing supervision and consultation. Having a theoretical basis for approaching clients, a 'map' for executing the first session and some particular techniques can also facilitate the process. The guiding principles are the backbone of good and safe practice. All these factors, including those of context, impinge on the therapeutic process. To practice therapy briefly requires an awareness of their influence, assists in a better appreciation and understanding of the client's circumstance and those that impinge on the therapist. Awareness of these factors helps prepare the therapist when meeting a new client. The end is also envisaged at the beginning within the opportunities and the restraints of the context and the pace of therapy. Chapters 8 and 11 examine the first and last sessions in greater detail.

8 Outline of the First Therapy Session: a 'Map' for Practice

> If therapy is to end properly, it must begin properly – by negotiating a solvable problem and discovering the social situation that makes the problem necessary.
>
> (Haley 1976)

Whatever the context or theoretical stance, some basic concepts and steps can guide the first interview. The first interview always has the potential for being the last session as understood in the terms of the approach outlined in this book. All sessions have a beginning, middle part and ending. As the session develops, the exact order and timing of the steps depend upon the flow of conversation, guided by the questions chosen by the therapist. These questions are fashioned in response to signs and symbols from the client that are the shorthand clues which guide the therapist to collaborate with the client in resolving or lessening his concerns. Clients, like travellers, are vulnerable to the elements in their surroundings. It is incumbent on the therapist to take the lead and set the tone for the session. The therapist picks up the signs and symbols to help the client reach his desired destination.

The ideas described in this chapter describe the first session with a new client. It includes an ordered number of practical steps that enhance the chance of making this first enconuter effective from an assessment and treatment perspective. These steps can be likened to the landmarks that help the traveller recognise which path to follow to reach his destination. Most experienced therapists, in different modalities, follow these or similar steps automatically and instinctively. However, in doing therapy briefly, special thought and attention is given to what to do, in what order and for what purpose.

The 'map' for practice can lead to:

- More effective use of each therapy session;
- Closer collaboration between client and therapist;

- Fewer misunderstandings about how therapy can help and its possible limitations;
- More accurate assessment regarding suitability of this therapy;
- Increased client satisfaction with therapy; and
- A clearer set of criteria against which the efficacy of therapy can be evaluated.

FIVE-STAGE GUIDE FOR THE FIRST SESSION

The first session can be divided into five stages:

1. Referral and preparation for the initial contact;
2. Meeting the client and starting the session;
3. Definition, clarification and assessment of the client's situation;
4. Decision-making for client and therapist and ending the session; and
5. Post-session reflection and tasks.

This five-step format is designed for the first session with an individual, but can easily be adapted for sessions with couples or families and for follow-up sessions. It is also useful when adapted for addressing problems in organisations. The principles are the same. Brief excerpts from different case vignettes are used to illustrate the points made and are integrated into the text of this and Chapter 11 devoted to endings and closure. For the sake of clarity a summary of the 'map' for the session precedes describing the stages in detail (Box 8.1).

Box 8.1 Summary of the 'Map' for the Session

Stage one: Pre-session consideration

1. think first and hypothesise (referrer, stage of life, context);
2. consider practical details (location, time, finance).

Stage two: Meeting and engagement

1. attend to practical arrangements;
2. begin the session;
3. engage the client;
4. identify concerns;
5. use language thoughtfully.

Box 8.1 (Continued)

Stage three: Gathering information and making an assessment

1. elicit more information;
2. identify beliefs;
3. give information as appropriate;
4. help manage concerns;
5. maintain professional boundaries;
6. make an assessment.

Stage four: Decision-making and ending

1. make decisions;
2. give time for client questions and comments;
3. obtain feedback;
4. discuss follow-up;
5. consider appropriate ending and interventions;
6. summarise session.

Stage five: Post-session tasks and reflections

1. record the session;
2. feedback to the referrer;
3. consultation and supervision.

Stage One: Pre-session Considerations

Essential tasks include receiving the referral, dealing with the initial client contact, considering practical factors (location, privacy, length of session, time available for the session) and addressing issues pertaining to the referring person. The steps include:

1. Thinking first (make a hypothesis or calculated guess) before meeting the client and starting the session (Selvini Pallazzoli *et al.* 1980). This exercise is a discipline that helps the therapist to anticipate some of the unique issues and problems for each client. In practicing a brief approach, issues that pertain to the referring person are considered as useful in starting the session in a more focused way. The important aspects to clarify about the referral are:

   • If the client has been referred, the referring person's perceptions of the client's problem;
   • What the referring person is requesting for the client (therapy, consultation) and is expecting the therapist to achieve;

- Agreement about the subsequent feedback to the referrer following the session; and
- If the client is a self-referral, establish how the client heard about the therapist, who else is aware that the client has made contact with the therapist and why therapy is being sought.

The hypothesis also takes into account the client's:

- *Stage of life* (age) and what milestones have been reached (leaving home, marriage, having children, adjusting to death and bereavement);
- The stage the client has reached in relation to *family* (married, single, divorced, caring for elderly parents, living alone or away from home);
- The particular *problem* (medical, work, relationship) and the stage reached in relation to the main presenting problem (recent onset, long duration);
- Any previous *medical* or *psychiatric problems*; and
- The social and cultural *context* of the client (ethnic, cultural, religious) and the setting of the therapy (educational, medical, employment).

2. Consider practical and other parameters about the *first contact* with the client including:

- Date, time and location of appointment;
- Reference as to how the referral came to the therapist;
- Details related to fees (if applicable);
- Issues related to confidentiality;
- Checking on the first contact made by the therapist by phone that the client is free to speak and is in a position to answer a few questions about the referral and his problem; and
- Defining parameters about the amount of information exchanged in the initial conversation when making the first appointment (an example of this was presented in Chapter 3).

Stage Two: Meeting and Engaging the Client (Start of Collaboration)

The first meeting is critical to client engagement. The outcome of the therapy depends on careful consideration of the issues and on how the session is conducted from the outset. The steps include:

1. Practical considerations (location, seating arrangements) may seem small issues but are important in starting the session well. These include:

- The location of the therapy session. The client needs an opportunity to express thoughts and emotions in an environment conducive to doing this. Interruptions might give a message to the client that time has not been allocated for him. However, sometimes the therapy takes place in less favourable conditions (at the bedside in a hospital or in a busy medical clinic). Drawing curtains around a bed in a ward does not eliminate sound from carrying, but it gives an atmosphere of trying to respect privacy. Providing thought has been given to achieving the optimum comfort and privacy, it is possible for effective therapy to take place under a variety of conditions. Engagement with the client is of prime importance, rather than having a 'perfect' ambience, even though this is clearly desirable.
- The positioning of chairs can also facilitate discussion. For example:

  (a) Placing them directly opposite allows for eye contact, but can be confrontational;
  (b) Sitting behind a desk can set a barrier between therapist and client;
  (c) Chairs placed at an angle to each other allow for eye contact as well as freedom to look away, and are therefore less confronting.

2. Begin the session by:

- Warmly greeting the client by name and clarifying how he wants to be addressed (surname, Christian name);
- Inviting the client to sit down;
- Clarifying:

  (a) Who you are;
  (b) Your place and involvement in the agency (if relevant);
  (c) Your task in relation to the client, for example:

      'I am a therapist, working as a clinical affiliate for the Employee Assistance Programme who you contacted for help.'

  (d) The purpose of the meeting, for example:

      'We are meeting to find out about your present situation and to consider what steps you might want to take next.'

  (e) The time available, for example:

      'We have fifty minutes together today.'

  (f) Note-taking:

      'I will be taking some notes during the session about our conversation and of the decisions that we take together at the end. Anything I write you can see or have a copy if you wish at any time.'

3. Engaging the client (build rapport and collaborate). Rapport is established with clients through a dialogue (talking, listening) as well as noting what is *not* said (being observant and receptive to the client's mood and non-verbal messages through body language). Rapport can be gained by conducting the session in such a way that the client begins to gain confidence in the therapist's leadership. The specific details in collaborating include:

- Taking the lead in opening the session (see Step 2);
- Asking those questions which facilitate a dialogue and encourage the client to tell his story;
- Accommodating to the unique style of the client can sometimes help to develop the therapeutic relationship, by using the words of the client or adjusting to a slower pace of an elderly person;
- Keeping a focus when confronted by difficult or challenging situations;
- Showing concern, but not being thrown by overt expression of emotion by the client (anger, tears, agitation);
- Being alert to clues from clients that are evidence of solutions, whilst they present examples of their problems. These clues, or grains of hope for a solution, often occur early in the session. Such evidence often contains the seeds of resolution of the client's problems. For example, a client might say that he feels out of control of his emotions and yet may be sitting telling his story quite calmly. Noticing his calmness and making this explicit can powerfully contribute to creating the moment when engagement happens and therapy begins to be emancipating. Such moments may herald not only the beginning but also the end of therapy! Extracts from a case are used to demonstrate some of these points.

  Andreas, aged 34, was referred by his general practitioner to the therapist for help in managing the breakdown of a long-term relationship with a woman eight years older than him. He came from a Greek Cypriot family who found his unmarried state at his age personally and socially distressing. He lived alone and worked in the property business. On arrival for the first session Andreas was so anxious and unfamiliar with the therapy situation that it was hard for the therapist to settle him enough to begin to tell his story. She decided to aim to do no more than try and engage with him, and was alert to clues that might help her in this task.

Therapist: To start our conversation, what would you like me to call you? Would you prefer Mr Vallas or Andreas?

Andreas: Please call me Andreas.

Therapist: Well Andreas, firstly, what is your understanding about why your doctor suggested we meet?

Andreas: He was worried about me. I have never been to a therapist. I'm not at all sure what you can do!

(By putting the question back to the client the therapist moved the conversation forward, and was able to engage the client by enlisting his views.)

Therapist: Did you have anything in mind to talk about in keeping this appointment today?

Andreas: I suppose I'd like to tell you about my problem and you to have some solution! Dr Black said that you would be able to help me.

(Using Andreas's words helped her to think about this challenge and to find a way forward that would take account of these factors.)

Therapist: Well I cannot be sure about solutions. However, it might be a start if you were to help me understand by beginning to tell me about your problem and what is it that you might like to achieve by the end of this session?

Andreas: I am still not sure.

Therapist: Well, as a start, try and tell me about some of those things that you are sure about.

Andreas: I feel so muddled. (He sobs briefly.)

Therapist: Is there anything in the muddle that you know you would like to unravel?

Andreas: Well, yes. (He looks at the therapist for the first time.)

Therapist: If you can begin to tell me what you want to unravel what might be easiest to start with?

Andreas: I suppose not really knowing what I want. When you put that question to me I suddenly realised that that is one big problem for me.

- Addressing and exploring expectations and views about therapy. Clarification of expectations about what therapy can achieve is an important step towards engagement and collaboration in doing therapy briefly. This exploration of beliefs and expectations about therapy is as important for those who have had experience, and may also hold fixed views, as it is for clients who have never experienced therapy. Questions can be used to explore the client's views, such as:

'What might you want to achieve by the end of meeting?'
'What are you expecting to happen in our meeting today?'

Some clients, such as Andreas, might know little about 'therapy'. Others might be expecting a particular approach, and yet others might have unrealistic expectations of how their dilemmas might be resolved. In doing therapy briefly, such expectations need to be identified and addressed from the outset. The initial focus is to gather information, but at a pace that engages the client and builds sufficient rapport to engender confidence. For example, the therapist gained Andreas's attention as she slowly pursued the issue of his feeling 'muddled'.

- Taking control and demonstrating this. It is not uncommon for clients to fear that 'things will get out of control'. The therapist should be able to contain the emotional situation sufficiently to allow the problem to be spoken about freely, and for the client to feel that there is no pre-judgement on her part. By being able to demonstrate this control the therapist shows the client how she will manage further discussion and emotions. For example, with couples, the therapist might direct the questioning to each in such a way that controls the flow of conversation and keeps the situation from becoming unbalanced. An example taken from a session with a husband and wife who feared that things would get 'out of control' is given to illustrate this point:

Therapist: Mrs Ngumi, what do you think your husband might want to discuss here today?
Mrs Ngumi: I don't know, why don't you ask him?
Therapist: I will ask him, but it is important to hear your views.
Mrs Ngumi: I know he hates rows and is afraid of what might happen here.
Therapist: Do you share your wife's views of this?
Mr Ngumi: I am not used to discussing our private relationship in public. She knows this!
Therapist: If your wife were to talk about the things that you don't normally talk about, what do you think the impact of that might be?
Mr Ngumi: My fear is that it might turn into a slinging match.
Therapist: It is my responsibility to see that you both get a chance to say what you wish. But it is up to you to decide what you want to raise here today.
Mr Ngumi: That's a relief! I wish she would listen for once!! I don't know how you can make her do that.

- Listening carefully and considering the client's responses is another important part of engagement. Listening is the therapist's 'radar'.

Active listening helps to pick up clues from what clients say, as well as noting what might not be stated but implied. The therapist may pick up clues to note when clients are avoiding, or having difficulty in bringing out feelings or concerns. Likewise, whatever the therapist says at the beginning of the session might give clues to the client as to how receptive or otherwise she is to the client's issues. For example, Mr Ngumi expresses anxiety about coming to therapy and of opening up the relationship with his wife for discussion. Attending to these issues rather than trying to overlook them can facilitate engagement in the early stages of the session. For example:

Therapist: I hear that you are not sure what might come out of our meeting. How would you like to start?

Mr Ngumi: Well today is a bad day. We started badly.

Therapist: Do you agree with your husband that this is a bad day, Mrs Ngumi?

Mrs Ngumi: (Mrs Ngumi looks at her husband briefly, and hesitates before replying.) Not so bad.

Therapist: Mr Ngumi did you know that your wife didn't think that it is such a bad day?

Mr Ngumi: That's what happens. We often see things differently.

Therapist: Mrs Ngumi, what do you think was so bad for your husband, that isn't so bad for you?

Mrs Ngumi: Well even though we were very tense this morning, I was sort of relieved that he was willing to come here.

Therapist: Mr Ngumi what do you guess was the relief for your wife?

Mr Ngumi: (Hesitates and looks at his wife for the first time.) I suppose she takes it that I mean to do something about our relationship and that I am not just running away.

- Being alert to both verbal and non-verbal clues facilitates a rapid engagement with the issues pertinent to the client. Verbal clues include pace of speech, clarity of expression and words chosen. Non-verbal clues include physical appearance, eye contact, sitting nervously on the edge of the chair or leaning back with folded arms, or other physical signs of distress (sweating, pallor, blushing, co-ordination). It is often from non-verbal clues that the therapist starts to discern that the client has difficulty in directly identifying something. The possible issue should not be assumed, or be based on personal prejudice or views. Facilitating the dialogue with verbal ('Tell me more') and non-verbal prompts (nodding, moving posture) is a way of helping to build rapport. For example, in the case of Andreas, the therapist noticed when Andreas had made eye contact with her for the first time.

- Keeping eye contact helps to engage the client. However, it has to be done sensitively. There is a difference between staring and keeping eye contact. Keeping fixed eye contact can be intimidating. By looking away, or straying off full vision, and then coming back when listening or asking questions can give emphasis to the points being made. It also gives the client an opportunity to withdraw when necessary. Returning to the case of Andreas. He was tearful, his speech was rapid and his sentences were sometimes disconnected as he struggled to explain his pain and distress. The eye contact was a moment of engagement.

4. Identifying the client's main concerns helps to:

- Achieve a sense of control by focusing on the main concern and setting small attainable goals. For example we continue with Andreas:

Therapist: Of all the concerns that you have mentioned – your anxiety, feeling out of control, the effect on work, losing the relationship with Dan, being on your own, fear of the future and the relationship with your family – which is of the most concern to you today?
Andreas: How I will face the future without Sue and Dan?
Therapist: Who would be hardest not to have in the future?
Andreas: Dan. Oh certainly Dan. It would be like losing a son.
Therapist: Which of your concerns troubles you least today?
Andreas: Perhaps my work.
Therapist: If losing the relationship with Dan and Sue is the most important, what about that situation do you find the most unbearable or anxious-making?

(The therapist has the structure of the session in mind. This helps her to keep an appropriate focus. Collaboration is achieved by asking the client about his wishes. She is trying to understand more about the pattern of the relationships and to help Andreas to be specific, as this will help him to feel he is more in control.)

Andreas: Well, I suppose, facing a future without a family of my own. How I will meet someone else? I have problems meeting new people. I worry what they think of me. (Andreas reveals a discomfort in his relationships with others, maybe a lack of confidence.)
Therapist: Do you know what they might be thinking?
Andreas: Not really, but I don't like looking different.
Therapist: What about you do you think people see as looking different?
Andreas: I don't know. Maybe nothing. I know I can be confident if I have to, but this relationship with Sue has taken all that confidence away from me. I need to break away. (Andreas gives the first clues as to what he might want in order to reduce his anxiety.)

5. Reflecting back client's actual words thoughtfully and purposefully is a technique that:

- Builds rapport with clients as it confirms that they have been heard, and helps the therapist to move at their pace. For example:

  Andreas: I feel very anxious.

  Therapist: You say that you feel anxious. How does feeling so anxious affect what you do?

  Andreas: It makes it difficult for me to concentrate on what people are saying. My anxiety blocks out whatever anyone is saying.

  Therapist: How much have you blocked out from our most recent conversation?

  Andreas: Not much. (The therapist is taking the discussion at Andreas's pace and his reply confirms that the pace is about right.)

  Therapist: So, your anxiety only sometimes makes it difficult for you to concentrate.

- Facilitates the discussion of sensitive or unfamiliar issues. Example:

  'You say that you fear rejection by your colleagues. What about this rejection do you fear most?'

- Helps the therapist to gain time when she feels stuck. Repeating the client's words enables the therapist to have a break to think and observe.

  'You say you are anxious all the time. Are you ever less anxious or not anxious at all?'

Stage Three: Gathering Information and Making an Assessment

The goal of this third stage is to make connections that help in the understanding of the client's problem. After gathering considerable information, it can be difficult for the therapist to decide how to proceed with the many strands that have been elicited from the client's story (see Chapters 3 and 4). Yet, it is necessary to move into a different phase of the session. The client and therapist can work together to set small achievable goals by including the following steps:

1. Begin to elicit more information in different ways about the problem. If there is more than one person in the session, try to gather information from all present about a particular issue. If the therapist is seeing an individual alone, eliciting his opinion of others' views can be explored

to assess how they might impact on the client and vice versa. The main areas of exploration include to:

- Define and redefine the problem and consider its origin and maintenance. This definition must be in accordance with the client's initiatives and desired wishes. It is the client's view of the difficulties, his ideas about why they occur and ultimately what he wants to achieve that are the springboard for change. Different questions help to define problems, for example:

  > 'Tell me how you see the problem?'
  > 'How does it affect you?'
  > 'When did the problem start?'
  > 'What is the worst thing about how you are feeling right now?'

- Help the client to be specific by asking him to give examples of how the problem has an impact on daily life (sleep, work concentration, eating, social activities with others, etc.). This helps the client view his problem in context and helps the therapist to assess the severity of the problem.

- Identify any critical events or changes that might have precipitated the problem (illness, death, changes in family or social life, occupational shifts). Questions about this can be woven into the conversation. For example:

  > 'What made you decide to seek help *now*?'
  > 'Tell me, have you had any recent events in the family such as illness, death or has anything else happened that you can remember that made you feel worse?'

- Consider the impact of the problem on relationships (family, friends, employers and other professionals) by addressing:

  > 'Who else knows about the problem?'
  > 'Who might be most affected and in what way?'
  > 'Who has been helpful and in what way?'
  > 'Who do you least want to be involved in your situation?'

This exploration can lead to rapid clarification of main concerns, and who is most affected by them. By linking the problem with behaviour and actions, the client is helped to view himself and others in relation to his problem. This is achieved through questions such as:

> 'When you are depressed how would it be noticed?'
> 'Who notices it?'
> 'What effect does it have on your wife?'

Prompts, in the form of questions, can help the client to think about his problem from another perspective. The following conversation was with a gay man whose work problems were also affecting his relationship with his partner. The therapist uses questions to link behaviour with relationships and beliefs:

Therapist: Who else knows that you have come for therapy?

Rickie: My partner. He insisted that I had to do something.

Therapist: Is there anyone else who you might want to be made aware of your problem?

Rickie: My parents, so they might understand better why I don't see them so often. I don't want to worry them and I'm not sure how my father might react.

Therapist: What reaction of his might concern you most?

Rickie: That he says 'pull yourself together' or asks whether I am gay.

Therapist: What effect does that have on you?

Rickie: It makes me feel more anxious and more hopeless.

Therapist: So when you are so anxious and feeling hopeless who notices it?

Rickie: My partner does and my colleagues at work might.

Therapist: Which of those do you worry about the most?

Rickie: My colleagues.

Therapist: What do they do to indicate to you that they have noticed that you are anxious?

Rickie: They try to pretend that they see nothing. It doesn't do to show anxiety in our organisation.

Therapist: Where do you think that belief comes from?

Rickie: My father believes that you shouldn't show your feelings. He learnt that from his father who was in the army.

It might be tempting for the therapist to offer interpretations at this stage of the session. It is preferable for clients to be helped to make their own connections and plans, as far as possible. This is achieved by using techniques and skills that help to bring the problem to the fore so that both the client and the therapist develop a clearer picture of the repetitive patterns of behaviour that keep the problem going, or make it seem intractable for the client.

2. Identify beliefs about the problem by using carefully constructed questions that uncover, with the client, areas of difficulty. Problems are often maintained because of firmly held beliefs. Solutions are unlikely to be considered unless the client wishes to move from the position in which he finds himself. Some therapists may feel tempted to suggest ideas about the problem presented by the client. Sometimes these suggestions may not be part of, or may even be out of

tune with, the client's beliefs. Therapy is unlikely to succeed unless a collaborative exploration is consistent with the client's innate wishes. Some general questions that help to uncover and address core beliefs include:

'What do *you* believe is the cause of your anxiety?'
'How do you think your partner believes you should deal with your anxiety about work?'
'What is your view about how therapy might alleviate some of your problems?'

The following dialogue extracted from a session with Dean, who had come to therapy to find ways of dealing with work-related stress, helps to illustrate the point:

Therapist: What are your thoughts about where this anxiety came from and your subsequent period of depression?
Dean: The more I took on at work the less I seemed able to think about what I wanted. I started not wanting to spend time at work or at home.
Therapist: Do you think anyone noticed this?
Dean: Well you know, I am always tired at night, and at work I sometimes can't face people. I try and hide it.
Therapist: What are your thoughts about how young men in your position, competent but pressurised, should be expected to cope with these pressures? (The therapist was tempted to offer an interpretation, but instead continued to explore beliefs, guiding the client to his own solution.)
Dean: Others seem to do it. I suppose by not worrying about what others think so much.
Therapist: What is it that you think others think about you?
Dean: That they look down on me. I don't have a university background like most of them. (Dean's beliefs had been uncovered and the therapist felt that she had some path to explore with him that might contain hope and restore confidence in his achievements.)

3. Give information when it is appropriate, depending on the therapy context. In medical, educational and social service settings there may be relevant information affecting the client's problem. For example, a child who presents to a school counsellor with the problem of bullying may be unaware that the school has an explicit policy for dealing with this problem. Some ways of giving information are more effective than others. If the client's knowledge and understanding is first explored through questions, it allows misinformation to be uncovered and then corrected, and the gaps in knowledge to be filled at the client's pace.

An example from a medical setting is used to illustrate giving information in a way to clarify understanding:

Therapist: Your doctor recommended that you have an HIV test. What do
   you understand about what that test involves?
James: I was so shocked I didn't listen to everything. I think it is to see if
   I have AIDS.
Therapist: That is not quite correct. It is a test to see if you have been
   infected with HIV.
James: I thought that means AIDS and that means death.
Therapist: So you think AIDS means death. What do you know about the
   treatments for HIV infection that are available now?
James: Not much. I never wanted to think about it.

(The therapist first explored the client's knowledge and then went on
to give information and elicited his main concerns.)

When people are anxious or afraid it is not uncommon for them to
miss what has been said. Thus, checking what the client has understood, at the end of a period of giving information, is important.

4. Help clients to manage their concerns and resolve or reduce problems.
   Once the client has identified main concerns, therapy is focused on
   how best he might manage them. It can be difficult to move into this
   stage if the client is still engaged in telling his story. However, in doing
   therapy briefly, it is an important step to be taken as it shifts the
   emphasis to focusing on decision-making. The therapist can facilitate
   this by:

   • Helping clients to view their problem from a different perspective.
     An example follows of helping Andreas to manage his concerns
     about his failing relationship with Sue:

     Therapist: What have you tried so far to lessen your difficulties?
     Andreas: I have tried to not phone her.
     Therapist: Can you say how much this helped?
     Andreas: Not much.
     Therapist: If not phoning doesn't help much, has anything else made any
        difference?
     Andreas: Yes, making myself think about the stress she causes me when-
        ever I do phone.
     Therapist: Who else knows about what you are going through now?
     Andreas: I have a friend. She knows everything. We talk. When I am
        alone I get into a panic over the slightest thing. My friend knows this
        and was the one who pushed me to get help.
     Therapist: So, you respect your friend's views?

Andreas: Yes, but in some ways she is too close to me to help. She gets upset when I am upset.

Therapist: Does anyone else know how you feel?

Andreas: My doctor. He gave me your name. (At this point the therapist knows that Andreas has a number of people around who are of some support and he is not isolated.)

- Identifying resources available to clients (how they have coped with past difficulties, how they might cope in the future, who is around to help) is another way of helping them manage their current concerns. Explore with the client any attempts he has made to deal with the problem to this point. These previous attempts give some clues as to the client's resources and can impact on the approach taken by the therapist. In some situations, there may also be other therapists involved who may influence the discussion and future plans. For example:

  'As you have already seen another therapist, how do you see our meeting in relation to the help you are seeking?'

An example from the session with Andreas illustrates his past coping strategies:

Therapist: Have you ever tried to cope with difficulties anything like this in the past?

Andreas: Yes, but I was much younger then.

Therapist: You might have been younger, but can you remember what helped you then?

Andreas: My pride. I used to pick fights at school. I wanted to be seen as tough.

Therapist: Is there anything now that you want to be 'tough' about?

Andreas: Yes, I don't want her to get the better of me and pull me down, affecting work and everything.

Therapist: Is there any way that you could show Sue you are tough?

Andreas: Yes, ending this relationship. If I knew how to do that I would be OK now.

- Using hypothetical, future-oriented questions (those that contain the words 'if', 'when', 'what if') can help clients think about the outcome they most fear and the possibilities for the future. Addressing such issues can be some inoculation against future negative outcomes by rehearsing possible options and solutions. Continuing with examples from the session with Andreas demonstrates the use of hypothetical questions.

> *Therapist*: If you continue to be caught up in a relationship with Sue, how might you see yourself coping, in say 3 years time?
>
> *Andreas*: I would be here talking about divorce!! Ultimately I couldn't continue. I have been close to thinking that ending everything as a way out.
>
> *Therapist*: How close are you now?
>
> *Andreas*: Not close but I feel trapped.
>
> *Therapist*: So if you were pushed to think of the smallest thing you could do to preserve yourself, feel less trapped and show Sue your toughness, what might it be?
>
> *Andreas*: I would stop giving her money every time she says she is 'broke'.
>
> *Therapist*: If you didn't give money to Sue what else might you do with it?
>
> *Andreas*: I'd not thought about it like that but yes, I would get out of some of the debts that are mounting up. I'd think of *my* needs first!

- Balancing reality with hope is another important strategy for managing concerns. This means being realistic about the nature of the problem, whatever it is, and its effect on relationships, whilst at the same time exploring the client's hopes and wishes. Many problems that clients bring to therapy cannot be 'cured', but they can be reduced in intensity or become less disruptive. Not all problems can be 'fixed' in a way that we want or expect. Therapy can help to free the client from this utopian belief or hope, that itself may be at the root of the problem (Watzlawick *et al.* 1977). Continuing with the example of Andreas, the therapist tries to balance reality with hope:

> *Therapist*: You say the hardest thing about breaking the present relationship with Sue is thinking that you will lose contact with Dan. Can you think of another way to manage a relationship with Dan?
>
> *Andreas*: I view him as my son. If I break with Sue, that will end.
>
> *Therapist*: You are right in a way, as Sue is his mother and can decide. However, what other way might you view your relationship with Dan other than as his 'father'?
>
> *Andreas*: He relies on me. I've been around since he was born. He is now 11.
>
> *Therapist*: So it sounds as if you have been a very good friend to Dan. Could you find a way of continuing that?
>
> *Andreas*: Yes, I hadn't thought of any other way forward. We go to football together, and I pay for his club.

- Mid-session interventions and reflections, as illustrated by the reframe to Andreas, are another strategy for helping clients manage their concerns (see also Chapter 3). Brief summaries and reflections of what has been addressed thus far can be used at any time in the session. The client may hear his story differently when it is presented back to him in this way. This is particularly important in working briefly as the ideas contained in the message may help clients re-evaluate their problem. Indications of the impact of these reflections are statements such as:

> 'I hadn't thought about it like that!' or
> 'I already feel better from having spoken to someone who doesn't react judgementally like my parents do.'

5. Maintain clear professional boundaries. Once the session is under way and rapport has been established, it is possible to cross boundaries from a professional to a less professional relationship, even in small ways (unguarded comments about the client, giving away personal information). The therapist may find it more difficult to maintain a position of some neutrality as the interview continues. Clients, like Andreas, may say quite explicitly that they seek to talk to a therapist because she is 'not involved in their situation' in the same way as friends and family members. Maintaining this position is vital for the therapeutic relationship and is a delicate position to maintain, especially when a high degree of collaboration is sought between client and therapist. This stance of neutrality can be facilitated by being mindful of the impact of what is said and what happens during the session. Sometimes clients ask personal questions or push the therapist for her opinion, for example:

Rose: How would *you* put up with pressure like that?
Therapist: I cannot say. Everyone's situation is different. But in my view you have shown strength and courage.
Rose: Well, do you have strategies for dealing with that pressure?
Therapist: Each person has to find what works for him. I suggest that you help me to understand better exactly how the pressure affects you, and what problems you face right now because of it.

Showing no surprise, asking questions and not giving an opinion are other ways of maintaining a professional stance that help clients to express whatever is troubling them most.

6. Make an assessment of the severity of the client's concerns towards the end of the middle stage of the session, before moving into the final stage (see also Chapter 4). This assessment is based on what is heard and seen in the session, on the client's emotional state and what he reports about his behaviour (drinking, drug-taking, sleeping habits, eating). Making an assessment comes at a point in the session when the therapist knows it is time to begin ending. In doing therapy

briefly, this is a very important moment for the therapist. Hypothetical, future-oriented questions that explore how clients might cope, and who else is around, are especially useful in helping to make an assessment. For example:

> 'If you were to make changes what might these be?'
> 'If things stayed the same how might you see your situation?'
> 'If things got better how would your work life be?'

If client suicide is a possibility, as in the case of Andreas, more detailed discussion is needed to clarify and assess the seriousness of the client's intent. For example:

Therapist: Andreas, you say that you feel very 'oppressed' by all your problems. Have you ever felt so oppressed that you thought of taking your life?

Andreas: Yes I have.

Therapist: Have you given thought as to how you might go about ending your life?

Andreas: Yes, with pills, but I don't feel that way now.

Therapist: What has changed this?

Andreas: I know it is wrong and there must be another way out.

Therapist: What other ways are you thinking about?

Andreas: Coming and talking has helped. I can see what I need to do, but as yet can't see how to manage it. Talking gives me ideas.

The assessment prior to ending may simply entail the therapist thinking through the session alone as a mental exercise. The assessment leads up to decision-making in the final stage with the client. In the case of Andreas, the therapist might reflect to herself:

> Andreas is under considerable stress and seems very much on the 'edge'. He has been in a relationship for 14 years that has led him to know that he cannot continue as he is. He comes from a Greek Cypriot background that expects children to marry and have family at a much younger age than he is at present, and in his case even to have an arranged marriage. At the same time he is not entirely unsupported. He is under the care of his family doctor who has prescribed antidepressants. He has come for help, and also has a female friend with whom he talks frequently. Nevertheless, he is very much involved in the relationship with Sue and her child Dan aged 11 years. He sees himself as Dan's father. Breaking the relationship with Sue means breaking with Dan, in his view. Andreas needs time to be able to view his situation as not 'hopeless', and to see that some freedom might help him to do the things he has been unable to do for many years.

Stage Four: Decision-making and Ending the Session

Knowing when to end a session or therapy is a key aspect of doing therapy briefly. For this reason a whole chapter is devoted to the topic of ending therapy (see Chapter 11). There are subtle differences applicable to decision-making and ending a session, and in bringing about closure to therapy. The issues specifically related to ending a session will be highlighted in this chapter. Different skills and ideas about endings and closure are reviewed in Chapter 11 and elsewhere in the book as this is such an important issue.

In doing therapy briefly, the details of ending the session well are as important as those attended to in beginning well.

1. Making decisions is integral to the collaborative process for both therapist and client. The therapist needs to be able to form an opinion by gathering and organising information about whether therapy should continue or not. Engaging the client in this process of decision-making respects the client's judgement about the right time to terminate therapy. The very process of decision-making can in itself change these decisions. The therapist should take a lead in this process. Both client and therapist have to make decisions. The decisions for the client include:

   - Whether or not to come back for more therapy and further sessions;
   - Whether sufficient progress has been achieved in the session;
   - What issues should remain private and which to share with others (referrer, therapist, family, friends, employers, GP);
   - How to best use the work done during the session; and
   - What might be a good time to end?

   Decisions for the therapist include:

   - Whether she is the right person to deal with the problems brought by the client;
   - How much additional time to give to the first session, if the context allows it;
   - Whether she considers that therapy should continue;
   - Who else, if anyone, should be involved in the therapy (family, couple);
   - With whom else to discuss the problem;
   - Choice of the most appropriate time interval between sessions. This depends on the theoretical stance of the therapist, but more importantly on the problem the client presents. Some therapists would consider a month between sessions a suitable time interval, to allow the interactions that took place during the session to take some effect. Yet others would require the client to come daily or weekly with

a pre-determined ending. In doing therapy briefly, there may be an interval of a week or more before the second session, in order to maintain rapport built up in the session. This would be decided with the client.

- The client can be involved in the ending and assessment of the appropriateness of follow-up by asking the client:

    'How has this discussion been?'
    'Was this sufficient for now, or do you need more of this session?'
    'If today was our only meeting, what has been achieved for you? What more do you think needs to be done?'

- What feedback will be appropriate for the referrer after this first session?

2. Giving the client time for any questions or comments is important prior to reaching the final stage of the session. The invitation to comment or ask questions:

- Changes the atmosphere between therapist and client, and clarifies that the session is coming to an end;
- Ensures that the client feels he has control and has a chance to raise or at least point out outstanding issues;
- Indicates that the therapist understands that there might be issues that the client might not have had an opportunity to raise. It is important not to bring to this part of the session issues that might open up new, contentious subjects. Thus, the invitation to the client to ask questions or raise other issues should be done in such a way that avoids a re-iteration of the session discussion. Nevertheless, the invitation should give the client an opportunity to say anything that has not been covered, and is still on his mind. For example:

    Therapist: Before we end, is there anything else that you think is important for me to hear from you? Or is there anything that you would like to say that we have not discussed so far?

In asking this question, the therapist should attempt to hear the issue and include it in the end of session summary, rather than addressing another complex problem late in the session when time is running out. Being able to hear the response depends on the nature of the issues raised and its relation to what has been discussed. The careful use of the word 'say' does not imply an agreement to address the issue raised. The therapist should keep in mind that earlier in the session a question was asked about the main concern for that time. The client has already had an opportunity to raise issues. In working briefly, there is recognition that, even within the session, there might be a shift in mood, as much as in the client's main concern. The questions are thus also a form of evaluation.

3. Obtaining feedback about the session towards the end of the session ensures that collaboration between therapist and client has been achieved during the session and that the client's concerns have been addressed. Obtaining feedback also helps the therapist to make a judgement as to whether one session is sufficient or not. Enquiring about issues not covered in the session is another way of obtaining feedback. Discussion of the time interval between sessions with the client, and eliciting their views, is another way of evaluating and assessing his engagement, ability to cope, as well as his view of therapy. Yet another approach to ending is to elicit the client's views about what impact the conversation might have had. Examples of questions include:

> 'What might you most want to tell your partner about this meeting?'
> 'If you were to take one idea away with you from this meeting what would it be?'
> 'Of all the things we have raised today which is the one that you might most think about again?'

Sometimes a question like the following helps to shift obstacles to difficult discussions.

> 'Is there anything from our discussion that you would rather not think about now or again?'

This is a linear question (eliciting a yes or no answer), which allows the client to reply in the way they wish.

4. Discussing what follow-up the client envisages and what the therapist can offer is important as it reduces the likelihood of unexpected phone calls or visits, and is a practical way of ending the session. If there is to be an ending and no follow-up this should also be clarified. Details about the follow-up include:

- Contact between sessions, if this is necessary, and how this can be done;
- Consideration of the time between sessions (If clients are seen too frequently they could be given a message that they cannot manage alone. On the other hand, if the time between sessions is too long the threads of help may be weakened.); and
- Discussion and consent about communication and feedback to the referrer.

5. Consider appropriate end of session interventions. These interventions can play an important part in ending when doing therapy briefly (Allman *et al.* 1992). Interventions can take the form of reflections, summaries

or even tasks that capture issues and relationships that arise during the session. To be effective, they must reflect the collaborative agreement between client and therapist about the client's problem. Interventions given at the end of the session can have different objectives. One is to make it easier for the client to leave the session, with a clearer indication of significant issues that have been discussed. This enables the client to evaluate the significance of the issues for himself. Practical suggestions can be used in messages by setting tasks. Such a task might be simply suggesting that the client with work-related stress lists for the next session the things he likes about his job, and those that he does not want to lose. He could also be invited to list those things that he does not like and would like to change. End of session messages should invite reflection and hopefully stimulate a change of perspective for clients.

6. Summarising the session. The therapist uses in the summary what has been seen and heard, and balances the client's identified strengths with any reported dilemmas or difficulties. The key element is respect for the client's situation, by emphasising, the client's strengths and capabilities. Highlighting perceived difficulties is a necessary part of a balanced summary. The summary should include the decision-making discussion and the final question or statement from the client. To be consonant with the client's view, the summary should only relate to what has been brought to the session. The summary should include actual phrases and words used by the client. Hearing these words repeatedly can make the impact more real for the client and is confirmation that the therapist has listened. The summary provides clients with an opportunity for reflection on actions, responses and the future. Included in the summary should be a reference to the follow-up arrangements, if any. An example from the first session with Andreas follows and it can be compared with the final summary in Chapter 11:

Therapist: From what I've heard and seen today you seem very stressed by the relationship with Sue, so much so that you have been forced to seek advice. You say you are out of control. However, it seems that you have been able to make decisions and have listened to your friend, your doctor and are seeking help. You have raised many different stressful aspects of ending this relationship, but have also given me an idea of how tough and determined you really are. In a strange way, your instincts have saved you from committing yourself to a longer-term relationship that has caused you such pain for so long. Your strong feelings for Dan will possibly help you to find a better and different way forward in the future, without breaking this special connection.

Andreas: (Nods in agreement.)

Stage Five: Post-Session Tasks and Reflection

Ending is a multiphased process. It includes all of the above and tasks to be completed post-session. Once the session has ended, the therapist might be tempted to only make a few notes and move on to the next client. However, careful recording and attention to detail will help prepare for the next meeting. It is also easy to forget details and issues to remember for the next session once the client has left and the next comes through the door! This final stage gives the therapist a chance to revise the hypothesis using the information from the session. The steps in this final stage include:

1. Recording the salient aspects of the session including:
   - Who attended;
   - The identified problems;
   - Areas of particular concern (alcohol, abuse, stress, depression, suicidal ideation);
   - Agreed future actions;
   - Assessment and issues to be raised in future sessions; and
   - Revision of the initial hypothesis.

   These notes should be made with careful thought about every word used. Clients have access to their records in the United Kingdom and may, at a later date, challenge what has been said. Thus, write with the thought in mind that the client might ask to see the notes and be sure that what is written reflects what the client has said. Using quotation marks is a way of doing this. For example, 'The client said he "hated" his wife', not 'the client hates his wife'. Recording that 'The client gave the impression of being very nervous as he was sweaty and fidgeted throughout the session' is preferable to saying 'The client was nervous.' The latter comment is making an assumption that could be misinterpreted or contested unless supported by evidence.

2. Feedback to the referrer is important from several perspectives. Firstly, it enables the therapist to review with the client the purpose of the referral and the original reason for the contact. Second, the feedback also clarifies future actions and facilitates more open communication between client and referrer (if this is appropriate for the future). Consider carefully whether the feedback is to be given by letter, verbally on the phone, face to face, or both. Also consider with the client whether feedback is to be given after the first, subsequent or last session. Consent must be obtained from the client at the start of the session, or at a later time, for this exchange of information with the referrer. Feedback might also pave the way for future referrals as it gives the referrer some idea about how the therapist dealt with the client.

3. Consultation and supervision are essential to the growth and development of skills and techniques that enhance and ensure the effectiveness of doing therapy briefly. Consultation is a means of reviewing what happened, how the therapist responded, and can serve to back up situations that are difficult, and those that could, in rare circumstances, lead to client–therapist disagreements. Regular supervision enables the therapist to gain other perspectives. This in turn enables the therapist to be as effective as possible in future sessions and with future clients.

CONCLUSION

Some of the aspects covered in this chapter may seem obvious. However, they are the steps that experienced therapists go through automatically, although not necessarily in the suggested order. Nevertheless, having them laid out step-by-step can help experienced therapists stop and consider what they are doing. Using a 'map' for the session ensures that every moment in the therapeutic encounter is taken seriously. Nothing is wasted.

Clarity about the aims of therapy can give therapists the confidence to focus on the tasks when dealing with client's problems and their complex repercussions for relationships. Having an outline or 'map' for the session enables the most to be achieved in a relatively short period of time. The focus is on how and where to begin, how to continue and deciding how and when to end sessions.

9 Working Positively and Briefly with a Teenager with a Serious Medical Condition: a Case Study

> Most therapists have conversations with people that lead to the view that they are suffering from some pathological, psychological, emotional, neurological or biochemical disorder...people tend to see themselves as sick and damaged. They often forget the resources, strengths and capabilities they have...
>
> (O'Hanlon 1992: 9, 137)

At no time is the above statement more true than when a medical label denoting illness or disability is attached to a person. The belief that one's personal identity is co-terminous with the illness or disability can often become entrenched. To create new ideas about self is a general objective of therapy (Rolland 1994). Such an objective becomes all the more challenging when a person has received a diagnosis of a serious medical condition.

This book has a particular focus on the nature of the context in which therapy occurs and the influence the context has on the nature of the work between therapist and client. The case described in this chapter has been selected for two reasons. First, to illustrate the role of brief therapy in a school setting where there is the added and complex problem of a serious medical condition that affects the physical, emotional and psychological development of a child. Second, to illustrate some of the therapeutic interventions described in the preceding chapters of this book. The implications for relationships when a child has a serious disability, within both the family and the child's peer group, are discussed. The temptation for anyone suffering from a serious medical condition is to allow such a diagnosis to dominate their life. Working within the non-pathologising school context affords the modern therapist the opportunity to avoid any unnecessary medicalisation of the young person's life.

To work briefly with such a young person in the face of very complex problems, as this case illustrates, can be both challenging and appropriate. In our experience, brief episodes of therapy are the treatment of choice for adolescents, especially within the school setting (Bor *et al.* 2002). Few young people would actively elect to spend many hours of their lives talking to a therapist: life is often too full of excitement and possibility for this! Any time-limited approach to therapy should always involve an awareness that work begun in the present may be continued at a future date. Also, it is our belief that any changes initiated within the therapeutic encounter take time to consolidate. This is reflected in the management of the spacing and timing of sessions.

The very natural urge to explore and experience life in all its dimensions that exists just as powerfully in the adolescent with an illness or a disability as in any other young person can be utilised by the therapist to work constructively with the young person. Such an approach does not exclude the acknowledgement of the inevitable loss and distress that accompanies a serious medical condition. Indeed, allowing time and space for the free expression of pain is an essential part of the therapeutic work. The therapist in a school has a particular freedom to explore such feelings, as the overall aim is not contaminated with the need to fix or to cure.

SETTING THE CONTEXT

The Referral

Sally was a 16-year-old girl who had been diagnosed as having Turner's syndrome about 18 months earlier. Turner's syndrome is associated with the absence of an X chromosome. This results in a female who is short in height, has 'webbing' of the neck, and whose ovaries do not develop (Harrison 1980). Sally attends College and was referred to the therapist by her tutor. Sally had a degree of mental impairment as is common in people affected with Turner's syndrome. Previously, her educational setting had been a 'special' school, that is a school for people with a range of disabilities – both physical and emotional and people who were 'slow learners'. Sally had been labelled as a 'slow learner'. She was in her first term in a new college setting. Sally had become distressed and the tutor brought her to talk to the therapist.

As discussed in Chapter 5, one must pause and reflect on the referral itself. Information on the referral system is essential to formulating pre-first session hypotheses (Selvini Palazzoli *et al.* 1980). The tutor said to the therapist: 'Sally is a lonely girl. She is a bit upset and she needs someone to have a chat with.' The implied meaning appears to be: 'Cheer Sally up, but don't upset her.' The belief underpinning this request might be: 'support and protect...emotionally, but don't upset by talking about the real issues pertaining to her disability'.

FIRST SESSION

Sally's appearance was characteristic of a person with Turner's syndrome. She was of short stature – almost dwarf like, with the typical 'webbed' neck. She apparently had poor eyesight as she wore glasses. She was dressed quite boyishly in jeans and had short cropped hair. She had blemished skin and was tearful. She presented a picture of distress and unattractiveness. The therapist found it difficult to comprehend what Sally said at times as she had difficulty in articulation.

The therapist began the session thus:

Therapist: Your tutor has some concerns about you; I'm wondering what these are and how you feel about being here?

In a time-limited context, issues have to be addressed immediately. The use of the questioning technique immediately invited Sally into a collaborative relationship to express her version of events and also to elicit her opinion about 'being sent' for therapy. It is more difficult for the therapist to form a therapeutic alliance if the person feels 'sent'. However, Sally told the therapist that she had wanted to come and talk.

Structuring the Session

The therapist proceeded to explain to Sally that they had around forty minutes to talk and that at the end of that time they could decide if they wanted to meet again. Phrasing it in this way ensured that Sally had a say in whether she wished to continue or not with therapy.

The 'normal' terms of therapeutic confidentiality were explained to Sally; the therapist took time to carefully explain possible exceptions to this in relation to disclosures of self-harm and that such information might have to be shared with others. If this had to be done, it would not be done without Sally's knowledge.

Introducing the elements of structure in the therapy process early in the interview was deemed appropriate by the therapist. Besides fulfilling the professional obligation, the therapeutic intent was that this might have a 'containing effect' on Sally's distress that was spilling out in her tears and her interrupted, almost incoherent, speech.

Sally's Story

Sally was upset, she said, because her mother was due to go away to Australia in about two weeks' time. Sally was going to stay with a friend of her mother's during her mother's absence. Sally had never before been separated from her mother. This came at a time of much change in Sally's life both as an adolescent and also as a student in a new college regime. From exploring her family history, it appeared that Sally had a small social network. Sally's parents had divorced ten years earlier. Her father was entirely absent from the family's daily life. Her father now lived in another town. Sally did not 'get on' with her two siblings. Apart from travelling independently to and from college each day and the contacts she had there, Sally's world was almost entirely centred on her mother. Throughout the session, Sally remained tearful and exhibited an almost 'toddler-like' speech pattern, obsessively repeating: 'I'm upset because my mother is going away.'

Therapist: Does your Mum know how upset you are?
Sally: Yes I've told her.
Therapist: What does she say to you?

From a brief therapy perspective, the therapist is always curious about the other's perspective. Questions that link beliefs to behaviour are always useful in helping the conversation to be specific.

Sally: Sometimes she gets angry with me.

Relationships can become uncomfortably close or very distant when illness or disability exists (Rolland 1994). Sally's mother may have been feeling 'engulfed' by Sally's distress. The therapist considered this a possible explanation for her angry outbursts towards her daughter. The therapist attempted to seek evidence for this hypothesis by asking:

Therapist: What makes your Mum angry at times, do you think?
Sally: I don't know.

Sally did not appear to have any sense that she might be contributing to the conflict and anguish that seemed to exist between her mother and herself. Sally was in a way so consumed by her own distress that she could not entertain another's perspective. When the therapeutic endeavour feels 'stuck', it is helpful for the therapist to look beyond the immediate situation to take account of the whole context of the child's life. Accordingly, the therapist asked Sally:

Therapist: How are your sisters going to manage while your Mum is away?
Sally: Hannah is going to a friend and Eliza is going to stay on her own at home and mind the cat. She is able to do things like that!

Out of this exclamation emerged a story of enormous loss and distress as Sally described her growing awareness of how her sister, who was two years younger than her, could do things that she was either unable or not allowed to do. Her sister was free to come and go as she pleased and have her friend's home or visit them as she wanted. Sally was never allowed to go out unaccompanied. She never had friends come to her house. Sally ended by almost crying:

Sally: It's so hard growing up.

Teenage years may be experienced as a time of challenge for many young people. For a teenager with disability, such challenge may be greater. When the therapist asked Sally what she most wanted to do, she repeated a few times: 'I want to explore the world.' However, this urge in Sally appeared to be largely discounted by the people about her because of her medical condition.

The pain of the loss of capability at this moment in Sally's life seemed all the more acute because of the impending loss of her mother. Sally's mother was to travel to Australia on the first anniversary of the death of Sally's grandmother. Sally found it painful to remember her grand-mother.

The therapeutic objective for this session centred around hearing Sally's story. To take the lead from Sally in terms of rate and pace seemed especially appropriate to this first encounter. Sally's story had to be told before it could be retold in a new way (Anderson and Goolishian 1995). Accordingly, the therapist encouraged Sally to talk freely throughout the session.

A few minutes before the session ended, the therapist asked Sally if she had found the conversation helpful.

Therapist: How have you found our discussion today?
Sally: It's been helpful.
Therapist: Could you say in what way has it been helpful?
Sally: Just talking; nobody ever listens to me.

The session seemed to provide Sally with the space to pour out her story of pain and distress. This seemed an essential first step in embarking on a therapeutic relationship with Sally. It was important to give Sally the option to decide whether she wanted to come back for 'more talking' or not. This was an attempt to recruit Sally as far as possible into a collaborative relationship with the therapist, where she had some control over the progress. Sally said she would like to come again.

Making a Contract

A contract to meet for five more sessions was agreed. Two of these sessions were arranged to span the interval in which Sally's mother was absent as Sally had indicated that this might be useful. Sally had said that what she most wanted to do was 'to explore the world'. The therapist, therefore, suggested to her that the next time they met they could talk about ways that might be helpful to Sally to 'explore the world'. This was an attempt to focus the therapeutic endeavour on Sally's own expressed goals. It was also a recognition and acknowledgement of the powerful urge towards self-expression and independence present in Sally in the face of the anguish arising from her disabilities.

Issues for Supervision following the First Session

One of the questions that arose from the discussion between therapist and supervisor was whether it was possible to work therapeutically with Sally, given her level of intellectual impairment. A certain degree of psychological ability is an essential attribute for a successful outcome to short-term therapy (Hoyt 1995). It was too early yet in the therapeutic endeavour to assess whether Sally could make use of the support on offer.

The other question discussed during supervision was if Sally's mother was aware that Sally was coming for therapy. Given Sally was 16 and had a serious disability, should her mother be informed that Sally was attending therapy? This is a complex question to address. A good starting point is always to begin the discussion by asking the young person directly.

SECOND SESSION

The questions that had been aired for discussion during supervision were in the therapist's mind at the beginning of the second session and were addressed immediately:

Therapist: Does your Mum know that you are coming for therapy?
Sally: Yes, she thinks it is a good idea.

The fact that Sally had communicated the fact that she was coming for therapy to her mother and was aware of her mother's perception of this was significant information for the therapist in her assessment of Sally's 'psychological mindedness'. It was indicative of Sally's ability to be reflective and to communicate.

During the second session, Sally appeared almost as distressed as she was during the previous session. She was tearful and talked repetitively about her mother's impending absence. At times her speech was again almost incoherent. The therapeutic objective remained the same as in the first session; allowing Sally the space and time to tell her story and to be heard. The pace during these two sessions was quite unhurried and illustrates one of the underlying principles of working briefly. To work briefly does not imply 'hurried' therapy.

Much of what happens in therapy is a matter of clinical judgement, executive skills, risk-taking and intuition on the part of the therapist. When the moment seemed right the therapist asked Sally:

Therapist: What does having Turner's syndrome mean to you?

When working with a person who has a serious disability, it is essential to address the main issues. This approach was contrary to the implied message of the referral: 'protect and don't upset'. It is also a principle of a focused approach to address the main problem early in the therapeutic encounter.

Sally: My hormones don't work right, that's why I'm always upset!

This response of Sally's was revealing in that it shed light on how the label of Turner's syndrome had taken over her life and controlled her very existence. She had abdicated responsibility for her life, attributing the reason for her constant upset to the presence of Turner's syndrome. At this moment in the therapeutic conversation, the stance of neutrality was particularly useful. Sound therapeutic practice must allow the client to define what is either good or bad news.

Therefore, the therapist felt impelled not to make assumptions about what the meaning of having Turner's syndrome signified to Sally. Accordingly, the therapist asked Sally to spell out in detail what having the syndrome meant to her.

Sally: My face is funny. My eyes are funny. My skin is odd. I've even had to have operations on my feet. I can't ever wear trendy shoes ... (Sally was wearing 'mannish' looking trainers) ... and I'm so small. I look odd.

Judging by these responses, Sally was not without real psychological insight as to the meaning of her condition with regard to her physical appearance. Furthermore, they denoted a level of understanding and sensitivity that might well go unnoticed by others. Sally was being treated with growth hormone and oestrogen therapy.

For a therapist working with clients with a medical problem it can be useful to have a basic understanding of the condition. It was important in this case for the therapist to have certain information about the course and 'treatment' of Turner's syndrome. One of the features of this syndrome is the absence of secondary sexual characteristics and infertility. For an adolescent, this could adversely affect her social development. It was important that Sally have as much information as possible about her condition. This would serve the dual purpose of acquainting her with the limitations attendant upon her condition and also to maintain some sense of hope. A discussion ensued between the therapist and Sally about her access to medical care and advice and of her understanding of the treatments she was taking. Some time was given to help Sally formulate certain questions she might ask of medical personnel as the opportunities arose. The therapist was satisfied that Sally was in touch with appropriate sources of medical advice and support. In any discussion of medical conditions, the therapist must disclaim any expertise in this area. The therapist's role is to guide the client in the direction of such expertise.

Throughout this phase of therapy Sally manifested much distress and tearfulness. Her story was 'pain saturated'. She lived most of her life within the four walls of her own house. Her urge to reach out and explore was curbed by her own anxiety and fearfulness and by her mother's very protective attitude towards her. Sally finished by exclaiming, in an agonised cry,

Sally: 'I'm so bored with my life.'

Many elements had converged over the last few months of Sally's life that had contributed to her distress. The diagnosis of Turner's syndrome had been made during that time. This timing is a common feature of Turner's syndrome, as frequently, only when the adolescent fails to achieve the pubertal growth spurt is the syndrome recognised. The adolescent then has to cope not only with the lack of the signs of physical maturing but also with the awareness that she is different to her peers. Sally had to contend with the 'pathologising' that inevitably surrounds the diagnosis of a medical label as well as her already established learning difficulties. The diagnosis came at a time when Sally was about to leave the protective environment of a special school to participate in the educational context of a College of Further Education.

School transition times can be a time of stress for all the family. For Sally's family the new information about her medical condition was an additional worry. It made the therapist wonder about Sally's mother's reaction. She might understandably be very anxious and concerned. Sally could possibly experience this as curbing and constraining, rather than caring and protective.

Risk Assessment

The imminent separation from her mother was a highly stressful event for Sally. At this point in Sally's life, the planned separation from her mother was 'bad news' for Sally. Given her level of distress, the therapist needed to assess its dimension in terms of a depressive episode and possible risk of self-harm. Sally's lowered mood seemed to be directly associated with the news of her mother's absence. The therapist established this with the referring tutor prior to the start of therapy. The therapist enquired about the presence of other somatic symptoms. However, Sally said she was eating and sleeping as normal and did not have thoughts about ending her life. Apparently, the acute anxiety Sally was currently experiencing in terms of her impending separation from her mother had also triggered intense psychological pain associated with the diagnosis of Turner's syndrome and its accompanying losses. At the time of this interview, in the judgement of the therapist, although her distress was profound, Sally did not seem to have any intent on self-harm. From everything she said, Sally's most profound urge was to live in a more productive and interesting way. Indeed her encounter with loss seemed to connect Sally even more deeply with her desire to live.

Progressing Therapy: Mobilising Client Resources

Given these circumstances and continuing along the same therapeutic path as begun in the first session, the therapist responded to Sally by asking:

Therapist: What could you do that would be most helpful to make your life less boring?

Such a question invites the child's own expression. The therapist makes no assumptions about this. It also instils hope and is entirely respectful as the assumption is that Sally knows how to make her life less boring. This is a critical moment in the therapy process. To help Sally marshal her own resources would be to effect a counterbalance to her feelings of inadequacy and impotence.

Sally: To go out more.

Accordingly, the therapist asked the following question:

Therapist: What can you do to make this happen?
Sally: I could ask Helen what she does in the afternoons after school.

This response from Sally indicated a leap forward in the therapy process. Sally had accepted the supposition that she was capable of working out what was the first step to take in trying to make her life less boring. It is also indicative of the developing collaborative relationship characteristic of this approach. At this point in the conversation, Sally's mood appeared to lighten. Her face brightened; she also began to smile and she sat more upright in her chair. These physical manifestations seemed to concur with the beginnings of some sense of mastery in Sally's life.

The therapist was aware that a range of evening activities for people with learning difficulties was available locally. Sally herself had come up with a suggestion for action that might lead her in the direction of utilising these services. The therapist encouraged Sally to begin her own enquiries with her friend, who also had to cope with learning difficulties, as to how she spent her leisure time. The therapist also shared her own knowledge of the local support groups.

The session ended with the therapist summarising the content of the conversation, checking with Sally what had been useful, positively connoting Sally's own idea to discuss leisure activities with her friend, Helen, and confirming with Sally the date and time of the next session.

The therapist also checked with Sally about the significance of the moment described above when Sally's face brightened by asking:

'Am I right, or is it my imagination at work, but you look different now than at the start of the session? You look brighter, more relaxed. Do you feel any of those things?'

Sally replied in the affirmative to these questions. Indeed her smile became brighter. As previously discussed in this book, to acknowledge such a moment in therapy can augment its therapeutic effect.

Intersession Reflection

The therapist had learned from Sally's tutor that Sally's mother had expressed great anger regarding the delay in the diagnosis of Sally's medical condition. She felt distraught because she said that she would have treated Sally differently had she known that Sally had Turner's syndrome. She now felt both guilty and inadequate about her care of Sally. This information could confirm the therapist's hypothesis that Sally's mother might be overly anxious and concerned in her behaviour towards Sally. What was eminently obvious was that Sally's mother herself was in need of support. In the particular context in which the therapist worked, the therapist could not invite Sally's mother to be part of the session. The therapist made the suggestion to the tutor that Sally's mother could be advised to make contact with the therapist in her local GP practice to talk about her feelings, as her reaction to Sally's diagnosis was wholly 'normal' and understandable. The therapist emphasised to the tutor that to 'normalise' Sally's mother's difficult feelings might have a beneficial effect. How else could a mother be in the face of such anguish?

THIRD SESSION

The therapy process with Sally up to this point had concentrated on Sally's pain of loss. Indeed the experience of loss in the present, coupled with anxiety about the future, might be paralysing for Sally, so that the only way the therapist might be able to address present difficulties would be in the context of the future. Talking to clients about their fears for the future is one of the most psychotherapeutic interventions in a therapist's repertoire of skills. Unless such fears are addressed they may grow into larger psychological problems that the person cannot handle. Accordingly the therapist asked Sally:

Therapist: What is your worst fear about the future?

The therapist asked the above question at a time when it felt appropriate. There was no sense of or need to push Sally into discussing matters she was not ready to discuss.

Sally: Living on my own; not being able to have children to be with me.

Sally indicated by such a response that not only was she ready to discuss the future, she clearly had given it thought. She also had the ability to identify the main issues. The therapist responded to Sally at this point by asking:

Therapist: Have you thought what you could do now to lessen this fear of being on your own in the future?

This is an example of a circular question based on the feedback in the session. It is a way of handing back responsibility for solution to the client. It is a clear example, too, of how solutions may be discovered in the course of the therapy conversation.

Sally: 'Oh yes, lots of things. Learning to cook and to iron and to use the washing machine, and learning to switch on the water heater.'

Sally was clearly doing her part in thinking through the construction of a solution.

The college course that Sally was presently doing was a course tailored to teach the students 'life skills' which included just such skills as Sally had mentioned. The course, as such, was positively connoted by the therapist so that Sally would feel encouraged to carry out her self-selected goals. The therapist, being impressed by Sally's thoughtful response, asked Sally:

Therapist: Do you think your sister thinks about the future as much as you do?
Sally: No.
Therapist: Why do you think that is so?
Sally: She's not so quick at thinking as me.

The therapeutic approach described here is characterised by an orientation towards solution and competence (Penn 1985). In this case, Sally had supplied an example of competence herself, which was more valuable than if the therapist had. The therapist prioritised it by responding:

Therapist: So you are quick at thinking.
Sally: (Face breaking into a smile) Yes.
Therapist: Do you think your sister knows that you're 'quick at thinking'?
Sally: No. She says I'm 'slow at doing'.
Therapist: So, you're slow at doing, but quick at thinking.
Sally: Yes.

Sally looked very pleased at this point in the conversation. The therapist wished to highlight this 'new story' about Sally as different to the 'dominant' one of disability and helplessness. She explored with Sally if there was any person in her life who could witness this 'quickness' at thinking. Without hesitation, Sally replied: 'Ruth, my Mum's friend. She knows that I'm quick at thinking.' The therapist believed that this moment was 'a pivotal moment' (Hoyt 1995) in the therapy process, that is a moment of change. Now, Sally had introduced a boundary between herself and the disability. Her new description of herself was as 'quick at thinking'. This was quite at variance with the old description of herself that was one of disablement. This is a clear example of how resources already present in the client, but hidden from view, can be accessed through therapy.

Earlier fears shared between therapist and supervisor about Sally's inability to be sufficiently 'psychologically minded' for her to benefit from the therapeutic process were not justified at this moment in time. Sally had achieved what might be described as a 'therapeutic leap'. When the client includes examples of his own abilities and resourcefulness in his descriptions of himself, it can help to embed new and positive patterns of thinking. The role of the therapist is simply to recognise such new descriptions and validate them.

The therapist is always curious about relationships. Remembering Sally's description of her mother, as often angry, the therapist asked Sally:

Therapist: Do you think your Mum worries about your being on your own in the future?
Sally: I don't know.
Therapist: Do you think you could talk to her about it? If you did perhaps she might be able to help you use the washing machine, the cooker and the other things you would like to know how to use?

The intended effect of this intervention was that Sally's dread of a future on her own needed to be addressed so that plans could be made in the present, which might ensure Sally's comfort and security in the future. This might also contribute to the mental well-being of her mother as well as that of Sally. Mother and daughter might both experience some sense of mastery and achievement in a very distressing situation.

The therapist also had some discussion with Sally with regard to what infertility meant to her. That meaning seemed to be about the fact that Sally would not have children to care for her in the future, rather than any desire to have children in their own right. Accordingly the therapist asked Sally:

Therapist: Do you think that children stay with their parents always? Your Mum left her Mum in Australia didn't she?
Sally: I suppose everyone is on their own sometime.
Therapist: I guess that is so.

The intervention was intended to normalise Sally's experience of aloneness. The third session was concluded with attention paid to the coming week in which Sally for the first time was going to be housed with a neighbour during her mother's sojourn in Australia.

FOURTH SESSION

The therapy work done in this session might be described as 'maintenance' work. It took place during the week of Sally's mother's absence, whilst she was relocated to her neighbour's house. Throughout the session, Sally seemed more relaxed in manner and said that it was better than she had expected to be away from home. Her guardian for the week had gone to some lengths to invite other young people into the house for Sally. Sally had viewed this positively and said: 'It's more interesting than being at home.' This was further evidence of Sally's ability to enjoy life.

The therapist asked Sally if she had been successful at gathering information about any leisure activities. Sally had made some effort in this direction. The therapist positively connoted this. The therapist risked asking Sally:

Therapist: What have you done during the week that has pleased and surprised you?
Sally: (Shyly) I've learned to iron my T-shirts.

Sally was proud of this achievement. The therapist congratulated Sally on her success and uncovered too that Sally had learned to improve her cookery skills. The therapist also positively noted the fact that Sally had been successfully living away from home.

This session concluded with a brief discussion that the next session was the last but one. Working in a time-limited context, the ending of therapy must be addressed as early as possible in the process. In this instance, the therapist was impressed by the fact that Sally had kept count herself and was fully aware of the fact that the next session was the second to last. This was further evidence of Sally's ability to collaborate in the therapy relationship. She had already accommodated to the ending of therapy. This in itself validated the brief episode of therapy in Sally's life, which seemed to have provided what was needed for now.

FIFTH SESSION

This session took place after Sally's mother had returned from holiday. Sally was reinstated in the family home. She arrived at the session positively radiant. She was wearing carefully applied gold sparkling eyeshadow. Her skin was much clearer and her face brighter. She began the session by responding to the therapist's remark on how different she looked by saying:

Sally: Things are not so horrible now.

Many things had happened to Sally since the last therapy session. Firstly, her mother had told Sally when she had returned that she and the rest of the family were going to Australia for the duration of the approaching college holiday. Sally was delighted with this news. When the therapist had asked Sally in an earlier session what she most wanted to do, she had replied: 'I want to explore the world.' In a sense this offer of a trip to Australia came just at the right time for Sally, dovetailing with her first experience of living successfully outside the family home. The therapist acknowledged this gain. A beneficial intervention can be to acknowledge positive events that occur in the client's life.

Sally was slowly gaining a new awareness of herself as autonomous. As evidence of this, she stated that because she was now 18, her mother no longer needed to accompany her on public transport. She was now ready to do that by herself, she said. Sally appeared to be gaining some controls over practical issues in her life. The label of disability appeared to be losing its hold over her life.

The discussion continued with Sally supplying further information about herself. She said, 'I'm a good judge of character. I'm confident. I'm not shy.' Unsolicited, Sally supplied a witness to this description of herself from her life: 'My old headmaster used to say that I'm confident.' A good measure of progress in therapy is when the client supplies positive descriptions of themselves.

Before the end of the session, Sally imparted the information that during her week's sojourn with the neighbour, she had begun to menstruate and that she had grown three centimetres in height. She exclaimed: 'At last my body is beginning to work normally! I've waited so long for this. I'm changing at last.' The hormone therapy was having a positive effect. Being empathic in this context seemed to require rejoicing with Sally over her 'normal' body functions. This the therapist did. The role of the therapy process in Sally's life at this moment was to provide a space where her achievements, changing body and good fortune were validated and acknowledged. Part of working from a systemic perspective and within a time-limited framework is to have an eye for the opportunities that life outside the therapy room bring.

The therapist asked Sally how she had found the session. Sally replied: 'I like talking! We're funny together.' This seemed to be her way of acknowledging that 'things are not so horrible now'. The therapist asked Sally if she wanted to have the final session in the coming week or if she would prefer to contact the therapist herself following her return from the holiday in Australia. This was to encourage Sally's own sense of being in control. Sally chose to contact the therapist some time in the future herself, once she had returned home after her holiday.

CONCLUSION

The final session did not take place. Sally's trip to Australia was extended. Sally had had control as to whether the 'final session' would happen or not. She chose not to utilise it. This in itself could be considered a positive therapeutic intervention. The possibility of future therapy had been discussed with Sally, should she desire it. This is a hallmark of working within a brief framework. The door is left open for the possibility of future work should the need arise. This feels particularly appropriate when working with young people and especially when working with a student with complex problems. Therapy, rather than being a permanent feature of life, is best saved for those times when the immediate way forward slips from the client's view.

The very structure that the time-limited therapy context imposes and the limited number of the sessions can provide a containing and stabilising framework for a child in distress following the diagnosis of a serious medical condition or having been given 'bad news'. Such a framework can provide the opportunity for the child to pause and reflect on their ideas of what the diagnosis means for them. Working thus is appropriate in the school setting. This may result in an altered perception of themselves in relation to the medical 'label'. In the case of Sally, she was able to create a new description of herself as 'quick at thinking'. This new perspective had profound implications for how she viewed herself in the future.

To work within a tightly structured framework with a child with a serious medical condition also acknowledges the fact that most change takes place outside the therapy room. One of the beliefs integral to this approach is that therapy initiates a process that is consolidated in time. Sally's problems had not gone away, but a new perspective of her own identity which was not co-terminous with her label of disablement had begun to emerge.

A new and different future could now be envisioned; a future that might not have been conjectured based on the first encounter with Sally, when she was characterised by her 'toddler-like' babble. In the final therapy session, Sally's speech was clear and coherent. She seemed appropriately adolescent in her renewed sense of hope and mastery of life. Therapy with Sally in the non-pathologising school context not only contributed to a successful outcome, but one could also argue that the work achieved was unique to the school setting. The presence of Sally's peers, which had once been a cause of anguish to her, had become real and revitalising role models for her to emulate. The school setting became the context for Sally in which she could create new connections and relationships beyond the world of her immediate family. This seemed to be symbolised by her gold eyeshadow, a feature of her peer group in the school, and her sense of anticipation of the future.

10 Getting Unstuck in Therapy: Adversity as Opportunity

The preceding chapters of this book describe what happens when therapy progresses seemingly without too many problems or obstacles. However, many therapists fear what is almost inevitable: that one day they will encounter a client who poses an issue or event with which they are not adequately prepared to handle. This chapter attempts not only to alleviate that fear but to change the perspective about feeling stuck altogether.

Historically, when faced with an impasse, therapists have termed the word 'resistance' – placing the blame or responsibility of the therapeutic impasse on the client rather than on the therapist. This is not to discredit such a concept or to suggest that it does not exist. A brief therapeutic approach as outlined in this book simply maintains that such a position may not be the most productive one for the client.

As such, this chapter attempts to shift the focus embedded in the concept of resistance: when an impasse is reached within therapy, the causal focus need not be placed upon the client. Feeling stuck with a client is better viewed as an opportunity than as a negative event. Clients are expected to have resistance to and ambivalence about change – without it there would scarcely be the need for therapy. Instead, a brief therapeutic approach recognises that when therapy stalls the onus for change falls upon the therapist and not upon the client. Responsibility suggests ownership and when we own something we have the power to do something about it.

This chapter aims to explore the various ways in which a therapist can positively approach any impasses that may occur in therapy and to embrace them as opportunities for change. Impasses are like road signs – they are indications that your direction or speed may need to change. Just as we appreciate the signs along the road as helpful indications of our journey, so too the therapist must learn to appreciate impasses as helpful indications of the therapeutic process. In this light, feeling stuck need not be feared but embraced as an opportunity that will ultimately contribute to a better therapeutic experience for the client.

WHAT IS 'FEELING STUCK'? HOW DO YOU RECOGNISE IT?

In order to capitalise on an opportunity, one must first be able to recognise that the opportunity is at hand. Thus, one needs to know what 'being stuck' is and what the indications are when it is present.

Feeling stuck '...in the therapeutic process can be defined as a block to progress either from the counsellor's or the client's point of view' (Bor *et al.* 1998: 155). No matter what your orientation as a therapist, goals for therapy should exist: cognitive-behavioural goals may be more explicit and well defined than Freudian goals, but a Freudian approach too will still have expectations about what represents progress. If those expectations are not being met or addressed, then even the Freudian counsellor can end up feeling stuck. Existential-phenomenological practitioners may face similar feelings when they are unable to sufficiently enter into the client's worldview and systemic therapists may at some point feel that they have exhausted exploration of the client's relationships and perceptions of situations and problems without a significant shift in feeling or problem focus. All therapists have expectations about what constitutes 'good' therapy.

Likewise, all therapists would agree that 'good therapy' is promoted when a therapist is able to recognise when she is feeling stuck. Such a feeling can occur at any stage of therapy and with any type of presenting problem. Moreover, therapy itself tends to oscillate between periods of positive evolution and periods of less noticeable progress. Rarely does progress just 'take off' from the moment of assessment and continue smoothly throughout the course of therapy. A competent therapist must be able to recognise the difference between naturally occurring 'slower' periods of therapy and moments of genuinely being stuck. Addressing the former case may disrupt the natural flow of therapy and may pressure the client to move more quickly than he is capable. In the later case, these moments must be addressed by the therapist for progress to resume in a timely manner. A brief therapeutic approach promotes an active handling of stuck moments as they are seen as potential catalysts for change.

Feeling stuck on the part of the therapist often manifests itself as feeling frustrated, bored or indifferent towards a client. As therapists, we are usually excited about the potential for change in a client (or within that client's environment) and are familiar with the sense of opportunity that each new client brings, both in positive transformation for that client and in our own opportunity to learn anew about the human spirit. When we find ourselves experiencing resistance towards a client, this is a key indication that we are encountering 'stuckness' and will need to reflect upon the processes taking place.

The therapist's feelings towards a client are an essential element of any therapeutic experience. They are a good measure of how this person is perceived by others and also if professional boundaries are being crossed. They allow you to bond with a client, gain sympathy and understanding, and to enter into a client's worldview. Thus, *your* feelings are a guiding force in every aspect of therapy despite our professional inclination to downplay their role. Brief therapy recognises this natural element of therapy and encourages honest reflection upon those feelings to help direct the therapeutic process. As a general check in your practice, from time to time you may wish to ask yourself:

- Have I become argumentative with any of my clients?
- Am I tired? Irritable? Frustrated? Bored?
- Am I lacking a sense of achievement with any clients?
- Am I distancing myself from any client?
- Have I become judgemental of any clients? (Bor *et al.* 1998).

When the answers to any of these questions are negative in nature (in other words, 'yes'), this is an indication that you may be approaching, or at, an impasse in therapy.

There are four main scenarios which may signify being stuck:

1. going over familiar issues without evidence of any progress in how the problem is viewed;
2. obvious boredom or missed sessions by the client;
3. the therapist not looking forward to a therapy session; and
4. the therapist becoming hostile or argumentative with the client.

The latter two scenarios reiterate the notion that negative emotions experienced by the therapist are a strong indication that something is amiss in the therapeutic process. When you recognise these feelings or behaviours being present, this is a signal that you must stop and reflect upon what is taking place.

Likewise, in the first two scenarios, you will also need to access the state of the therapeutic process. However, in both these instances the behaviour of the client, as opposed to that of the therapist, will be the key indication that an impasse in therapy may be occurring. When a client repeatedly goes over the same information or focuses on a particular

event without any signs that such information is being emotionally pro-
cessed or reworked, this may signal that you have hit therapeutic doldrums.
Missed sessions, especially those which occur repetitively, with increased
frequency or without proper notice, are also events which should give the
brief therapist pause.

Boredom in sessions or a lack of interest in engaging in the therapeutic
process is cause for concern as well. Although many clients do not initially
arrive at therapy with a great deal of hope about their current situation,
most are at least willing to participate in the search for a solution or for
some alleviation from their distress. Boredom and a failure to engage
signal a lack of participation in the fundamental process of therapy.
Most therapists would agree that little progress is ever gained with clients
who are reluctant about therapy. Boredom is a form of reluctance. It may
be subtler than a client who outwardly expresses his ambivalence about
being in therapy, but boredom is a way of saying 'I do not care about
being here. This process with you does not interest me.' It is thus a sign
that something needs to change.

However, a note of caution in all these situations must be raised.
As a responsible and proactive therapist, one must remember that what
may be 'stuck' for you may not always equate to being 'stuck' for the
client. However, therapy as described in this book is a process of
mutual engagement, and it is likely that your feelings as a therapist will
reflect the feelings of the client. In your assessment of being 'stuck', you
must try and separate your emotions and goals from that of the client.
Repetitive discussion of a problem may in some instances be exactly
what the client needs in order to reframe it for himself. A lack of
interest in therapy may signal ambivalence, but for some clients just the
act of coming to therapy regardless of the amount of participation is
a sign of progress. Missed sessions are not always a sign of resistance.
Sometimes clients will miss consecutive therapy sessions for legitimate
and unavoidable reasons and in such instances the therapist must
remain open and supportive. Any frustrations that you as the therapist
are feeling must be addressed in order to further therapy. However, one
must always consider the possibility that your frustrations with the
pace of therapy may be just that: *your* frustration and not the client's.
Professional practice will demand that you are able to separate the two.
As a check, when you are feeling frustrated, indifferent or bored, ask
yourself:

- Does my frustration stem from a goal that I have set and not the
  client's goal(s)?
- Am I frustrated with the pace? Does the client appear frustrated/
  bored/indifferent as well?

- Is there anything occurring in my personal life that may be causing stress, such as health issues, relationship difficulties or too much work?
- Is there pressure from an outside source that is impacting my practice?

Your answers to these questions will help direct your course of action.

A DIFFERENT PHILOSOPHY ABOUT BEING STUCK

Difficulties or obstacles in therapy are a natural part of the therapeutic process. The client who does not pose a challenge is a rare one. Clients are in therapy precisely because they are having a difficult time in their lives or are struggling to define themselves as a person. They are in our offices because they are seeking help in a process. To assume that you will know precisely what to do in each and every case and will do it effortlessly and with confidence is irresponsible. A good therapist therefore will acknowledge that difficulties will arise *as a matter of course* and as such the responsibility for tackling those difficulties lies with the therapist. If difficulties are viewed as part and parcel of the therapeutic process, then the task of managing those problems will naturally fall to the therapist; it is part of the therapist's job. One cannot expect the client to manage the therapeutic process.

This approach is a departure from the traditional viewpoint. Freud coined the word 'resistance' to describe when a client did not move forward with therapy as expected by the therapist. Thus, from the beginning of psychological practice, the client has often been seen as the bearer of responsibility whenever progress has not been made. A brief therapeutic approach suggests that, at the very least, this is not a useful standpoint and it may even be negligent. Quick (1996: 4), in her overview of brief therapy, sees the therapist as 'an active agent for change who deliberately initiates the change process'. If you view the therapist as a catalyst for change, then failure to change by the client is a malfunction of the catalyst rather than a stoppage by the client as suggested by the term 'resistance'.

Moreover, the therapist is not a neutral observer, even within the most client-directed therapies. All relationships are circular and nowhere is this more important to acknowledge than in the therapeutic setting. The environment in therapy is co-created by therapist and client. In a brief approach if one arrives at a place in therapy where progress is slow or at an impasse, this is an indication that the stance taken by the therapist needs to be examined. This is not to say that the client is free from responsibility for creating the impasse. A brief approach simply takes the position that in a circular relationship where the therapist is, by nature, more active in consciously shaping the environment, it is then the responsibility of the therapist to shift the approach when resistance is present.

As therapists, no matter which underlying theory underpins our practice, we must remember that it is the relationship with the client that is the single most important factor in determining the client's outcome. Study after study suggests that the empathy and bonding experienced by the client with the therapist is critical to the success of the experience. A solid, collaborative relationship is a necessary element for sound practice, especially when working briefly.

This is important to reflect upon when we consider the ideas of being 'stuck' and 'resistance'. From the perspective of working briefly, being 'stuck' suggests that something within the therapeutic relationship is not working. As we are trying to honour and build a stronger therapeutic relationship, brief therapy takes the view that it is more beneficial to own the responsibility for that situation. If we own it, we are in a better position to then control it. If we place the responsibility on the client, we risk the possibility of damaging our relationship with the client rather than strengthening it. Consider the difference between a therapist saying 'You are having a problem with therapy' and 'I am having difficulty helping you reach your goals.' Which is more helpful for the client? Of course, these words would rarely, if ever, be spoken to a client but the philosophy with which we approach a problem will set the tone for the therapeutic alliance.

An 'important premise of [a brief] approach is that multiple views of reality exist...[and] that [these] "views" of reality are all we can know, and perhaps all that exist' (Quick 1996: 3). To be 'stuck' suggests that we may have not yet sufficiently entered into the world of our client – that we have not yet fully grasped our client's 'reality' and its implications. This means that when we are stuck we have an opportunity to better connect with our client and to build the therapeutic relationship. Rather than seeing a stuck point in therapy as a breakdown in the therapeutic process, we can see it as a place where we can strengthen the bond and understanding between ourselves and the client.

A client's reality is also created and maintained by the environment in which that client lives. As Quick (1996: 3) notes 'problems are not single entities that exist within a single individual; rather, they result from interactions between individuals'. One must remember that no matter how out of the ordinary a client's behaviour may seem, it is understandable in conjunction with the reality of the client. If a client seems to be thwarting progress or is indifferent to change, as therapists, we must consider that such action is reasonable given the client's reality. Thus, if we feel blocked by the client's behaviour or do not understand it, we must contemplate the possibility that we have not sufficiently measured the implications of the client's reality. In such cases, we are stuck not because the client is lacking, but because we are lacking the insight into the client's reality. Of course, this does not imply any individual therapist is capable of understanding every client's reality. The skill that is being identified here is the ability to recognise the 'state of stuckness' and as a therapist to take responsibility for it and action to address and resolve it.

This view of being stuck is a somewhat radical departure from what has been accepted in the past. Indeed, it may not feel comfortable to the therapist to be responsible for an impasse and part of us may resist such a notion. Certainly, there are clients who are more difficult to work with than others. The brief therapeutic approach as described in this book simply suggests that it is more beneficial to approach an impasse with the philosophy that the therapist has a responsibility to manage the situation and to alter her approach accordingly. Little is gained by viewing an impasse as the 'client's problem'. As the client has come to you seeking help with a problem, any obstacles in moving forward are part of that problem – part of the therapist's commitment to the client.

Thus, when the therapist feels 'stuck', a brief therapeutic approach offers two main insights:

1. the responsibility in managing/moving through the impasse rests with the therapist. This does not exclude eliciting the client's help and views of what the next steps might be; and
2. that responsibility is an important and pregnant opportunity.

Being stuck may be frustrating your practice but it should do so only in the same way that a good conundrum challenges your mind: it may be difficult at first, but the rewards of breaking through far outweigh the effort given.

WHAT COULD BE WRONG? THE FIRST LINES OF ENQUIRY

Simple problems call for simple solutions. In fact, even the most complex of problems often have a simple solution. As such, when one is feeling stuck, the first line of attack is to start with the most obvious and straight-forward approaches. With a conundrum you would first try to tackle it by going through the simplest lines of reasoning. Indeed, some brain-teasers are difficult just because a person often fails to examine the simplest solution first. Likewise, when you are feeling 'stuck', some simple strategies may be all you need to overcome the therapeutic impasse.

Review

A review of your notes and/or tapes is always good practice, even when you are not feeling stuck. In times when you are feeling blocked, it is critical. This review should include, but not be limited to, the referring letter, the client's medical history, your assessment notes, subsequent session notes and any other letters or notes received relating to the client. You may also want to reference any learning materials, class notes or books which have guided your practice. Such an examination often helps to refresh one's memory about techniques or theories that can be easily forgotten in one's daily work.

When reviewing your notes, ask yourself:

- How did the referring letter set the initial framework of my work with this client? Did it assume something about the client which may be untrue or counterproductive?
- What was my initial assessment? What would be my assessment now? Are they in conflict? Are they too similar, that is, could a different initial assessment have been made?
- Is there a medical condition present which has not been addressed? Has a medical condition been given too much attention? Could it be a distraction from a broader issue?
- Do my session notes have a theme? What part of my session notes have I ignored? What does the 'fine print' of my session notes suggest?
- Have I incorporated the information from other letters into our work? Have these letters/notes from outside sources influenced the direction therapy has taken? Is that direction valid?

During this review, try to formulate a different picture of your client than the one you have now. You may even want to form a mental image of a client that is entirely different from your client's just to help you see your client in a different light. The purpose of such an exercise is to try and start 'fresh' with no pre-conceived notions about the client. Sometimes our mental image of a client is so strong that it does not enable us to think laterally about the client. Of course, visual cues are extremely important in building a complete picture of a person but when you are stuck, creating a client that is less 'real' may free up your mind to think in an alternative direction.

Also, pay close attention to any advice or comments offered by the referring agent and medical practitioners involved in the case. Input from other sources can be invaluable but it can also prejudice our view of a problem from the outset. For instance, consider this actual referral from a doctor at a general practice health centre:

Dear Therapist,
   Could you please meet with Mrs Gerwen, a lovely, active client of mine who has been experiencing bouts of depression? These appear to be

caused by her relationship with her son that has become strained due to his drug use. She is not presently on any medication.

Thank you, the referring Dr Newport

Mrs Gerwen arrived at the assessment meeting tearful and shaky. She indeed appeared to be depressed and the therapist began a cognitive-behavioural treatment programme. Progress, however, was slow and the therapist began to have doubts about the efficacy of such interventions with this particular client. Something appeared to be 'off'. In the end, Mrs Gerwen dropped out of therapy after breaking into the therapist's office and stealing the therapist's purse. Mrs Gerwen was actually the person with a drug problem.

This assessment was missed because of the tone set by the referring letter. The words 'lovely' and 'active' prejudiced the therapist's view so that Mrs Gerwen's fidgeting and intensity was overlooked. The tearfulness and shakiness were interpreted along the doctor's viewpoint as depression-related rather than being caused by an outside agent. Drug use was not considered given that, according to the referring letter, Mrs Gerwen's relationship with her son had become strained due to his use. This set the tone that Mrs Gerwen was against drug use and that assumption prevailed throughout the course of therapy. No doubt, Mrs Gerwen had given this information to the doctor and he cannot be blamed for passing it along. But, as a therapist, one must be very careful about the information gathered from outside sources. It is both a valuable, indispensable resource and a resource that can unknowingly hinder the therapeutic process. As such, whenever one feels stuck, a good overview of conversations and diagnoses gathered from other sources is essential. A useful approach is to play 'devil's advocate' with such information and to reformulate an assessment of your client as if that information was erroneous.

Outside Support

Another important strategy when you are feeling stuck is to make use of your supervisors, peers and work colleagues. Besides providing a general check and support base, your supervisor's role is also to guide you through the more difficult aspects of your work. In other words, one of your supervisor's main functions is to help you when you do not know what to do, that is, when you are stuck! Bringing a client's case to a supervisor does not necessarily imply that the therapist failed to discern his role in a problem; it is difficult to observe and be objective about a process in which one is a part. In fact, a brief therapeutic approach maintains that the use of a supervisor when one is feeling stuck is to actually discern one's role rather than being perceived as a failure for doing so. It is a sign that the therapist is aware of some of her limitations and has the professionalism to act positively in relation to this understanding.

The very act of describing a client's case to another individual can help to sort out the different dimensions of a problem and to clarify the various maintaining elements. Thus, to simply review a case with your supervisor, peers or work colleagues can often help to shift an impasse. This network of individuals is qualified to offer feedback and an informed perspective that may enrich your understanding of a problem. Whenever you reach an impasse, the possibility of such a review should always be considered.

In addition, not only can this group of individuals add perspective, but they can also help you to determine if a client's case is beyond your level of expertise. The ability to recognise such a situation is critical to professional practice. No matter how much experience or training a therapist may have, the possibility always exists that a client may be beyond your skill level or may benefit from more specialised care. Knowing when to refer is a crucial part of brief therapeutic practice. It maximises both your time and the client's. Therapy cannot remain brief if a client is in the care of a therapist who is not able to manage a case appropriately. Hence, when you do feel stuck, you must consider the possibility that the impasse is an indication that the client is beyond your skill level. In such cases, one would need to refer either to another therapist or to another type of professional specialist. Knowing what your boundaries and limitations are is vital to effective brief practice.

Assess Problems and Goals

Brief therapy also demands that within each case you have a well-developed sense of 'the problem' and 'the goals'. In any approach to therapy, you must be able to formulate a sense of direction as, indeed, it is when this direction is thwarted or changed that we may experience feeling stuck. When stuck, take the time out to review both your problem definition and your goals. Goals need to be manageable in size and collaboratively defined between client and therapist. When too big or vague, they become difficult to achieve. Increasing the specificity of goals makes them less universal and, as a result, more manageable (Quick 1996). In brief therapy, goals should be small, specific and significant. When collaboratively defined goals are real for the client, this helps to keep therapy on track. An impasse can often be shifted simply by reducing the size of change that is expected.

At one level, being stuck suggests that something assumed about the problem is incorrect. The problem is somehow different or more complicated. Therefore, another useful strategy in a brief approach is to ask yourself what you have presumed about the problem. Focus on the problem definition:

- Who developed it? How does the client describe it?
- What is assumed within that definition?
- What does the client believe others understand about the problem?
- What solutions have been attempted? How do you know about them?
- Have you asked your client in what way it is a problem for him? Is there a hidden meaning to the problem?
- Are you 'buying into' the problem?

As Walter and Peller (2000: 36–37) point out, 'If we enter a relationship assuming ahead of time that we know what is right or best for our clients, then we are already closing off possibilities, as well as our ability to be open and understanding. As soon as we assume we understand, then curiosity ceases'. Whatever we assume about a problem limits our understanding of it. Working alongside the client and eliciting his views on the problem helps to cut through our assumptions and hopefully makes therapy more appropriate.

Clients sometimes switch goals and problems as well. Continual direction changes in therapy can be frustrating as little progress is ever made when goals remain elusive. If your client does switch goals, a brief approach recommends that you address such change. You may ask your client, 'Last time we talked X seemed to be the greatest frustration in your life. Today Y seems to be of greater concern. What happened? Is X still troubling for you?' (Quick 1996). This simple and direct approach will allow you and your client to prioritise issues and tackle them in order of importance.

When stuck, you may also want to try measuring the amount of success achieved so far. Conversation about positive changes that have already taken place can serve to highlight what might be helpful in the future. Often as therapists looking for the larger picture, we may not always recognise or appreciate what has given comfort to a client on a smaller scale. When you are feeling stuck, you may want to try asking your client:

> 'I was wondering what elements of our work together so far have you found most helpful? Sometimes when we understand what has worked best for you, it helps us to create similar, but larger, changes for you in the future.'

Such an approach may help spur conversation in a positive direction.

As we have already discussed, another solution-focused strategy in brief therapy is the 'miracle question' (Quick 1996) and in times of difficulty, it can be very useful in shifting the tone of therapy. In brief, the miracle question asks: 'Suppose that one night, while you were asleep, there was a miracle and this problem was solved. How would you know? What would be different? [What would you do differently?]' (de Shazer 1988: 5 as found in Quick). This is a question that opens countless possibilities as it removes the normal boundaries we tend to draw around a problem. It is a question that lifts obstacles.

No matter what a client's reply to this question may be – whether possible or impossible – it makes available a scenario where the client can imagine a different state of affairs. The follow-up questions then produce a mental exercise that forces the client to step outside of the current reality of his situation. Sometimes, client and therapy can become so mired in the present time that movement away from the problem and towards a solution is too encumbered. The miracle of the 'miracle question' can allow client and therapist to bypass that reality and to mentally move into a more positive space where constructive ways of being are created. This exercise is a variation of the two impasse strategies defined above: outlining specific goals and focusing on success. The miracle creates a successful situation and the follow-up questions define strategies for maintaining that situation. Those strategies can be seen as goals.

Finally, whenever one is faced with an impasse in therapy, one must reflect upon the timing of such an event. Just as one may regularly ask the question, 'Why now?' during an initial assessment, that question is also pertinent when one is feeling stuck.

- Are events occurring in the client's life that may be causing added stress? (that is, a birthday, back to school, the anniversary of a loss).
- What time of year is it? The holidays? Shorter daylight hours?
- Is a deadline imminent for the client such as a move or a job change?
- Where are you in therapy? Is treatment ending soon?

All of these questions address factors which could be contributing to or creating an impasse.

GOING DEEPER: THE SECOND LINE OF ENQUIRY

Once you have reviewed your notes, discussed the case with your supervisor/peers/colleagues, examined your goals and successes, posed the miracle question, invited the client's view of the impasse and/or considered the timing of the impasse, you should be well past feeling stuck, right? Hopefully, but as experience will show, this is not always the case.

Straightforward approaches are essential to consider but they may not always reap the change needed. Sometimes more complex issues involving the process of therapy will need to be explored. Many of these avenues are a 'deeper' level of the strategies outlined above.

Hidden Fears and Benefits

For instance, this chapter began by redefining 'feeling stuck' and the concept of 'resistance'. Emphasis was placed upon therapist responsibility in the management of an impasse and understanding that a client's behaviour must be seen as functional at some level within his environment. The idea of resistance towards therapy was thus downplayed. Yet, clients can and do at times thwart progress whether consciously or unconsciously. This can create an impasse that is resilient. It is hard, to say the least, to shift an obstacle in therapy when the client continually replaces each obstacle with another one.

In a brief therapeutic approach, although the client may be actively trying to resist change, the therapist is responsible for understanding and tackling that resistance. In such cases, the fears of the client may not have been adequately addressed. If you detect 'resistance' from your client, ask yourself:

- What benefits does this client receive from his behaviour? From the current situation?
- What fears may the client have about change? What will he possibly lose?

The answers to these questions are real and compelling issues. No matter how distressed a client may seem, the client has also survived by using some of the behaviours you may be trying to change. It is a very real possibility that the changes you are trying to make in a client threaten the client's identity or sense of control in a situation. Remember, in a brief approach, all behaviour can be seen as functional given particular circumstances.

Case Example: Mrs Jones

Mrs Jones is a 27-year-old mother of two children, aged four and two. Her husband, Mr Jones, recently suffered a work-related injury which left him partially paralysed and her own mother had been bedridden on and off over the past five years. Mrs Jones was referred to therapy for depressive symptoms. At her assessment she complained through tears that she simply could not manage caring for so many people. Her husband's injury was overwhelming for her and she felt she could not cope with the changes she would have to make in order to adjust to his new needs. She felt the care of her two children and her mother would suffer. Mrs Jones complained of insomnia and an inability to concentrate, both of which added to her fears about being able to cope.

After acknowledging and accepting the difficulty of her situation, the therapist and Mrs Jones began a cognitive-behavioural programme in which Mrs Jones was counselled on how to recognise and challenge depressing thought patterns. Her successful coping skills in the past were highlighted and new management techniques were introduced. These included making use of lists, a schedule, neighbours and local support facilities.

At first, Mrs Jones appeared comforted by these new techniques. However, Mrs Jones failed to submit application forms for assisted day care for her children despite expressing interest in the extra time such care would provide her. Mrs Jones also found fault with three consecutive nurses granted to her by the local health authority. She turned each one out of her house after less than a week each, complaining they were all incompetent. Her depression seemed to deepen with the added stress caused by the nursing situation. The therapist then arranged for Mrs Jones to speak with a money-managing specialist. Mrs Jones failed to show up for her appointment explaining the following week that her mother had been 'sick' that day.

The therapist began to feel stuck in his work with Mrs Jones. They just could not seem to catch a break with the nurses and something always seemed to 'pop-up' when Mrs Jones had the opportunity to work with a specialist. At this time, the therapist began to hypothesise that Mrs Jones might have been fearful of implementing such changes into her routine. Could such support be threatening Mrs Jones in any way? What were the benefits of the current situation for Mrs Jones?

Careful exploration along these lines led the therapist to discover that Mrs Jones's sense of worth was derived from the care she gave to others. Her role within her family since she was a child was to care for other individuals – first her younger brothers and sisters, then her father when he was dying and now with her mother and her own family. As an adult, she received attention and kind words of encouragement from friends and neighbours who recognised the difficulty of Mrs Jones's situation. With the addition of her husband's injury she became stuck between being able to effectively cope with the situation and afraid that if she did accept outside help, her own work would be devalued. She worried that if others could do her job, her own value, and thus self worth, would be diminished. In recognising these issues the counsellor was able to shift the focus of therapy away from added resources and towards a programme that strengthened Mrs Jones's self-esteem. When Mrs Jones began to believe that people would appreciate all of her care efforts, including managing a team of caregivers, and that people valued other aspects of her personality such as her wit and enthusiasm, her reservations about outside care dissipated.

If you do suspect that your client has hidden fears or is benefiting from his current mode of behaviour, then you will need to tailor your approach accordingly. With a client who is fearful of change, you will need to find the balance between initiating change and preserving the therapeutic bond. This may mean addressing such issues directly, switching the focus of your interventions or simply allowing the client more time to adjust to the changes taking place. Only experience will tell which course of action is appropriate for each client.

At times, the most effective and efficient direction will be to speak directly about your apprehensions, that is, 'Mrs Jones, I am worried that not only are you feeling overwhelmed by the current situation, but also that you may be fearing a loss of identity and control which is quite common in circumstances such as your own. How do you feel about having other people help you care for your family? Does the thought frighten you in any way?' At other times, you may have to be subtler by steering around such impediments without your client being consciously aware of the direction change. In the example given above, the therapist, following a cognitive-behavioural course of therapy, might have begun schema work with Mrs Jones starting with homework assignments aimed at building her self-esteem. In either case, the course of action chosen will be the one that maximises time and reinforces the therapeutic relationship.

If a client admits to feeling apprehensive about change or the direction of therapy, a good approach is to explore the consequences of those fears. Ask your client:

- What is the worst possible consequence of the presenting problem? What will happen if this problem is not addressed?
- What are the worst possible consequences if the problem is addressed? What could you lose?
- Has any part of those consequences started to take place? How likely is each?
- Is there a middle ground between the two outcomes?
- What is the least that can be done to initiate change? (Bor *et al.* 1998)

Because hidden motivations and fears can interfere with progress, '...it is particularly important to consider the client's "position". "Position" encompasses values, beliefs about self and others, and the "language", literal and figurative, that is spoken' (Quick 1996: 5). One must consider with the client his 'position' when collaboratively formulating a therapeutic plan. If you have not already explored this, this may be the reason you are feeling stuck.

Role-play

At such times, a good tactic is to start 'walking in your client's shoes'. *What exactly does it feel like to be him?* Role-play in your mind being your client. Have conversations with people in his life, responding not as you would respond but as you believe your client would respond. Consider his social context: what pressures are put on your client due to finances, family, culture, gender, life cycle and peers? How would these pressures effect the decisions your client has to make? How would changes made by your client be perceived/received by these forces? Most importantly, with each of these questions, extrapolate several levels to the problem. Think about what may happen not just as an immediate response to your client's actions but several responses 'down the line'. You may also want to build a type of flow diagram that illustrates the interrelatedness of the various pressures on your client.

Case Example: Kevin

Kevin was a 23-year-old Latino man referred for anger management issues. He worked for a shipping company helping direct packages in the central warehouse facility. On several occasions at work he had become violent with his managing supervisor and had to be restrained by his colleagues. Witnesses to the situations testified that his anger had not been provoked. When Kevin did not respond positively to anger management techniques, the therapist began to feel stuck as Kevin needed his job as a condition of his immigration status and as a consequence of his finances.

When the therapist attempted to 'role-play' Kevin in his mind, the therapist discovered that he knew very little about Kevin's 'position' in life. As such, he began to expand the boundaries of his questioning and found that Kevin worked with his girlfriend's brother, Juan. Juan had actually praised Kevin for standing up to his boss and not backing down 'like the other gutless workers'.

This bit of information eventually led the therapist to understand some of the complexities surrounding Kevin's problem. Juan was passing on information to Kevin's girlfriend about 'what a man' he was at work. Her last boyfriend had apparently failed to protect her from a jealous, previous boyfriend. Kevin's family expected him to marry soon and had questioned his 'manhood' when his previous girlfriend had left him. During a very public fight, she had chastised him about his failure to satisfy her sexually.

Thus, Kevin's outbursts at work actually elevated him in the eyes of his girlfriend. This was important to Kevin as his relationship with his family would be affected if he lost his girlfriend. He feared that another break-up would cause him to lose respect and then status within his household (he had two younger brothers who were already fathers).

These relationships surrounding the problem needed to be considered in the therapeutic process. Kevin's 'position' on his anger encompassed values unique to his social and familial situation. These issues were not discovered during assessment as Kevin had stated that he 'needed to manage [his] anger better in order to keep [his] job'. When the therapist 'stepped into Kevin's shoes' and used some of the anger management techniques they had discussed, the therapist realised that such efforts diminished Kevin's sense of 'manliness'. His 'position' had not been integrated into the problem approach. With this new frame of reference, the therapist was able to better connect with his client and develop some strategies that respected the dynamics of Kevin's situation.

Spinelli (1994) in his seminal work, 'Demystifying Therapy', suggests that the hallmark of effective therapy is to be able to enter into your client's world and to then expand the possibilities within your client's reality. No matter what philosophy directs your therapy, when you are stuck this is a fruitful attitude to adapt. Thinking as if you were your client and working with the web of relations in his life is an exercise that can only expand your understanding of a problem. As suggested before, we can only really 'know' our own reality. Yet, to manage and make sense of the world, we are constantly projecting our own view of reality onto others. When we become stuck, a good strategy is to try and minimise this process and to actively search for ways in which a client's reality is different than our own or the 'norm'. At the very least, such an exercise will allow you to gain a larger and richer picture of your client.

Language

The language we use in relation to a problem also defines how we, and our client, will see and understand it. Thus, when we are stuck, we must also reflect upon the language being used. Language sets the tone for the therapeutic environment as well as the tone for the problem. Just as we choose words carefully when setting up the relationship between therapist and client, we must also choose our words carefully when speaking about the problem. Therapy is health care through talking. The quality of the language therefore determines the quality of the therapy.

Everything said during a session has an impact and may alter perceptions. Problems exist in a language used between people and are unique to each dialogue. For example, consider these two possible responses to the statement, 'Ugh. This is just a huge problem':

Therapist: You're right, that really is a huge problem!

or

Therapist: Wow, that does sound a bit difficult.

Although both confirm the complexity of the situation, the first response keeps the problem definition at the same level: it's huge! The problem now exists as a huge entity between client and therapist. The second statement, however, acknowledges the seriousness of the task while turning the severity level down a notch. Within this dialogue, the problem is characterised somewhere between 'huge' and 'a bit difficult'; this is a small change but one that is real.

These are the types of language changes that are essential in a brief approach. Consider this conversation:

Client: I just cannot do anything right for her. Every thing I seem to do is wrong. I just cannot see how this marriage is ever going to make it. I'm not meant to be married. It's just too much hard work.
Therapist: Can you think of a time when it was working for the two of you?
Client: Yeah sure. I mean I would not have married her if things were always this way. When we first got married we would do lots of things together. I'd be rushing home to see her and she'd be rushing out the front door to meet me.
Therapist: Sounds fun. Could you think of something you could do that would make her want to rush out to meet you today?

The client's language is initially very negative both in the present and when talking about the foreseeable future. The therapist responds by moving away from the negativity of the future and focusing on the positive aspects of the past. Notice that the therapist asks if the relationship was at some point working 'for the two of you'. By using this phrase, the therapist is able to underline that the marriage is about the two of them and not just about one person's views. The client has just expressed that his actions do not seem to be working within the marriage. The phrase 'the two of you' reaffirms that whatever solutions are explored, they must be workable solutions for him as well.

Also notice that the therapist then asks the client if he could do something that would make his wife rush out to meet him *today*. This one word injects hope into the present. Change is possible today: something can be done today. The therapist does not comment on marriage being hard work but rather refers to their marriage in the past as sounding fun. The implication is that marriage can be something other than hard work. Such an implication has arisen directly from the therapeutic dialogue. The therapist does not 'buy into' the problem. At times a client may need to hear that marriage is work, that it takes effort and isn't always a breeze. But, to reiterate what the client is already feeling here may just solidify his belief that marriage is difficult and he is not up to the task. The therapist's approach is one that uses language wisely. He does not refute the client's feelings but is able to create a more positive atmosphere with the simple use of the words 'fun' and 'today'. The client too has contributed to this possibility by his description of the early days of marriage being 'problem-free'. The choice of words and careful attention to language helps to 'seize the moment' and to change an impasse into an opportunity.

These are not big changes. They are small and subtle but effective. When stuck, a therapist must check to see if she is using language wisely. Good questions to ask yourself are:

- Am I using words that convey hope?
- Does my language indicate that change is occurring already?
- Am I empowering the client with my words?
- Am I listening carefully to what the client is saying?
- Does my language help to 'downsize' the changes that need to be made?

Small modifications in the language of therapy can create an entirely different atmosphere. It can cultivate an environment that is ripe for change. As such, language is a powerful tool when facing a therapeutic impasse.

Examine the Philosophy behind Questions

Language can expand or limit our experience. Each approach to therapy has its own language. As Walter and Peller (1992: 1) note, '[t]he questions that developers of therapy models ask contain presuppositions within them. Therefore, by their very asking the questions, the developers pre-select directions towards particular answers or classes of answers'. Strasser and Strasser (1997: 2) continue, '... any therapy is a philosophy, in the sense that it contains fundamental assumptions, however implicit, of how therapists view their own world and how they conduct their lives'. The questions and statements of any given mode of therapy direct the course of therapy.

Being stuck suggests that something about the direction taken is incorrect. Thus, when faced with an impasse, one must examine the questions being asked. While such questions open up avenues of discussion, they also steer the client away from other avenues of discussion. This, of course, is the point of most questions. A therapist tries to gather pertinent and revealing information while minimising the amount of extraneous details. But when at an impasse, it is only logical to consider that another avenue of discussion is needed to overcome the impasse.

A useful exercise, therefore, is to examine the questions you have been asking. Exploring the language of a question works at a detailed level, while consideration of the question as a whole looks at 'the larger picture'. What picture are you building with the questions you have been asking? Could you create a different picture with different questions? To help answer this, write down three to five of your most frequently asked questions or phrases. What do they presuppose?

For instance, consider the following two consecutive questions:

1. What did you think to yourself when that happened?
2. How did that make you feel?

The first question implies that the client's thought process is an important factor in the situation being discussed and that the client's response will give insight into the problem. It also assumes that the client is aware of his thought process. This line of questioning gives value to an individual's thoughts and even suggests, with the second question, that the thoughts are helping to generate the client's feelings. This is a perfectly valid and useful line of questioning.

Yet, many other questions could be asked: When that happened, how do you think person 'A' felt? When that happened, what did that remind you of? When that happened, what emotions did you feel? When that happened, were you more or less apprehensive about the future? These questions direct attention to relationships, to past experience, to emotions and to the future respectively. These are equally valid and useful lines of questioning – even within a single philosophy of therapy. To focus on the thought process can be very direct and informative. However, with a client who is out of touch with his feelings, such a line of questioning may only yield 'more of the same'. A more useful line of questioning with such a client might be to close one's eyes and focus on the emotional experience of that situation. With a client who is very much focused on himself, questions that help the client to speculate about other people's feelings might be more pertinent.

When you review your list of questions, think to yourself, 'When I asked this question, what question didn't I ask? What was valued with this question and what was devalued?'. Think of your questioning as doors in a fun house: when you step through one door, other doors become available, but at the same time, the previous set of doors is now out of sight. When you get stuck, you might need to go back to the main room of doors and choose a different approach.

The Therapeutic Bond

A brief approach to therapy requires a strong foundational bond between client and therapist. Without it, the opportunity for change is diminished. If a positive bond is considered essential for change, then a period of little change may indicate that the bond needs reviewing. Two things need to be considered:

1. Is the relationship between therapist and client repeating a pattern?
2. Is the relationship a positive one?

Often clients enter therapy with long-standing patterns of interaction. Indeed, when a client initially starts therapy, part of the assessment is based upon the client's style of interaction with the therapist. A therapist partially understands her client and the problem at hand through the client's behaviour and reactions in session.

A useful strategy therefore is to reflect upon the therapeutic relationship. Does the relationship repeat a pattern of interaction that is problematic in the client's life? If the relationship does mirror others, the therapist must remember that she has contributed to that relationship. Whatever the client's style of interaction, the therapist is in part responsible for the type of relationship that has been built. Thus, from a brief perspective, it is a useful exercise for the therapist to examine the process that has taken place. Whatever the therapist's responses have been, they are helpful in illustrating how others respond to the client and how ineffective relationship patterns are maintained. To overcome an impasse, a therapist may need to free herself from the interactional style of the client.

At some point in dealing with a therapeutic impasse, the therapist must also consider that the styles of the client and of the therapist are simply incompatible. No one therapist is right for every single client. The skilled therapist can recognise when a relationship with the client is not suitable for change and then refer that client to other qualified professionals. This is a professional, and respectful, course of action.

When a therapist is stuck, the problem may simply be that the client does not like or have a high opinion of the therapist. In such a scenario, the therapist is responsible for determining the correct course of action. It is possible to work with a client who does not like his therapist, but the approach taken will be one that differs dramatically from a situation in which the client and therapist are amicably bonded. It may also be possible to change negative feelings that a client has towards a therapist into positive ones. However, this change cannot be made unless the therapist is well aware of the client's feelings. A brief strategy requires that a therapist direct the therapy according to the relationship formed.

Finally, the therapist may want to address the meaning of being stuck with the client. If the client is feeling stuck or bored within therapy, to discuss this difficulty may be of great relief to the client. Many clients have expectations that their problems will be resolved quickly. When they encounter difficulties or when therapy moves slower than expected, some clients may take this as another indication that their problems are insurmountable. They can lose heart. Thus, to address the impasse may relieve some of their worries. It may also allow clients to voice fears or frustrations they have been having. Many clients are reluctant to admit that they are finding the therapeutic process difficult. Therapy is believed to be something that is supposed to make them feel better. When they do not find comfort in it, clients may be reluctant to say anything because they fear that voicing such frustrations might make matters worse.

Thus, directly addressing an impasse to the client can 'clear the air'. It can be a freeing experience for the client. Be careful and considerate with the approach:

> Susan, I have felt recently that our work may not be moving as quickly as you would like or that you may be feeling frustrated with our work. Sometimes I feel as if I am not connecting with your expectations. Is this something you feel as well?

One note of caution: although openly addressing an impasse can be an effective and efficient way to manage the situation, it can also escalate the impasse if approached inappropriately. With some clients a direct approach will only heighten the tension within the therapeutic setting. Always carefully consider the impact such a statement may have upon the client. One of the advantages of addressing the impasse to the client is that some responsibility for its resolution can be shared with the client.

Doing something Different

As a final strategy, a therapist may consider simply doing something different.

> [D]o something different, may seem painstakingly obvious. However, how often have you heard the old proverb, "If at first you don't succeed, try, try again?" Our culture has reinforced the notion of persistence in spite of procedures not working. (Walter and Peller 1992: 6)

Sometimes therapy can become so centralised around finding a solution that the client and therapist are unable to 'find the forest through the trees'. In such circumstances, a paradoxical solution may work best. Instead of continuing to focus on the problem, move away from it and simply discuss something else. The power of this approach is similar to searching for a word 'on the tip of your tongue'. When a person cannot remember a certain word, but is aware that he knows it, usually moving onto a different subject instead of continuing to actively search for the word will allow the person's mind to find that word. After a period of time the person will just find the word popping into his mind. When a therapist is stuck, but is confident that a solution or workable approach can be found, moving away from the problem may allow the mind to find the answer.

Similarly, the therapist can suggest that the client take a different approach to the problem as well. De Shazer (1988: 7) writes, 'all that is necessary is that the person...*does something different*, even if that behaviour is seemingly irrational, certainly irrelevant, obviously bizarre, or humorous'. If the seemingly rational behaviours towards a situation have not been working, then an irrelevant or irrational approach may actually produce change. People notice things that are out of the ordinary and respond to them. You probably would not look twice at a man walking down the street with a brown hat on his head but you would probably take a second glance at someone with a monkey balanced on top. You would probably even change your facial expression. Brief therapy maintains that change can happen at any moment and with the smallest, and perhaps irrelevant, beginning. Although 'do something different' may be the last strategy suggested in this chapter, it is by no means the least important.

CONCLUSION

By engaging in the therapeutic process, therapist and client are seeking change. In a sense, the client is 'feeling stuck' in his life and the therapist is helping to generate change. Similarly, when a therapist is 'feeling stuck' in her work, the therapist must generate change within her therapy. A therapist cannot ask something of her client that she is not willing to do herself. However, from a collaborative viewpoint, it is appropriate for the therapist to elicit the client's help in resolving the therapeutic impasse or, at the very least, give the client the option of sharing his views on the feeling of 'being stuck'.

Yet, at times, change for a client will be inappropriate. Behaviours and patterns of interaction and thought, even though they may be dysfunctional, are a way of managing the world. Therapists should always respect a person's defences and consider the possibility when stuck, that change at the current time is not possibility. No matter how frustrated a therapist may become with a client, one must remember that each client interacts with the world in a manner that has been molded by his particular environment, each is looking for a solution that eludes him, and each enters into therapy with hope for change. Fundamentally, it is the client's choice to change or not to change.

As therapists, being stuck is never a comfortable place in which to find ourselves. Discomfort exists within any test that we face. However, brief therapy suggests that any such discomfort is actually a sign of potential growth and therefore should be embraced as an opportunity for change. Challenging clients are ultimately the ones that teach us most about our skills as therapists. They force us to broaden our thinking and to be more flexible. Instead of fearing an impasse, therapists need to actively manage them and to recognise the possibilities embedded within them. Such a philosophy is necessary both for the growth of the client and for the growth of the therapist.

11 Endings and Closure in Therapy

Termination of therapy depends upon the definition of the problem and contract or agreement to deal with it in therapy. Conventionally, the end of therapy is when clients do not define themselves as having a problem, or when the therapeutic context does not define itself as being helpful any more. The aim in doing therapy briefly is not necessarily to solve all problems presented by the client but to find a different way of viewing one or two chosen problems, and thereby set an example for managing other difficult issues. Ultimately, the aim is to restore the client's normal capacity for competence in managing problems, or instil new ideas about how to do this better. The methods by which this can be achieved, of course, are many and varied. As in all other phases of therapy, when applying a brief approach, careful thought needs to be given to what is said and at what stage in the therapeutic process. Endings, in any therapeutic approach, are a time when review and evaluation of the effectiveness of the therapy are brought to the fore.

One of the necessary skills in doing therapy briefly is knowing when and how to end therapy. This skill is equally important whether ending after one session, during a series of meetings with the client, or in the course of a session. The therapist working briefly is guided in this decision about closure by theory, experience, inviting the client's opinion and watching for the signs from the client. Endings can be initiated by the therapist or by the clients. Working collaboratively means that both client and therapist have a part to play in the decision about ending. In the best of situations, this decision to end therapy should be at a moment when both the therapist and the client agree that the client feels emancipated from his problem or troubled feelings and is able to continue alone.

The phase of ending with the client is of vital importance to the effectiveness of doing therapy briefly. Few books focus in detail on how to bring about closure in therapy. They appear to give more attention to the beginning phases of therapy and psychopathological meaning of problems or symptoms. We devote a whole chapter to ideas about endings and closure, as it is a vital punctuation mark in doing therapy briefly. The therapist is actively planning for ending from the start of the contact irrespective of the approach used, although with different aims and timescales. The concept of doing therapy briefly in itself encapsulates the idea that the start and the end of therapy as being very closely connected. If both stages are carefully planned and executed, in tune with the needs, capabilities and competencies of the client, they form the beginning or continuation of how the client might manage problems alone in the future. Thus in starting therapy, the end is envisaged, whether it is a one-off session or the end of a number of contacts.

Some theoretical ideas about endings in brief therapy are put forward in this chapter. These include taking feedback from the client. Issues relating to ending in the context of brief therapy are discussed and some techniques particularly applicable for termination are reviewed. Finally, a more detailed outline or 'map' for the closing stage of therapy than that suggested in Chapter 7 is proposed. The outline contains the steps (signs and symbols) that herald the end of therapy and help the therapist to pace it appropriately.

SOME THEORETICAL CONCEPTS: SIGNS AND 'CLUES' FOR ENDING THERAPY

Knowing when to end is a key aspect of doing therapy briefly. Important turning points in a session can be blurred by too much discussion. Knowing when to stop therapy is something that requires skill and expertise that develops over time with practice and increasing confidence. To allow therapy to over-run can dilute the impact. The negotiation between client and therapist about ending is in itself a vital part of the process when working briefly. It is the act of emancipating the client from therapy.

There are many therapeutic approaches to ending therapy. Terminating therapy is an event that has meaning for the client and for the therapist. Endings, as traditionally understood in many modes of therapy, have the potential to evoke for both client and therapist feelings of grief, loss of the relationship and disbelief (that the client can cope alone), as much as relief (that the commitment and the emotional stress of discussions is over). These reactions are very similar to those of any loss. In doing therapy briefly, the overriding aim is to help the client leave with a feeling of work accomplished and of work well done. Competence that might have been absent or unclear at the time of seeking help may hopefully be reinstated. If this is achieved, the feelings the client departs with may be those of relief, even excitement, renewed hope, new energy and not just the negative ones outlined above. The aims of the therapy must be clear from the outset. If the client expects a 'cure', this imposes almost an impossible burden on the therapeutic system and demands that the therapist assume a position that is beyond her expertise, towards omnipotence. It also invokes a medical model conceptualisation of problems and their resolution.

The therapist working briefly is alert to the possibility that every session may be the last one. The concept of ending is in the therapist's mind from the beginning. The possibility of a session being a 'one-off' is used in the formulation of the initial hypothesis and influences how the session is conducted. As such, each session needs to be both contained and beneficial on its own so that the client has the greatest possible chance of walking away with something of value. The idea of naming a session of therapy as a 'consultation' includes the notion of collaboration that may help to engage the client from the very beginning and hence contributes to the appropriately timed ending of therapy. This differs from longer-term treatment where a series of sessions, possibly over months or years, is considered necessary to effect change. Every theoretical approach to therapy (psychoanalytic, client-centred, systemic, CBT among others) infers an end point whether this is short, medium or long term. The therapeutic orientation of the therapist influences how endings are conceived and executed from the therapist's point of view. The end point as such, in therapy is a theoretical construct from the therapist's point of view. The end point of therapy from the client's viewpoint is more a point of transition on which many aspects of a practical, social and psychological nature, have influence.

The subject of termination of therapy is a critical issue in all models of therapy. Different models approach it differently. The objective of working briefly is to make the therapist redundant in the client's life as therapeutically and ethically as possible and with due attention to time. It follows, therefore, that the issue of when and how to end therapy and the possibility of terminating therapy at any moment in the therapeutic process informs the theoretical conceptualisation that underpins working briefly. It influences and shapes the structuring of the whole course of therapy. The steps that lead to ending are expanded and outlined in greater detail in this chapter. A number of factors have a bearing on this end point in therapy. They are listed in Box 11.1.

Doing therapy briefly is often to do with helping clients move from one fixed view of their problem to taking on another perspective, thereby freeing up their own natural coping strategies and resources. Once the client indicates (either by saying so, or through his actions) that he has regained or reunited himself with his own capabilities, the therapist knows that it is the time to begin to 'get out' and terminate the therapeutic relationship. Therapeutic skill is required to do this in a collaborative way

---

Box 11.1   Factors that Determine Ending in Therapy

- The therapist's experience and competence;
- Views about the problem and psychopathology;
- How therapy has progressed;
- The general context and particular setting with its demands and constraints (waiting lists, number of sessions, etc.);
- The expectations of the referrer, client and therapist;
- Feedback from the client about how he has managed the problem through self-reports and behaviour;
- Ideas about the ability of the client to deal with problems and therapy;
- The beliefs of the therapist (whether she feels a need to 'be there' at all stages to help the client, or abdicate some responsibility to the client to cope alone with some problems);
- The extent to which the therapist can tolerate ambiguity, emotional displays, uncertainty and other difficult processes that arise when dealing with people in distress; and
- Financial resources of the client and equally the financial or emotional needs of the therapist (if appropriate).

---

with the client. If the client feels that he is contributing to the decision to end, this in itself endorses and enhances his renewed sense of competence. The client is encouraged to use his own capabilities to deal with other difficulties that may be of less importance.

Therapists working in a time-sensitive way need to be alert to the responses from the client that indicate a wish or readiness to terminate therapy. Such responses include:

- Direct verbal feedback from the client. This is a significant and important way to ascertain when it is an appropriate ending time. This feedback can be elicited at the end of sessions or even during a session. For example:

  'From our discussion so far, what things have been helpful?'

To positively frame questions is useful in our experience. Clients who have found some of the experience unhelpful will soon let the therapist know! Each session can end with an evaluation by asking open questions such as:

  'What would be one thought that you might take away from today's discussion?'

- Noticing that a tension has left the dialogue and that the client appears more relaxed, which may be demonstrated by the client saying:

   'I feel better today.'
   'It has been a good week.'

Equally it may be manifested in a more relaxed body stance of the client.

- Clues for the therapist to pick up that the client might have gained enough from the therapy might include noticing a loss of concentration on the client's part during the session, and the client looking for new issues or just making statements that are less direct and clear than the examples above. The therapist must be alert to such signs and find a way to help the client move to the position of ending therapy. The therapist may enquire:

   'It may be that we've dealt with the main issue that was affecting you and it feels as if there isn't much to talk about today.' or
   'Have we said as much as we can about this matter for now?'

Such questions appropriately timed usually bring a sense of release and permission to leave therapy for the client.

- The physical presentation of the client may have changed during the process of therapy. He might smile more or not be so flushed and sweaty during the session. These may be clues that he is more relaxed and less anxious.
- Last minute cancellations and missed appointments can be a more common (and inconvenient) indication that the client no longer needs, or wishes, to come to therapy. This may indicate that a truly collaborative relationship with the therapist has not occurred. When working collaboratively, the topic of when a client might wish to end therapy can be included in the discussion. For example, asking a client early on in therapy:

   'How will I know that you feel ready to end therapy?'

- If a successful collaborative way of working has been established between therapist and client, the client may feel free to say:

   'I was wondering if I couldn't stop coming for now but I would like to see you in a fortnight or month's time just to check all is well.'

Such a statement might well indicate a renewed sense of competence. It might, of course, indicate other undisclosed issues, such as time or money pressures. In either instant, the therapist working briefly should take note and encourage the client to try things alone with less frequent sessions or by stopping. The client can always come back at another time which can be positively conveyed. In doing therapy briefly, the door is not closed forever. The client may return if this is necessary. All therapies have a trial-and-error component and firm guarantees can never be given irrespective of the length of the course of therapy.

- The therapist may sometimes experience difficulties in keeping the conversation going, alongside sensing a different atmosphere in the room. These too are clues that the therapist should not ignore and might usefully address to the client. In some approaches to therapy, the client gets better and therapy continues beyond the point where it is helpful to the client. Working in a truly collaborative way can minimise the chance of this happening. The therapist is always alert to signs of a lack of or a breakdown in collaboration. In a collaborative relationship, the decision to end therapy is mutually arrived at, by both therapist and client.

CONDITIONS OF TERMINATING THERAPY

Terminating when the problem has been resolved is the preferred basis for ending therapy. The client might simply say that the problem has gone away and that he feels ready to end therapy. Other clients are less direct and may be unsure about whether or not to end therapy. In using a brief approach, the therapist should take the lead in suggesting that the possibility of ending therapy can be considered at any point. This gives the client permission to discuss the issue of ending. Some will welcome the suggestion of termination. Other clients may respond that they still feel unsure about stopping and fear a recurrence of being unable to cope.

The client who has experienced a relief from painful feelings or resolution of a problem may fear a return or exacerbation of the symptoms. Careful thought should be given before offering any reassurance. Complete reassurance that the problem will not re-occur should not be given. However, reality can be balanced with hope. The therapist might respond by saying for example:

'Things do go up and down. However, you have overcome the problem once and from what I've heard from you, you should be able to find ways to do so again.'

This is an example of a cautionary message on ending therapy. Yet other clients, even if pleased with results, will express concern about terminating and will want to be able to contact the therapist in case of need. Whether or not doubt is expressed, most clients feel some uncertainty. The therapist can reduce this uncertainty by suggesting to clients that it can be a normal part of the change process for the problem to re-occur temporarily. To arrange a review meeting for some time in the future can help support the client through the ending. A 'final session' can be 'given' to the client as insurance, to take place when he chooses. In our experience, the offer of the 'optional' final session is rarely taken.

Some clients express gratitude for the help and support of the therapist in resolving their problems. The therapist may be put in a 'one-up' position or a position of competence in relation to the client. For those who work collaboratively, this can be a disadvantage as it may disqualify the client's own accomplishments. It thereby defines the client as less in control of events and more vulnerable to other unforeseen problems. It is important to acknowledge this gratitude, but in a way that acknowledges the client's contribution to his improvement.

> 'You said it was a relief to talk to someone outside your circle of friends and family. You used the time well to balance up your difficulties with what you are able to manage well.'

Or more directly the therapist can ask:

> 'Tell me what *you* have done to bring about this improvement?'

This question helps the client to track his role in the process of change. This in itself helps to consolidate the improvement achieved.

Terminating when the problem is partially resolved is another scenario around ending. Sometimes therapy is terminated at a time when the client's problem may not be fully resolved such as the client with a chronic illness or disability. This need not indicate that therapy has been ineffective. The therapist and client might come to an agreement that enough has been achieved for now.

Terminating when the presenting problem is not resolved is a more challenging scenario for both the client and the therapist. The client's concern may not always be fully resolved when therapy ends. In most time-limited therapy, the number of sessions may be prescribed by the context. There may be the impetus then to progress to the resolution of the problem within a finite number of sessions and to use therapy time to the optimum. However, even in more open-ended therapy the client might terminate when the problem is still unresolved. Time is never 'endless' as such.

Part of what we attempt to 'teach' in this book is that assessment skills are an integral part of the therapeutic process. This includes acknowledging as early as possible to the client whether the therapeutic context is appropriate for the current problem, given its limitations. Discussing this might in itself be the trigger to introducing a new perspective. The therapist might start by saying:

'I have the impression that you still are experiencing the same difficulties although we have had a number of conversations already. What are your views about this?'

Some clients might respond by refuting this. Rather than getting into a debate about the details of the problem, it can be helpful simply to review the contact by asking, for example:

'Tell me then what aspects you found helpful, and is there anything that might have made it difficult for you in dealing with your problem?'

This question might help the client to review his experience of the therapy, but also shows that the therapist is willing to hear about the aspects that were difficult for the client. It is a way of demonstrating respect for the client's opinions and of attaining a collaborative ending to the therapy. Following such a discussion, when the problem has apparently not been resolved, clients might themselves instigate termination through statements such as:

'I would like to see how I can manage alone. If it does not work, I will call you.'

Rather than discussing the client's reasons for the statement, the therapist might respond in a way that allows the client to have an easy departure.

'Yes, I think that would be worth a try. You might find that you can manage. It is always best to test the water for oneself.'

The therapist's statement can evoke a response of relief freeing the client to express some uncertainty. The client might say, for example:

Client: As we are about to end, have you got any further suggestions for me?

The therapist might respond by saying:

Therapist: What suggestion from me might be the one that would be most helpful for you for when you are alone?

Client: I know you can't give me the answers. Perhaps just urging me to think before I panic about what it is that I am worried about. That helped before!

Therapist: It sounds to me that you have just said it clearly to yourself!

Some clients know the problem has not been resolved but are satisfied with some progress towards resolution of the problem. The client might say, for example:

> 'Things have been a little better recently, and I have demands on my time so I wondered what you thought of me terminating therapy for now.'

The therapist would be prolonging treatment unnecessarily when the client feels he has already achieved sufficient for his current needs. However, it is always appropriate for the therapist to attempt to understand the reasons for the client's desire to end now. In our experience, the timing has to be right for the client to address his problem. The present may not be the right time for doing this. In this regard, a client can always be invited to return to therapy when he feels ready to work on his problem.

In contrast to the above examples, some clients will say that the problem that they came with is resolved, but that they would like to continue with therapy to consider another problem. The therapist working briefly then has certain options. The preferred first choice would be to re-enforce the work that has been done, and consider with the client how this work could help deal with the more recent problems. To extend a contract already negotiated without very careful consideration could undermine the whole notion of working within time constraints. It may be appropriate in a few cases to refer the client to another expert for further work and ongoing therapy. Therapists doing therapy briefly recognise that their approach might not be appropriate for every client. It is important to emphasise that although we work briefly, this does not preclude long-term therapy for those clients who need it. However, we always start with the expectation that therapy will be brief, until persuaded otherwise. Using a brief approach minimises the risk of client and therapist being drawn into a situation when there is a loss of clarity and focus. It also minimises the possibility of the client becoming dependent on the therapist.

Unplanned endings occasionally happen in all therapy. Unplanned endings have many meanings. Some unexpected endings can encapsulate the moment when therapy has been effective. The most welcome unplanned ending in doing therapy briefly is the moment when there is a recognition that therapy has been effective and the client is emancipated from his problem.

The therapist and client, working collaboratively, know then that therapy can terminate. This is an exciting moment, easy to recognise and act upon for the alert therapist. This recognition may be explicitly stated by the client, thus:

'I had never thought of it like that before!'

Such an exclamation suggests that a useful and enlightening connection has occurred for the client and heralds the beginning of the end of therapy. Many factors, of course, have to be assessed before an agreement is made to end therapy. Clients 'dropping out' of therapy unexpectedly can leave unanswered questions about the effectiveness of the therapy. These unexpected 'dropouts' are less likely to happen if a truly collaborative relationship is set up and the client's opinion is constantly elicited about the continuance of therapy. For example, we have found it good practice to ask at the end of each session:

'How do you feel about meeting again?'

If a real consensus about this decision is arrived at, then dropping out without explanation, on the part of the client, is less likely to occur. In summary, whatever the conditions of ending therapy, responding to client actions, wishes and beliefs needs careful thought. A client might ask:

'If problems arise again, can I call?'

A possible response might be:

'What sort of problem would you face that you might not be able to handle or about which you might consider telephoning me?'
'What from our sessions might you use to handle another problem?'

At the same time it is important not to hold too rigid views about working with the client again in the future should the going get too difficult. After all, treating therapy like a visit to the doctor is entirely appropriate. Working together to solve the problem is not a guarantee that the client will not need to consult the doctor again if a problem arises in the future. A client returning to the therapist at a later stage is not necessarily a sign of failure. On the contrary, it may signal confidence in the relationship with the therapist and her skills. The therapist working briefly need not have a sense of failure about this. Sometimes, the fact that the client returns to therapy again after some time with the same problem should itself be the subject for therapeutic discussion.

'MAP' OR OUTLINE FOR ENDINGS

Clarity about how to end therapy is just as important as having clarity about how to start therapy. The following steps are suggested as a guide for terminating therapy. In a modified form, they are similar to those used to end every session.

1. Think first and hypothesise about the ending. Factors to be considered in the hypothesis include:

    - The life stage of the client (any significant changes since starting);
    - The stage in relation to family (single, separated, married, elderly care responsibilities, children);
    - The stage of the presenting problem (enduring, resolved, partially resolved);
    - The context (any differences from the start of therapy); and
    - Any recent events in the client's life that have contributed to change.

2. Introduce ideas about ending in the initial engagement during the first session and in exploring the client's expectations of therapy. For example:

    'We have up to six sessions. We can decide together how many might be needed as we go along.'
    'If you were to think about how things would be if the problem was not so acute how would it be?'
    'We have one session left – how might you like to use it?'

3. Make decisions with the client about when therapy should end, as this is integral to the collaborative process. Engaging the client in this process of decision-making not only alleviates any discrepancies in timing the end but also respects the client's judgement about terminating therapy. Agreement needs to be reached between therapist and client as to what communication there should be between the therapist and the referrer. Both client and therapist have to make decisions towards the end of therapy. The decisions for the *client* include:

    - Whether he is confident to stop therapy;
    - Whether sufficient has been achieved;
    - Are there issues resulting from the therapeutic process to share with others; and
    - How to best use the work done during the session.

    Decisions for the *therapist* include:

    - Whether she considers that therapy has been sufficient;
    - How best to give the client an open door and respect achievements made so far;

- Who else the client might usefully involve after ending (professionals, family, colleagues);
- How to balance reality with hope if not all problems have been resolved; and
- What feedback, and in what form, will be appropriate for the referrer?

These are some questions that therapist and client might have to consider. In working collaboratively, the client must be involved in assessing the appropriateness of the timing of the ending. The decision to end should only be made when feedback from the client has been taken.

4. Weave ideas of ending into the body of the session. Examples of questions to stimulate thought and change perspective include:

   'If you were not able to be here, with whom else might you discuss your worries?'

   'If you thought it was time to end these sessions how might you go about doing it?'

5. Give the client time to raise any questions or comments prior to reaching the final stage of the therapy session. Sufficient time needs to be allocated before the session finishes so that new or contentious issues that are raised are not unattended. The invitation to raise issues of importance to him can contribute to giving the client a sense of control towards the end of the therapy. The therapist might say, for example:

   'Before we end is there anything you would like to say, or any comments you would like to make?'

As discussed in the previous chapter careful use of the word 'say' does not imply an agreement to address the issue raised.

6. Assess the signs that therapy needs to end, or that more might be needed, as the session progresses. Notice any signs that might give clues as to when is the right time to end, as discussed earlier in this chapter. The signs appear as information is exchanged between client and therapist, and as collaboration is established. For example, if the client keeps introducing different topics, ceases to discuss the presenting problem, or says that he is feeling much better, the therapist might be alerted to the appropriateness of terminating therapy.

   'I get the impression that you are less anxious about returning to work. Am I correct?'

   'I hear that you feel ready to try things alone now, and seem to have found ways to help you to do so. What is your view about this?'

7. Consult the client for his views about ending. A range of questions can be useful including the 'miracle' questions. For example:

   'If the problem was not here now, how would things be for you in other areas of your life?'
   'What would have to happen to make you know that things were improving?'
   'If you were to end the therapy before your problem was completely resolved, how might you manage?'

8. Consider tasks and techniques appropriate for endings. These include:

   • Providing summaries early in the session, in the middle or at the end;
   • Using rating scales for the client to indicate where they feel they are in terms of mood, progress in dealing with their problem and so on;
   • Being clear about tasks that help to ensure that doing therapy briefly is effective (ascertaining signs that the client is ready to leave, enhancing confidence and capabilities, and changing perspectives);
   • Reframing the problem in a way that suggests possibilities as well as distress associated with the problem; and
   • Sending summary letters to clients and referrer (as appropriate).

9. Evaluating each session, during the session and at the end of therapy, is integral to doing therapy briefly. Give the client the rationale for evaluating what has happened. One should also monitor the overall effectiveness of the therapy. The client's views are a vital part of this process. Immediate verbal feedback is useful and can be obtained by asking:

   'Would you suggest one thought that you might take away from the session/sessions?'

   However, more systematic research using questionnaires and other methods should be considered (Bor and McCann 1999).

10. Discussing what follow-up, if any, the client envisages and what the therapist can offer is important. In working briefly the client may have had only a few sessions and might at another time want to return. A review session offered for the future sometimes is reassuring for the client. If there is to be an ending and no follow-up, this should also be clarified.

11. Summarise, after the previous few steps, what has been seen and heard during the course of therapy. Strategies used in the final summary have to be carefully considered. The key element is respecting

the client's strengths and capabilities. However, a cautionary note: if an emphasis is only placed on the positive aspects of the client's situation, the client may feel that his real concerns have not been sufficiently understood or have been denied as being important. Thus, highlighting perceived difficulties is also part of a balanced summary. The summary should include the decision-making discussion and the final question or statement from the client. The summary is a way of the client hearing the therapist's perceptions. To be consonant with the client's view, the summary should only relate to what has been brought to the session. The summary should include actual phrases and words used by the client. Hearing these words repeated can make the impact more real for the client and is confirmation that the therapist has listened. In the last session, the summary may well be what the client takes away, thus careful choice of words is important. An example from the case of Andreas as described in Chapter 8 follows:

Therapist: From what I've heard and seen through the sessions we have had together, you have come a long way. Despite the difficulties you have managed to keep up the relationship with Dan whilst changing your relationship with Sue. You have fears for the future and still seek a close relationship with a woman who might be the mother of your children. What you have experienced and learned from these changes, you have said will help if you feel low in the future. It has been a good experience to see you using the toughness that comes from your youthful years during this difficult phase in your life. All this seems to have helped you to live through the uncertainties at work.

Andreas: (Looks up.) I feel quite differently now and find myself looking forward to the future. I'm trying to enjoy each day and am spending money on myself. It has helped me being able to talk to you and not feel that I am stupid or going mad. I have even bought myself some new clothes, which is something that I haven't done in years.

12. Ending is the final action taken by the therapist. Think carefully about how to finally end and part from the client. Such considerations include actions such as standing up at the end of the session, shaking hands, or using only a verbal exchange such as 'Thank you' or 'Good bye', and finally seeing the client to the door. Consider the moments of parting from a practical as well as theoretical point of view. The main considerations are:

- Body language (shake hands, embrace, stand up). If, for example, the client is touched or even hugged, it could give a message that the therapist will miss them, or might be giving a confusing message about friendship; and

- Words that are used for the final moments. Everything that is said has an impact. The parting words can re-enforce or undermine the client's competence. For example,

'Good luck.'
'I wish you well.'

These statements can be interpreted both negatively and positively.

13. Closing the notes is a very important final step in all therapy. In brief therapy, it is a vital part of completing a short piece of work. The recording should include notes about the final session, what issues were resolved, those still outstanding and how the client decided to continue. The contents of case notes and letters should be discussed with the client, to reduce misunderstandings. Consent must be given for discussion with others.
14. Feedback to referrer must be done with the client's consent. Feedback might help the referrer to be more in tune with the client's wishes and concerns, and thus re-enforces the benefits of the therapeutic experience.
15. Consultation and supervision provide an essential opportunity for the therapist to review her contact with the client and this helps to enhance future practice with other clients.

CONCLUSION

Therapy is a journey embarked upon by the client. In using a brief approach, the key elements are envisaging the end at the very beginning, recognising and acting upon the moments that indicate to both therapist and client that sufficient change in perspective has occurred and the client is emancipated from his problem. Ending in such a way that the client leaves, recognising and able to use his own capabilities, is the main objective. In doing therapy briefly, this journey is viewed as a joint venture between therapist and client. The signs and symbols referred to in these last chapters are the points on the 'map' that help chart the territory, making the journey shorter and less hazardous for both client and therapist. The pace varies, but the goals are clearly indicated on the 'map'. At the start, the end is always in view and this conserves time, a precious commodity for our 'travellers'.

12 Evidence-based and Time-limited Therapy

The current and future context of the UK NHS is for evidence-based and time-limited interventions and treatments. There is an increasing demand for therapists working in a range of clinical settings to conduct research emphasising an assessment of workload, audit and quality assurance. We live and work in an age where many factors such as socio-economic pressures, information, technology, cultural influences and increased client awareness directly impact on the practice and delivery of psychotherapy. Such influences require and demand a modern response from us as therapists. The model and concept of managed care, as developed and implemented in the United States can serve as a valuable guide and blueprint for responding to these demands, not only in the NHS, but also in other contexts such as in organisational settings, in educational institutions or in employee-assisted programmes in the UK. Almost all therapists will need to adapt their practice to some extent in order to respond to these challenges and demands. The key in making such changes is to remember that the ultimate goal of managed care is to provide care efficiently and effectively.

As previously mentioned, context is the backdrop for therapy. All therapeutic practice is defined and structured by the context in which it takes place. Without a clear understanding of our work environment, our ability to creatively and effectively implement the philosophy of brief therapy, as developed in the modern workplace and described in this book, is compromised. Recent changes in this environment may come as a challenge to our traditional mode of working. However, these pressures need not be viewed as a yoke or straightjacket, but rather as a fruitful opportunity to take a refreshing look at how we practice.

THE EVOLUTION AND DEFINITION OF MANAGED CARE

Today's therapy context does not require that we abandon all that we have learned or hold dear in our practice. Instead, it means learning to practice differently and shifting the client–therapist relationship into the modern era. This shift requires that the client–therapist relationship be characterised by parsimony, connectedness, genuineness, passion and honesty rather than aloofness, a top-down attitude and a 'therapist knows best' stance. To understand the need for these changes and to meet them effectively, we must first examine the backdrop on which most therapeutic practice takes place today: the managed care environment. Knight (1998: 43) has stated:

> It is difficult to define managed care given its continuous modification and contradictory perceptions of it. Because managed care is shaped by fluid market forces, its structure and focus change frequently and swiftly, sometimes faster than one can absorb.

'Managed care' is a term of the health care industry in the United States that gives rise to many different definitions and perceptions. Its precise meaning is rarely clear, given that the industry changes so rapidly and that the term is used loosely in a variety of different settings. However, no matter how illusive the definition may be, a clear understanding of the implications that managed care may have for one's practice is fundamental to effective and professional care. Such knowledge is essential to the future of psychological services within the managed care system. Only by understanding the environment in which one works can one hope to forge a solid respect and appreciation for the services one provides.

Managed care generally refers to a system of health care delivery in which a third party, such as within a health trust or as covered by private health insurance, is responsible for providing access to health care services and, in most cases, subsequent payment of those services. Increasingly, primary and secondary health care providers (e.g. primary care counselling services and hospital psychology departments) offer evidence-based, time-limited therapy in a way that is similar to that done in managed care. Managed care organisations are businesses and, subsequently, are run like most other businesses (Powell 2000).

One implication of this is that a third party, and one which is not involved in the daily practical provision of care, will be responsible for many of the decisions which will determine the quality and quantity of care. From this perspective, therapists working within the managed care environment today have an immense opportunity. Instead of focusing on the drawbacks and frustrations inherent in the managed care environment, therapists need to be leaders, both in working within the system and in being a force which drives the system to be more efficient and powerful. One must remember that 'the goal of managed care is to encourage consumers, providers and payers to all become accountable for the wise use of limited health care resources' (Powell 2000: 3). This is a worthy goal and one that few professionals would question as being beneficial. Instead, the debate will centre on which paths and which policies are the most compatible, compassionate and cost-effective to meet this aim.

Therapists may, at times, prefer paths and policies that apparently conflict with the choices made by those agencies that devise managed health care policy. Therapists tend to be client-focused while policy makers are system-focused. This has led many therapists to regard managed care with a measure of caution or suspicion. Managed care dictates to them how much and even how (i.e. evidence-based techniques and practices) to dispense care, even though the policy makers may have little in-depth knowledge about the practice of psychological care. It is incumbent upon us as therapists, therefore, to work with those who manage us, to enlighten them as to what we do and to engage with them as we might with the client so that a clear consensus about the nature and practice of psychotherapy emerges.

Therapists have an opportunity to set the pace for future care within that system. Only by being visionary with one's approach can therapists direct change that benefits the client and forges respect for the practice of psychological care. Therapists need to work with that system so that they can effect change that benefits both client and system. A brief therapeutic approach is a primary tool that can be used to achieve this goal.

THE EFFECT OF MANAGED CARE ON THERAPEUTIC PRACTICE

All working environments influence the type of care that is given, as we have previously stated. In a hospital versus a private office, in a group versus an individual, in a prison versus a walk in clinic, in a drug rehabilitation centre versus care offered by one's employer: the care given in all of these will take on a life as determined by the context. A managed care environment is no different: it impacts on the relationship with the client from the moment a client is referred for care. As such, the pace of therapy has to adapt accordingly and therapists have to work with and contribute to the sometimes conflicting preferences of clients, nurses, doctors, teachers, administrators and policy makers. By definition, managed care will impact upon the life cycle of therapy. The responsibility of the therapist is to ensure that this occurs in as positive a way as possible.

The single most important influence managed care has on therapeutic practice is simply that the preconditions for and the extent of therapy is neither likely to be determined by the practitioner nor by someone directly involved with the client. However, one must remember that the goal of managed care is to distribute a limited amount of resources as effectively and efficiently as possible to as many who require the service and to keep the wait to see someone to a minimum. The demands placed on policy makers are considerable and complex, and to lose sight of this challenge is to operate from a perspective that will benefit neither client nor practitioner. Hence it is the responsibility of the therapist to discover new ways of working within these constraints that positively benefit the client.

The good news is that after demonstrating the ability to curtail costs, managed care organisations are also now being asked to prove that such cost containment does not come at the expense of quality. They must show that their policies actually improve the quality of care dispensed (Knight 1998). Once again, for the creative practitioner, this is an opportunity to forge progress. If therapists can work effectively within the current system and provide consistent data which makes evident 'what works with whom', then future practitioners will find themselves in a much different and, indeed, more supportive work environment. A brief therapeutic approach allows therapists to work within the current system, ultimately providing the data necessary to consolidate the therapist's place in the medical setting and to make the changes needed for quality mental health care.

To work within the current system, the traditional goals sought by therapists may have to be reworked. Just as a man thrown overboard from a boat finds that he no longer needs to visit paradise island. He simply needs to stay afloat until he finds any land whatsoever, so too, today's practitioners may find that their goals have changed as well. The conventional aim to 'cure' a client or to address every problem may need to be modified in order to stay afloat in the current health care environment.

Today's therapists may find that the attainment of apparently small goals will result in surprising and welcome gains for the client. Some changes in specified areas may be sufficient to 'unblock' the client and restore normal coping. Rather than trying to focus on long-term change or breaking maladaptive lifelong patterns of interaction with every client, therapists need to effect change that is meaningful for some clients yet achievable within the current context. When this approach is underpinned by the belief that the client is competent, it gives the practitioner a positive springboard from which to work. Each new client should therefore be approached as if a brief approach may work. If this proves not to be the case, at least the extent of the problem will have been more fully assessed and the pros and cons of another approach can then be discussed with the client (and managed care providers). In other words, the therapeutic approach can be seen to have been selected on the basis of evidence rather than solely on the therapist's 'preferred approach'.

Today's therapists have been challenged to discovering what is efficient and what works. It is sobering to remember that managed care is replacing a system that was equally, if not more, problematic: a system where costs and approaches used precluded many from receiving necessary care and yet, where costs associated with delivery were generally high. By re-establishing new goals for the client, therapists have managed not only to survive in a challenging environment, but also to discover new ways of working efficiently and effectively.

One must remember that, like the man who survives his ordeal in the ocean and finds himself stronger because of it, as therapists we may ultimately find our practice stronger because of the difficult challenges we face today. Few practitioners relish the idea of 'downsizing' their goals for their clients. Yet, this may be just the exercise needed to determine what lies at the core of each of our therapeutic styles. What we view now as necessary may in the end seem extraneous. Perhaps only by being forced to 'pare down' our expectations can we re-evaluate our practice and ultimately find expectations which are better, more achievable, more valuable and more durable than those we hold today. Whilst 'paring down' invokes the idea of less happening in therapy, this is not the case with brief therapy; brief therapy should not be misunderstood as 'therapy lite'. Therapy that is brief should be intense so that more is covered in a shorter time, whilst respecting the client's need for and capacity to engage and change.

This is an enormous shift in thinking for both client and therapist. Most clients arrive at therapy with the idea that their care will be a protracted event and/or that they will need to delve deep into their past to solve today's problems. From the outset then, not only do therapists need to manage their own expectations about change, but they will need to address and engage with those of the client. Managed care demands this shift, and fortunately a brief therapeutic approach can provide the framework to achieve it. How to engage with the client whilst working within time constraints has been described in detail in the previous chapters of this book.

MEETING THE CHALLENGE: ENGAGING WITH THE SYSTEM

More immediate goals, eliciting and discussing expectations, increased collaboration and frequent feedback contribute to meet the challenges of today's therapy environment. A more active and broadened role for the therapist within the system can also help to accomplish one's goals. Just as improved collaboration is necessary to work with the client, collaboration is equally critical to working within the managed care environment. Therapists can no longer work in relative isolation. Working within managed care means that one is part of a system. This means that therapists will need to take on additional roles both to advocate better care for the client and to achieve a more enduring and respected position for mental health professionals in general. To meet the challenges of today's health care context, therapists will need to be a:

Team Player – Perhaps more than anything else, therapists in a managed care environment need to recognise and work with the other professionals surrounding them. They must liaise with the doctors, nurses, social workers and specialists involved in their client's care. They will also need to communicate with hospital managers and practice administrators. All of these individuals influence not only the care given to an individual client but the assessment of client's suitability for therapy in a given context.

As such, therapists must understand the role that each person plays and then identify how each person can best contribute to their client's care. Without constant communication between the therapist and these individuals, a client's care can be compromised or overlaps in care may occur. In an environment where efficiency is of primary importance such shortcomings need to be avoided. Being a team player is paramount to working effectively within the system.

When clients arrive at therapy, one of the assessments often made is 'Does this person have a support system? Does he have family and friends on whom he can rely?' Therapists recognise that the connections an individual has with others are critical to healthy functioning. The same is true for therapists within managed care: the degree to which a therapist is connected to those around her will reflect how well that therapist is able to function within the managed care community. To this end, the therapist must be adept in identifying and possibly engaging others within the client's social and family milieu in addressing the problem. Skills in working with families, small communities and couples are valuable to the therapist who in the past has focused on one-to-one sessions.

Negotiator – As outlined above, the managed care environment is not a perfect system. It has its flaws that will inevitably bring about frustration for therapists trying to achieve optimal progress for their clients. As such, therapists will need to be able to negotiate. They will need to be able to present a client's case, argue for certain treatments and make appropriate compromises when needed. Managed care organisations face tremendous challenges in distributing care effectively to a population whose demands far exceed their resources. Its managers and administrators are forced to make compromises daily in order to handle the demands placed upon them.

Therapists will need to do the same and to do it diplomatically. To negotiate effectively, one must begin by doing one's homework. A therapist must know exactly what her client needs and be able to document why. She must also try to understand why any current restrictions on such care exist. When a therapist addresses the problem to others, she must make sure to clearly state the problem, the goal and what she feels is needed to solve that problem. A therapist may also wish to put her case in writing as this helps to clarify issues and serves as a reference for all those involved. Finally, a practitioner must be realistic about her goals. She needs to be viewed as one who understands the difficulties of the work environment and, thus, simply asks for what the client *needs*. With this latter reputation, when a therapist does ask for more exceptional care, her requests will more likely be heeded.

Expert and Educator – The managed care therapist must be an expert in her field. The environment requires that therapists keep up with new treatments, theories and the latest improvements in their fields, through both seminars and educational text. Therapists also need to be aware of the alternative treatment options available for clients and to access their effectiveness and appropriateness. Not only is such information vital to optimising the care given to clients but it is also necessary to drive the managed care market in the most beneficial direction. They also need to be clear about what does not work and be willing to explain this to either the client or managed care administrators, as it would be wasteful and potentially unethical to proceed with therapy where there is simply no evidence that it can work. This stresses the importance of an initial consultation with a new client in order to assess suitability for therapy (see Chapter 5) before embarking on a course of sessions.

Without the input of highly informed therapists, managed care can never maximise the care it dispenses. Therapists must educate decision-makers about the mental health field so that informed decisions can be made. The administrators and managers of managed care do not have the time to become experts in every field. They need help from those dispensing care to make the most prudent and effective decisions. The more knowledgeable a therapist is, the more likely her opinion will become highly regarded and useful in the decision-making process.

Professional – Being professional means practising to the highest standards and taking responsibility for the outcome. It means being accountable for one's work while also being dependable and conscientious. Therapists must be able to back up their decisions with research, documentation, expert opinions and well-thought out case plans. Nothing in a managed care environment is haphazard (although it may feel that way to you at times!). Similarly, nothing in one's own work should appear to be disorganised. The professional therapist acts with care, pays attention to details and is accountable for the decisions she makes.

Client Advocate – Although a therapist may act on behalf of her client *during* each session, a therapist within managed care must also act on behalf of her client *out* of each session. The therapist is the only voice for the client within the system and that voice must be heard. In today's environment, silence is neglectful. Because managers and administrators who do not specialise in giving care run managed care, practitioners must speak out to ensure that the needs of the client are heard. Therapists '…are the pivotal, prime movers of the managed care environment. Their presence adds humanity to an otherwise overwhelming system' (Powell 2000: 5–6).

As such, therapists must be active in their role within the system. They must speak out on what is best for each individual client and on what is best for the future of client care as a whole. They need to protect the privacy and confidentiality of clients. This can often get lost in a large system where numerous individuals have access to, and may be involved in, the care of a client. Moreover, therapists need to be proactive in coordinating client care and making sure that each client does not get 'lost' within the system. Managed care can be impersonal and, as a result, it is the responsibility of the practitioners to maintain and fortify the personal care that is needed in the mental health field.

Evaluator – Therapists must constantly evaluate:

1. the progress of each individual;
2. the care given to clients in general; and
3. the effectiveness of the system in meeting client's needs.

As in any environment, therapists must continually assess the status of each client. A person's health and needs will fluctuate and the competent professional must determine the amount and type of care desired at any given time. This responsibility is heightened in the managed care environment where resources are limited and in high demand. This may mean requesting feedback from the client more often as well as updating and reviewing notes on a more regular basis.

The system will also require that practitioners evaluate the overall quality of care given to clients. Therapists also need to follow up with clients after therapy has ended. They need to secure information about how well clients continue to progress, what clients found helpful, the aspects of therapy clients did not enjoy and what clients believe would be helpful to them in the future. Standardised measures of affect, such as those for depression and anxiety, should be considered as well as questionnaires designed to measure the specific services of a practice (see Du Plessis and Bor 1999).

The more documentation a therapist can provide to managers about the level of service given, the more influential that therapist can become in directing the future of managed care. The importance of evaluative measures in the managed care context cannot be overstated and, as such, therapists are wise to personally oversee this aspect of care.

In addition, therapists will also need to monitor the waiting list for their services. While evaluations may show that therapists are meeting the needs of their clients, the needs of those who have not yet been seen must also be considered. A practice is not providing an adequate level of service if many are left in distress while only a small percentage of clients receive care, no matter how outstanding that care may be. If waiting lists are unduly long, therapists will need to implement measures to remedy the situation. Assessment sessions, well before more prolonged treatment, is an option as is shortened consultations for select clients. Solid data documenting the demand for increased psychological services should be provided to managed care administrators. This is the type of information they will need to make sound decisions about the distribution of resources.

To fulfil these roles, five characteristics in particular will aid therapists:

1. flexibility;
2. resourcefulness;
3. curiosity;
4. commitment; and
5. communication.

Curiosity is also paramount. In an environment where decisions are being made by those not directly involved in care, policies and rules need to be questioned and understood. Therapists must find the balance between accepting the difficulties administrators face and speaking out against the injustices faced by their clients. They must maintain a genuine curiosity concerning what is most beneficial for their clients both in the short and long term.

This characteristic will not only add to a practitioner's ability to be resourceful, but it will also aid in maintaining a practitioner's commitment to providing the best level of care to her clients. Therapists in managed care need to remember that they are the pioneers of their day. Just as the early practitioners of psychology met frustrations but persevered in the face of scepticism, today's practitioners must persist in the face of limited resources and bureaucratic red tape. Only by maintaining a strong commitment to the health of their clients can they forge a long-lasting and respected place for the mental health professions.

Finally, and most importantly, therapists should strive to communicate effectively with their co-workers. Managed care has its own goals while therapists have theirs. Only by communicating can therapists hope to make manage care understand their needs. This may mean, amongst other things, that the therapist needs to learn the language of business. Managers and administrators cannot be expected to create perfect policies without being educated on what constitutes good care. Therapists are in the best position to provide this information.

CONCLUSION

We do not live in a perfect world and although we may try and work our way towards such a place in therapy we should also accept, and deal with, the reality of our present work context. Brief therapy is an approach that can help with this process. By engaging differently with the client and more proactively with the system, therapists can make great progress in a difficult environment with a sizeable number of clients who seek therapy. Mutual respect and communication between all parties is essential – between client and therapist as well as between therapists and the care giving system. By maintaining one's commitment, professionalism and creativity, therapists in any type of managed care context will also maintain the integrity of client care.

Therapy has potentially a secure and exciting future but only if it is responsive to the wider context in which it is practised. It is our belief that therapists in a wide range of settings can apply the ideas in this book. This is not to say that the approach described here is prescriptive or suited to every therapist, client, context and problem. Built into this model of working is an accommodation for the individual therapist's own way of working with their skills, expertise, life experience and training developed over a period of time. It is of course incumbent upon each therapist to continually develop her own unique competencies through ongoing professional development and supervision. This is equally true for supervisors themselves and all those who manage therapists, that they should be aware of continuous professional developments in the field of therapy. The objective of it all is to learn to elicit what is best *in* and *for* the client.

References

Allman, P., Bloch, S. and Sharpe, M. (1992) 'The end-of-session message in systemic family therapy: a descriptive study', *Journal of Family Therapy*, 14, pp. 69–85.

Anderson, T. (1996) 'Language is not innocent', in F. Kaslow (ed.), *The Handbook of Relational Diagnosis*, New York: John Wiley & Sons.

Anderson, H. and Goolishian, H. (1995) 'The patient is the expert: a not-knowing approach to therapy', ch. in S. McNamee and J. Gergen (eds), *Therapy as Social Construction*, London: Sage.

Barkham, M. and Shapiro, D. (1990) 'Brief psychotherapeutic interventions for job related distress: a pilot study of prescriptive and explorative therapy', *Counselling Psychology Quarterly*, 3, pp. 133–147.

Bateson, G. (1972) *Steps to an Ecology of Mind*, New York: Balantine.

Berg, I. and Miller, S. (1992) *Working with the Problem Drinker*, New York: W.W. Norton.

Bloom, B. (1992) *Planned Short Term Psychotherapy*, Boston: Allyn & Bacon.

Bor, R. and McCann, D. (eds) (1999) *The Practice of Counselling in Primary Care*, London: Sage.

Bor, R. and Miller, R. (1991) *Internal Consultation in Health Care Settings*, London: Karnac Books.

Bor, R., Miller, R., Latz, M. and Salt, H. (1998) *Counselling in Health Care Settings*, London: Cassell.

Bor, R., Ebner-Landy, J., Gill, S. and Brace, C. (2002) *Counselling in Schools*, London: Sage.

Budman, S. and Gurman, A. (1988) *Theory and Practice of Brief Psychotherapy*, New York: Guilford.

Budman, S. and Gurman, A. (1992) 'A time-sensitive model of brief therapy: the IDE approach', in S. Budman, M. Hoyt and S. Friedman (eds), *The First Session in Brief Therapy*, New York: Guilford.

Byng-Hall, J. (1995) *Rewriting Family Scripts*, New York: Guilford Press.

Combrinck-Graham, L. (1987) 'Invitation to a kiss: diagnosing ecosystemically', *Psychotherapy*, 24, pp. 504–510.

de Shazer, S. (1985) *Keys to Solutions in Brief Therapy*, New York: W.W. Norton.

de Shazer, S. (1988) *Clues: Investigating Solutions in Brief Therapy*, New York: W.W. Norton.

du Plessis, P. and Bor, R. (1999) 'Evaluating counselling in primary health care', in R. Bor and D. McCann (eds), *The Practice of Counselling in Primary Care*, London: Sage.

Gergen, K. (1994) *Realities and Relationships: Soundings in Social Construction*, Cambridge, MA: Harvard University Press.

Gill, S. (1999) 'The competent patient', ch. in R. Bor and D. McCann (eds), *The Practice of Counselling in Primary Care*, London: Sage.

Goss, S. and Rose, S. (2002) 'Evidence-based practice: a guide for counsellors and psychotherapists', *Counselling and Psychotherapy Journal*, 2, pp. 147–151.

Haley, J. (1976) *Problem-Solving Therapy*, San Francisco: Jossey-Bass.

Harrison, R. (1980) *Textbook of Medicine*, London: Hodder and Stoughton.

Hewson, D. (1991) 'From laboratory to therapy room: prediction questions for reconstructing the "new-old" story', *Dulwich Centre Newsletter*, 3, pp. 5–12.

Howard, K., Kopta, S., Krause, M. and Orlinsky, D. (1986) 'The dose–effect relationship in psychotherapy', *American Psychologist*, 41, pp. 159–164.

Hoyt, M. (1995) *Brief Therapy and Managed Care*, San Francisco: Jossey-Bass Publishers.

Hubble, M., Duncan, B. and Miller, S. (1999) *The Heart and Soul of Change: What Works in Therapy*, Washington DC: American Psychological Association.

Kadera, S., Lambert, M. and Andrews, A. (1996) 'How much therapy is really enough?', *Journal of Psychotherapy: Practice and Research*, 5, pp. 132–151.

Keeney, B. (1979) 'Ecosystemic epistemology: an alternate paradigm for diagnosis', *Family Process*, 18, pp. 117–129.

Knight, W. (1998) *Managed Care: What it Is and How It Works*, Maryland: Aspen Publishers.

Koss, M. and Butcher, J. (1986) 'Research on brief psychotherapy', in S. Garfield and A. Bergin (eds), *Handbook of Psychotherapy and Behavior Change: An Empirical Analysis*, 3rd edn, New York: John Wiley.

Koss, M. and Shiang, J. (1994) Research on brief psychotherapy, ch. in A. Bergin and S. Garfield (eds) *Handbook of Psychotherapy and Behavior Change*, 4th edn, New York: John Wiley & Sons.

Malan, D., Heath, E., Bacla, H. and Balfour, F. (1975) 'Psychodynamic changes in apparently untreated neurotic patients. II. Apparently genuine improvements', *Archives of General Psychiatry*, 32, pp. 110–126.

McGoldrick, M. and Gerson, R. (1985) *Genograms in Family Assessment*, New York: W.W. Norton.

Miller, S., Duncan, B. and Hubble, M. (1997) *Escape from Babel: Toward a Unifying Language for Psychotherapy Practice*, New York: W.W. Norton.

Mooney, K.A. and Padesky, C.A (2000) 'Applying client creativity to recurrent problems: constructing possibilities and tolerating doubt', *Journal of Cognitive Psychotherapy: An International Quarterly*, 14, Nov 2.

Mooney, K. and Padesky, C. (2002) 'Applying patient creativity to recurrent problems: constructing possibilities and tolerating doubt', *Journal of Cognitive Psychotherapy: An International Quarterly*, 14, pp. 149–161.

O'Hanlon, H. (1992) 'History becomes her story: collaborative solution-oriented therapy of the after-effects of sexual abuse', in S. McNamee and K. Gergen (eds), *Therapy as Social Construction*, London: Sage.

O'Hanlon, B. (1998) *New Possibilities in Brief Therapy: Collaboration, Inclusion, Validation and Change*, London: B.T. Press.

Penguin English Dictionary (2002) London: Penguin Books. 'Context', p. 180.

Penn, P. (1985) 'Feed forward: future questions, future maps', *Family Process*, 24, pp. 299–310.

Powell, S. (2000) *Case Management: A Practical Guide to Success in Managed Care*, Philadelphia: Lippincott Williams & Wilkins.

Purves, D. (2003) 'Time limited practice', ch. in W. Dryden and R. Woolf (eds), *Handbook of Counselling Psychology*, 2nd edn, London: Sage.

Quick, E. (1996) *Doing What Works in Brief Therapy*, San Diego: Academic Press.

Rogers, C. (1951) *Patient-Centered Therapy*, Boston: Houghton-Mifflin.

Rolland, J. (1994) 'In sickness and in health: the impact of illness on couples' relationships', *Journal of Marital and Family Therapy*, 20, pp. 327–347.

Sackett, D., Rosenberg, W., Gray, J., Haynes, R. and Richardson, W. (1996) 'Evidence-based medicine: what it is and what it is not', *British Medical Journal*, 312, pp. 71–72.

Seligman, M. (1995) *What you Can Change . . . and What you Can't*, New York: Ballantine.

Selvini Palazzoli, M., Boscolo, L., Cecchin, G. and Prata, G. (1980) 'Hypothesizing, circularity, neutrality: three guidelines for the conductor of the session', *Family Process*, 19, pp. 3–12.

Selvini Palazzoli, M., Boscolo, C., Cecchin, G. and Prata, G. (1980) 'The problem of the referring person', *Journal of Marital and Family Therapy*, 6, pp. 3–9.

Shotter, J. (1998) '"Living moments" in dialogical exchanges', *Human Systems: The Journal of Systemic Consultation and Management*, 9, pp. 81–93.

Spinelli, E. (1994) *Demystifying Therapy*, London: Constable.

Steenbarger (1992) 'Duration and outcome in psychotherapy: an integrative review', *Professional Psychology: Research and Practice*, 25, pp. 111–119.

Strasser, F. and Strasser, A. (1997) *Existential Time-Limited Therapy: the Wheel of Existence*, Chichester: John Wiley.

Strong, T. (2000) 'Six orienting ideas for collaborative therapists', *European Journal of Psychotherapy, Therapy and Health*, 3, pp. 25–42.

Talmon, M. (1990) *Single Session Therapy*, San Francisco: Jossey-Bass.

Van Emmerick, A., Kamphuis, J., Hulsbosch, A. and Emmelkamp, P. (2002) 'Single session debriefing after psychological trauma: a meta-analysis', The Lancet, 360, pp. 766–771.

Van Trommel, M. (1983) The intake procedure placed within a systemic context. *Journal of Strategic and Systemic Therapies*, 3, pp. 74–86.

Walter, J. and Peller, J. (1992) *Becoming Solution-Focused in Brief Therapy*, Pennsylvania: Brunner/Mazel.

Walter, J. and Peller, J. (2000) *Recreating Brief Therapy: Preferences and Possibilities*, New York: W.W. Norton & Company.

Watzlawick, P., Weakland, J. and Fisch, R. (1977) *Change: Principles of Problem Formation and Problem Resolution*, New York: W.W. Norton.

Weber, T., McKeever, J. and McDaniel, S. (1985) 'A beginner's guide to the problem-oriented first family interview', *Family Process*, 24, pp. 357–364.

White, M. (1995) 'School and education: exploring new possibilities', *Dulwich Centre Newsletter*, 2(3), pp. 51–66.

White, M. and Epston, D. (1990) *Narrative Means to Therapeutic Ends*, New York: W.W. Norton.

Zeldin, T. (1998) *Conversation: How Talk Can Change Your Life*, London: The Marvill Press.

Index